# POLITICAL TOLERANCE

### AND

# AMERICAN DEMOCRACY

# POLITICAL TOLERANCE

## AND

## AMERICAN DEMOCRACY

**John L. Sullivan**

**James Piereson**

**George E. Marcus**

**The University of Chicago Press**

Chicago and London

The University of Chicago Press, Chicago 60637
The University of Chicago Press, Ltd., London

© 1982 by The University of Chicago
All rights reserved. Published 1982
Printed in the United States of America
89 88 87 86 85 84 83 82    5 4 3 2 1


*Library of Congress Cataloging in Publication Data*

Sullivan, John Lawrence, 1945–
  Political tolerance and American democracy.

  Bibliography: p.
  Includes index.
  1. Political psychology.   2. Toleration.
3. Democracy.   4. Civil rights—United States.
5. Public opinion—United States.   I. Piereson,
James.   II. Marcus, George E.   III. Title.
JA74.5.S94        306′.2′0973        81-16406
ISBN 0-226-77990-4        AACR2

JOHN L. SULLIVAN is associate professor of political science at
the University of Minnesota. He is the coauthor (with Stanley
Feldman) of *Multiple Indicators*. James Piereson is assistant
professor of political science at the University of Pennsylvania.
George E. Marcus is professor of political science at Williams
College. Sullivan and Marcus are coeditors of the journal *Political
Methodology*.
[1982]

# Contents

*Preface*                                                      ix

**1   Tolerance and Democracy**                                 1

The Concept of Political Tolerance    2
The Limits of Tolerance    7
Democratic Theories and Political Tolerance    10
Summary and Conclusion    23

**2   Political Tolerance and American Politics:
The Empirical Literature**                                     26

Communism, Conformity, and Civil Liberties    27
Tolerance and the Democratic Creed    33
Changing Levels of Tolerance, 1954–1978    44
Alternative Strategies for Measuring
   Tolerance    46
Attitudes and Behavior    49
Implications for the Study of Tolerance    51

**3   A Profile of Political Tolerance in the 1970s:
Implications of a Different Approach**                         54

Changing Levels of Political Tolerance:
   The Stouffer Items    54
A Content-Controlled Measure of Political
   Tolerance    60
The Twin Cities Samples    63
The Content-Controlled Measure:
   The Problem of Validity    70
A Framework for the Analysis of Political
   Tolerance    76
Appendix 3-A    81

**4**    **Pluralistic Intolerance: The Distribution of**
**Target Groups in American Society**      **82**

The Problem of Intensity    83
Pluralistic Intolerance    84
The Distribution of Target Groups    85
Social and Political Bases of Target Group
    Selection    92
Levels of Tolerance for the Different Groups    106

**5**    **The Social Sources of Political Tolerance**      **110**

The Dependent Variable:
    Degree of Political Tolerance    111
Education, Social Status, and Tolerance    114
Gender and Tolerance    126
Race and Tolerance    129
Aging, Generations, and Tolerance    131
Religion and Tolerance    135
Urbanization and Tolerance    139
Region and Tolerance    141
Conclusions    144

**6**    **The Psychological Sources of Political Tolerance**    **145**

Maslow's Need Hierarchy and Tolerance    146
Socialization, Authoritarianism, and Tolerance    150
Dogmatism and Tolerance    153
Social Learning Theory and Tolerance    156
Conclusions    160

**7**    **Political Explanations of Tolerance**      **163**

Some Limits to the Analysis:
    The Political Context    163
Objections to Target Groups    165
Tolerance and Ideology    175
Political Threat and Tolerance    186
Tolerance and Political Involvement    194

## Contents

Support for the General Norms of Democracy    202
Summary and Conclusions    207

**8    A Multivariate Model of Political Tolerance    209**

A Model for the Analysis of Political
  Tolerance    210
Parameter Estimation    214
Internal and External Threat    226
Alternative Types of Perceived Threat    228
Political Elites and the Processes of Political
    Tolerance    231
Social Tolerance    237
Tolerance and Stouffer's Content-Biased
    Measures    239
Summary and Conclusions    240
Appendix 8A. Statistical Procedures    241

**9    Political Tolerance: Implications for Democratic
Theory    248**

Summary of Findings    249
Implications for Democratic Theory    254
Concluding Comments    263

*Bibliography*    266

*Index*    275

# Preface

This book is the product of a collaborative venture among the three authors which spans many years of sharing and sifting ideas and criticisms. Needless to say, we share equally in whatever credit or criticism the book is due. Although each of us took initial responsibility for different parts of the book, the entire manuscript has been repeatedly reviewed, discussed, and revised by all three authors. The result is a book that, though it may bear some of the inevitable marks of collaboration, was strengthened considerably by a productive and profitable partnership.

During the course of the project we fell into the debt of several people whose assistance made our work easier. We thank Robert Holt and Richard Dawson, in particular, for their encouragement during the early stages of the project. Professors Robert Jackman, Jane Mansbridge, John Aldrich, and Christopher Achen read all or parts of the manuscript, and gave us many helpful suggestions for improving it. Helen Rieselbach edited the manuscript in her customarily skillful way, and her efforts made the arguments that follow more intelligible. The assistance of Paul Sheatsley, who supervised our national survey for the National Opinion Research Center, is also gratefully acknowledged. Finally, we owe a special debt of thanks to Professors Stanley Feldman and Michal Shamir, who served as research assistants on the project and whose efforts above and beyond the call of duty are reflected throughout the book.

We acknowledge the financial assistance of the National Science Foundation which supported our research through a grant (SOC 77-17623) to the University of Minnesota. Williams College was also very generous in its provision of funds for research, travel, and clerical assistance.

Some of the results reported in this book have already been published, as follows: material in chapter 3 is taken from John L. Sullivan, James Piereson, and George E. Marcus, "An Alternative Conceptualization of Political Tolerance: Illusory Increases 1950s–1970s," *American Political Science Review,* 73 (1979), pp. 781-794, © 1979 by American Political Science Association; and "Political Intolerance: The Illusion of Progress," *Psychology Today,* February 1979, pp. 86-91, © 1979 by Ziff-Davis Publishing Company; in Chapter 5, from George E. Marcus, James Piereson, and John L. Sullivan, "Rural-Urban Differences in Tolerance: Confounding Problems of Conceptualization and Measurement," *Rural Sociology,* 45 (1980), pp. 731–737, © 1980 by Rural Sociological Society; in chapters 5 and 7, from James Piereson, John L. Sullivan, and George E. Marcus, "Political Tolerance: An Overview and Some New Findings," in *The Electorate Reconsidered,* edited by John C. Pierce and John L. Sullivan (Beverly Hills, Cal.: Sage Publications, 1980), © 1980 by Sage Publications, Inc.; and in chapter 8, from John L. Sullivan, George E. Marcus, Stanley Feldman, and James Piereson, "The Sources of Political Tolerance: A Multivariate Analysis," *American Political Science Review,* 75 (1981), pp. 92–106, © American Political Science Association.

Williamstown, Mass.        J.S.
January 1981        G.E.M.
        J.P.

# Tolerance and Democracy

1

Democracies may be distinguished from rival forms of government by the degree to which they permit opposition both to the democratic regime and to the leaders who happen to be in power at a given moment. Since democratic regimes allow and even encourage opposition, they must always face the problem of deciding what forms of opposition to tolerate and how far such tolerance can be safely extended.

Although it sometimes appears, during periods of satisfaction and complacency, that the problem of how much tolerance is acceptable has been overcome, some new threat usually surfaces, bringing these questions to the fore once again. American history is littered with controversies over the legitimacy of radical opposition to its liberal regime, beginning as early as the Revolutionary War when supporters of American independence had to decide the fate of those who had remained loyal to England, and continuing to the present controversies over the rights of ideological groups on the left and the right. Such questions were raised again recently by the American Nazi Party's attempt to stage a uniformed march through the Chicago suburb of Skokie, which is the home of several thousand survivors of Nazi concentration camps. An ordinance designed to prohibit their march was passed by the Skokie village council, and this was in turn challenged in the courts on the ground that it violated the rights of free speech and assembly guaranteed the Nazis under the First Amendment. The litigation on the issue, which was finally decided in favor of Nazis, aroused considerable controversy over the meaning of tolerance and the range of legitimate dissent in a democratic society.

This book is an investigation into the character of American opinion on the subject of tolerance for ex-

1

tremist political groups. The responses that are summarized below were culled from some 1500 interviews that were conducted in the spring of 1978. Those who were interviewed represent a cross-section of the American population, and their responses to our questions represent a cross-section of American opinion. Because public opinion on many questions is volatile, we have taken some care to separate the more permanent and fundamental elements from the transitory and the unimportant elements. The object of this enterprise is to say both something precise about the character of American opinion and something general about the character of American democracy.

The book begins and ends with these general formulations, and our empirical concerns are addressed in the middle chapters. Because the concept of tolerance is controversial and often loosely used, it is necessary first to clarify its meaning and its theoretical relationship to democracy. These questions will be taken up in this chapter and the next one, after which we turn to the empirical issues.

## The Concept of Political Tolerance

Tolerance implies a willingness to "put up with" those things one rejects or opposes. Politically, it implies a willingness to permit the expression of ideas or interests one opposes. A tolerant regime, then, like a tolerant individual, is one that does not restrict, much less suppress, ideas that challenge its basic principles.[1]

In a narrower sense, tolerance is closely associated with the idea of procedural fairness. An important element of liberal political theory is its emphasis on the distinction between the substantive issues of political conflicts and the procedural rules by which conflicts are resolved. Though liberal societies may be divided by intense conflicts, they can remain stable if there is a general adherence to the rules of democratic or constitutional procedure. Tolerance in this sense implies a commitment to the "rules of the game" and a willingness to apply them equally. Therefore persons are tolerant to the extent they are prepared to extend such constitutional guarantees—the right to speak, to publish, to run for office—to those with whom they disagree. Similarly, a fully tolerant regime applies such norms equally to all.

Whether a fully tolerant regime is desirable or, indeed, possible is another question. Although most of us believe that tolerance is "good," there may be circumstances under which even the principle's most ardent defenders would be prepared to compromise it to preserve some

1. This definition, and the discussion that follows, owes a great deal to Bernard Crick's (1973: Chapter 3) thoughts on tolerance and intolerance. Jane Mansbridge provided valuable comments on this chapter.

more important value. It is, therefore, unrealistic to elevate the concept of tolerance to an unbreachable virtue.

Nevertheless, in studying tolerance, certain problems inevitably arise from the tendency to use the concept in a hortatory manner. Since most political analysts believe that tolerance is good, they define tolerance so that none of their own actions can be construed as intolerant. As a consequence, it is difficult to provide a neutral definition of tolerance, but it is necessary to try to do so if the problem is to be studied with any degree of detachment.

Another difficulty with the concept of tolerance is its often confusing relationship to such related notions as religious toleration, "democratic" norms and attitudes, "open-mindedness," or freedom from prejudice. Though these notions are connected with tolerance, matters become confused when all are lumped together. Some clarity may be gained, therefore, by distinguishing among these several concepts.

## Tolerance and Toleration

The modern concept of tolerance developed out of the theory of religious toleration, as it emerged from the religious controversies in seventeenth and eighteenth century England. Thus, *toleration* is closely identified, both historically and theoretically, with religion, while *tolerance* more commonly applies to struggles among political doctrines. As a doctrine, religious toleration sought to remove religious opinions and religious conflicts from the political realm. Religious struggles among the various Protestant sects, and between Protestants and Catholics, could not be resolved peacefully so long as the parties insisted that the state enforce their doctrines. Because religious dogmas embodied fundamentally different ways of life, "true believers" were often prepared to engage in substantial sacrifice and strife to have their doctrines triumph.

As a solution to religious conflicts, toleration was, in an important sense, a "Protestant" contribution, since proponents of toleration argued that religion is a matter of private conscience requiring no political mediation, a view that the established church could not accept. Defenders of toleration believed that political authority should be confined to the affairs of this world, and consequently were led to narrow the scope of politics. Locke, in his *Letter On Toleration,* made the critical point:

> all the power of civil government relates only to man's civil interests, is confined to the care of the things of this world, and hath nothing to do with the world to come (1963: 23).

The eventual acceptance of this doctrine, at least in England and America, marked an important turning point in the development of liberalism, for it provided an early basis for limiting the sphere of the state and for distinguishing the public from the private in a way that enlarged the domain of the private. Freedom of religion, now institutionalized in liberal democracies in the separation of church and state, resulted from treating religious doctrine and practice as private rather than public matters.

Many now argue that political freedom rests on the same grounds as religious freedom. Freedom to hold political beliefs is seen as similar to freedom to hold religious convictions. Sometimes this claim is based on an interpretation of John Stuart Mill's argument in *On Liberty* that "private regarding" actions are beyond the reach of the state. If political opinions and practice do not harm others, then the argument is very plausible, but political doctrines inherently affect others. If one quietly disagrees with the religious beliefs of others, it can be said to be a private matter; but if one politically agitates against the principle of religious toleration, it is necessarily a political question.

In a more complicated and indirect sense, one consequence of extending this argument for tolerance is to make political doctrines a matter of private belief, defusing them to make them compatible with liberal politics. For this reason, some contemporary radicals denounce the notion of tolerance as a subtle means liberal regimes use to disarm challenges. Marxism, for example, is substantially less threatening when viewed as a private opinion rather than as a call to reorganize society (see Wolff et al., 1965), being in this way "liberalized" in the same way that Catholicism was "protestantized" through religious toleration. In this sense, tolerance (like toleration) is not merely a principle but also a powerful political weapon in the liberal arsenal.

*Tolerance and Prejudice*

Since tolerance refers to a willingness to "put up with" things that one rejects, the term presumes opposition or disagreement. Thus, tolerance means something other than indifference. The problem of tolerance arises when there are grounds for real disagreement. Tolerance, therefore, is not merely the absence of prejudice. We sometimes say a person without prejudice is very tolerant, while those who are prejudiced are necessarily intolerant. Yet this need not be so. The prejudiced person may in fact be tolerant, if he understands his prejudices and proceeds to permit the expression of those things toward which he is prejudiced. As Crick (1973: 64) observes, "Toleration need not imply the absence of prejudice but only its constraint and limitation."

The concepts of tolerance and toleration presume a political situation in which controversies exist, people disagree, and people may be prejudiced. Given these facts, people are urged to be tolerant; they must agree to disagree.

Some notions from social psychology may be useful here. "Attitudes" are frequently defined in terms of three different elements: (1) beliefs about an object; (2) evaluations of that object; (3) behavioral orientations toward the object. People may combine such elements in any number of ways. They may, for example, combine stereotyped beliefs about an object with positive evaluations and positive behavioral orientations, or with any other combination of the two.

A "prejudiced" attitude is commonly said to combine (1) stereotyped beliefs about a group, (2) negative evaluations of the group, and (3) a predisposition to act negatively toward the group. It is sometimes argued, as noted, that the reverse of a "prejudiced" attitude is a "tolerant" one; the tolerant individual does not hold stereotyped beliefs or negative evaluations of groups and is generally disposed to act positively toward them. Jackman (1977) questions this view. Even if people hold generalized beliefs about other groups that lead to negative evaluations, it does not follow that such beliefs will lead to hostile actions. People may combine strong norms of tolerance with generally negative feelings about some groups, in which case they must be said to be prejudiced but tolerant. Thus, the prejudiced person may be either tolerant or intolerant, depending on what action he or she is prepared to take politically. Given our definition, in fact, the issue of tolerance or intolerance does not come into play *unless* one holds negative beliefs or evaluations about the group or doctrine in question.

## Tolerance and "Democratic" Norms

Another source of conceptual confusion lies in identifying tolerance with "democratic" norms or attitudes. For example, Prothro and Grigg (1960) and McClosky (1964), in studies discussed in Chapter 2, asserted that tolerance is a fundamental principle of democracy that citizens are in some way obliged to understand and accept. Thus they imply that citizens who are not fully tolerant are "undemocratic" or at least hold undemocratic beliefs. Moreover, they suggest, democratic systems may be in danger if large numbers of their citizens do not accept the principle.

However, few theorists of democracy have argued that full and universal tolerance is a requirement of a functioning democracy. Madison, for example, analyzing republicanism in *The Federalist*, seems to rely more on conflict and diversity structured by a constitutional order than on the universal acceptance of a norm of tolerance. (See the section on democratic theories below for a fuller discussion of these points.)

In addition, the implementation of universal tolerance could in some circumstances threaten the existence of democracy. To some theorists, universal tolerance requires tolerance of undemocratic groups, if these groups act within legitimate channels. Since the argument is based on principle (tolerance is "right" or "democratic") rather than on prudence (tolerance is safer or easier than intolerance), intolerance seems to be unjustified even in the face of an extreme threat by an undemocratic movement. Though one may by definition link tolerance and democracy, as a practical matter the two may be at odds.

*Tolerance: Measurement Approaches*

Tolerance can be, and has been, studied in various ways. First, it has been studied in relation to particular groups, such as communists or socialists (Stouffer, 1955). Such studies focus on attitudes toward particular dissenting groups, with tolerance implicitly understood as "tolerance for" the group or groups in question. Such inquiries serve a legitimate purpose, and through them we have learned a great deal about the extent to which the American public is tolerant of particular dissenting groups. However, these studies do not assess tolerance as a general attitude or disposition to permit the expression of opinions or interests that one opposes. In studies of attitudes toward, and tolerance of, a particular group (such as communists), it is unlikely that all respondents oppose the group equally. Thus one precondition that our more inclusive definition of tolerance requires—opposition toward the group in question—will exist for some respondents but not others. Therefore, the conclusions of such studies bear more directly on the *group* than on tolerance in a more universal sense.

Second, tolerance has been defined as acceptance of certain abstract norms of democratic procedure. The chief weakness of studies that try to address the problem at this level (McClosky, 1964) is a tendency to use abstract formulations of tolerance that do not incorporate the element of opposition implicit in the concept. In contrast to the studies that erred in tying the operationalizations of tolerance to a specific context, i.e. to attitudes toward a particular group, these latter studies have lacked any context whatsoever; respondents were merely asked to express support for general principles. Although a respondent may, in general, agree with the principle of majority rule, when the principle is applied to a specific group, the respondent's willingness to apply the principle depends on his attitude toward that group, on the form of that group's challenge to majority rule, and so on.

As we shall see, these two approaches are sometimes confused, most typically when researchers study tolerance for particular groups and proceed to draw conclusions as if they had studied tolerance as a general or inclusive attitude. In the present study, tolerance is investigated in this more inclusive sense, although we attempt to solve the problem of context. This perspective inevitably leads to the questions that we now ask about the desirability of tolerance and the role of tolerance in democratic theories.

## The Limits of Tolerance

As noted, most previous studies presume that tolerance is desirable, and many writers have implied that it provides the most fundamental prerequisite for democracy. Those who accept these assumptions have been alarmed at the results of public opinion studies showing that large numbers of Americans are intolerant of extremist political groups. Stouffer (1955), for example, in his study of public attitudes towards communists, found that large majorities believed that admitted communists should not be permitted to speak publicly or to teach in public schools. Given the above assumptions, such findings imply either that the United States is not a perfect democracy or that, if it is, tolerance is not a true requisite of democracy.

Logically, tolerance might be defended on two grounds: that it promotes the individual and social "goods" linked with the pursuit of truth, or that it is part of a package of inalienable individual private rights. Those who hold the first view argue for the open competition among political ideas and beliefs. In the United States, the value of tolerance and of the "free market of ideas" is often traced back to, and defined in terms of, Jefferson's theories. There is, for example, his frequently cited statements in "Notes on the State of Virginia" (1944) in defense of religious freedom:

> Reason and free inquiry are the only effectual agents against error . . . They are the natural enemies of error and of error only . . . It is error alone that needs the support of government. Truth can stand by itself (p. 158).

In addition, there is this clear statement from his first inaugural address, written in the wake of the battle over the Alien and Sedition Acts:

> If there be any among us who would wish to dissolve this union or to change its republican form, let them stand undisturbed as monuments of the safety with which error of opinion may be tolerated where reason is left free to combat it (p. 333).

Jefferson seems to say that the surest safeguard against error is the free trade in ideas. Tolerance of conflicting opinion is thus the best way to find the truth.

J.S. Mill, in *On Liberty,* elaborated this point, arguing that an open competition of ideas contributed to the dual ends of efficiency and individual self-development. Open competition among ideas provided the best opportunity for finding correct, and efficient, solutions to its problems. J.S. Mill also expected such competition to develop the character of citizens by making them more active, thinking beings.

As a practical question, the problem of defining the limits of tolerance has been faced most squarely by the U.S. Supreme Court in attempts to construe the First Amendment to the Constitution. Since the Court did not decide any free speech or free press cases under the First Amendment before 1900, the judicial doctrines in these areas have been modern ones. Justice Oliver Wendell Holmes has been the most forceful modern advocate of the belief that our constitutional system is based on, and thus requires, free circulation of political ideas. In his dissent in the case of *Abrams* v. *United States* (1919), he argued:

> If you have no doubt of your premises or your power and want a certain result with all your heart you naturally express your wishes in law and sweep away all opposition. To allow opposition by speech seems to indicate that you think the speech impotent, as when a man says he has squared the circle, or that you do not care wholeheartedly for the result, or that you doubt either your power or your premises. But when men have realized that time has upset many fighting faiths, they come to believe even more than they believe in the very foundations of their own conduct that the ultimate good desired is better reached by free trade in ideas—that the best test of truth is the power of the thought to get itself accepted in the competition of the market, and that truth is the only ground upon which their wishes safely can be carried out. That at any rate is the theory of our Constitution (p. 630).

Holmes's view, once controversial, is now part of the conventional wisdom. He does not argue, as do many of the writers cited earlier, that tolerance insures stable democratic government; rather, he argues that the will of the people ought to prevail. If allowed to choose freely, the people will choose something approximating the good. But he also faced the clear implication of his argument—that doctrines he hated might prevail in the "free market" of ideas. He acknowledged this in his dissent in *Gitlow* v. *New York* (1925):

> If, in the long run, the beliefs expressed in proletarian dictatorship are destined to be accepted by the dominant forces of the community,

the only meaning of free speech is that they should be given their chance and have their way (p. 673).

Though persuasive and widely accepted, this argument has its weaknesses. Are the citizens of a democracy obliged to tolerate those who, if they prevailed, would destroy the practice of tolerance? If tolerance is among the highest values in democratic regimes, does it make sense to tolerate those who threaten this very principle? These questions raise what might be called the "paradox of tolerance," because they suggest that a defense of tolerance may require some degree of intolerance.

Critics of the "free market" argument are quick to point to this paradox as its chief flaw. If intolerance should prevail in the free market, then the principle of tolerance would be defeated.[2] As Crick (1973: 64) argues, tolerance "is a value to be held among other values—such as justice, and liberty itself, but also order and truth; it can never always be right to be tolerant; there are occasions on which we should be intolerant."

One might wonder, of course, where the line between legitimate and illegitimate dissent falls, and what kinds of dissent are to be permitted on the grounds of principle and what kinds are to be discouraged on the grounds of prudence. To show that these questions are not just abstractions, we need only refer to the debate occasioned by the attempt of the American Nazi Party to stage a march in Skokie, Illinois, an episode mentioned earlier, which became the subject of an exchange between George Will, a syndicated conservative columnist, and Anrieh Neier, national Chairman of the American Civil Liberties Union, which defended the Nazis. Will, citing Berns, argued that there is no constitutional obligation to tolerate groups, like the Nazis, that would indicate violence, do gratuitous harm to the feelings of other citizens, and perhaps overturn the constitutional order itself. Neier, on the other hand, cited the appropriate quotation from Jefferson ("Reason and free inquiry are the only effectual agents against error") and argued that the only defense against intolerance is always to allow the right of dissent. By example, tolerance will demonstrate the superiority of democracy over Nazi docrines. Thus, the right of the Nazis to march in Skokie is guaranteed by the First Amendment.

It is difficult, and probably pointless, to say who won the argument. The Nazis do not hold out an attractive banner, and even the purest doctrine might be tarnished when brought to their defense. But an important principle was at stake, one that has often protected dissent from the left. The Nazis won in the courts, but at the same time the

2. On this whole point, see Berns (1976).

American Civil Liberties Union lost thousands of members, who resigned in protest.[3] Liberal opinion, which has usually defended the principle of pure tolerance, was split by the issue. By the time it was over the episode had generated some healthy reconsideration of the meaning of tolerance and the First Amendment.

The distinction between tolerance as a principle and tolerance as prudential can be clarified, in part, by its relation to other values. If tolerance is seen as a central feature of a democracy, then it ought not be compromised. The principle is pure and cannot be compromised. This argument parallels that made on the nature of free speech (e.g. the A.C.L.U. position). A breach in the principle destroys, or at least weakens, the claim of the regime and of the society as to its democratic character. However, tolerance can be seen as one of *many* important values. And, while the importance of tolerance must be respected, other important values may require accommodations by placing limits on the extent of tolerance to be practiced. Some restraints are thus justified if they are likely to preserve a balance between tolerance and other values.

The principle of tolerance remains controversial. Thoughtful people are divided in their views about the limits of tolerance in a democratic society. One way to clarify the role that political tolerance plays, or ought to play, in the political process is to show how different versions of democratic theory justify and incorporate the principle. In the next section we explore three common versions of democratic theory, each of which addresses the question of how important the principle is and how it may be sustained.

## Democratic Theories and Political Tolerance

To discuss the role of tolerance in democratic theory requires defining the latter, a difficult task given the number of theorists who have struggled with the problem and the numerous disagreements among them. In his attempt to specify the "democratic" position on tolerance of anti-democratic minorities, Mayo (1960) found little guidance from classical democratic theorists. Reviewing the work of Hobbes, Locke, and Mill, he concluded that intolerance in the name of tolerance *may* be, and *can* be, legitimate from the standpoint of democratic theory itself.

Part of the problem Mayo experienced in specifying the role of tolerance in democratic theory resulted from his seeming assumption that

3. Gibson and Bingham (1979) have recently completed a study of the responses of A.C.L.U. members to the Skokie controversy.

there is a single democratic theory. As noted above, there are many different versions of democratic theory, and the importance and role of tolerance differ for various theorists. In this analysis, we make three distinctions regarding democratic theory, without attempting to delineate carefully their historical context. We label these versions of democratic theory, with some trepidation, "liberal democratic theory," "conservative democratic theory," and "federalist" (or "constitutional") democratic theory. We include the third version, federalist democracy, mainly because it has requirements for political tolerance that differ significantly from most other liberal democratic theories.

### Liberal Democratic Theory and Political Tolerance

The major intellectual currents in eighteenth century England produced liberalism, the primary elements of which include the autonomy of the individual, the primacy of secular existence (as exemplified in utilitarianism), and the search for progress (Macpherson, 1977). Utilitarianism was not at the outset democratic, but some elements of its internal logic, along with accidents of history, led eventually to the advocacy of democracy by the elder Mill and the philosophic radicals.

The liberal idea of the autonomous individual meant more than that man should be free from the grip of tradition, dogma, and authority. It meant, after J.S. Mill in particular, that liberty was crucial to the development of human capacities. Individual autonomy linked the liberalism of the British tradition to the later enlightenment, with its similar claim that human progress would result from an unfettered human spirit. Support for the idea of tolerance followed from the enlightenment beliefs in reason, truth, and progress. Dogma, religious and political, restricted both the search for truth and free expression.

The development of the conception of individual autonomy reflected in part the decline of the universal church and its weakened ability to maintain the dominance of its doctrine. To proclaim the right of each individual to be a personal judge of matters religious and political was to declare the failure of the Church to control acceptance of its doctrine. Mill expanded this argument, asserting that only through personal exploration and experience could an individual find fullest human development. The liberal view of tolerance was broadened to say that any expression, so long as no harm is done to others, *should* be tolerated. Beginning with *religious tolerance,* the general argument was advanced that no existing religious or political institutions could or should impose religious homogeneity of belief and expression.

The liberals, then, saw toleration as a desirable protection of individual autonomy. They also believed toleration, encouraging the open competition among ideas, would allow the "truth" to emerge. Although we cannot apply Mill's analysis directly to the modern situation without wrenching his arguments violently out of their context (since Mill was advocating individualism in Victorian England), we can see in these arguments the germ of "the free market place of ideas." The modern liberal, following Mill, believes that a free market of ideas will compel wrong opinion to yield to the power of fact and argument. Suppressed opinions may ultimately be true, whereas the authority claiming infallibility may assert false ideas. Tolerance is to be valued, therefore, on both moral (individual rights) and pragmatic (truth will emerge) grounds, precisely those Mill advocated.

In modern times, the major liberal concern has been to protect the rights of unpopular political groups, since in most modern democracies the right of religious liberty has not been threatened. So although the precise concerns of modern liberalism differ from Mill's, as they must, given the vastly different historical context, the grounds for tolerance are essentially unchanged. Tolerance is central in liberal democratic theory, and although it may be legitimately limited, it must be broadly protected in order to preserve the liberal character of society.

### The Liberal Solution to Political Intolerance

The idea of human progress, as noted, was used to justify and legitimize liberalism. In both *On Liberty* and *Considerations on Representative Government,* John Stuart Mill argued that freedom develops human intelligence and personality. Rational thinking and the exercise of political responsibilities will gradually improve human nature and the human condition. Progress is more than the increase in material wealth provided by industrialization. Material wealth fosters human development, meeting the needs for clothing, housing, and food, so that man can develop higher capacities, and reducing fundamental conflicts resulting from great inequities of wealth. More importantly, human development also follows from the exercise of rationality (fostered by the increasing availability of education) and participation. Such development must be active, following from the actual exercise of judgment and experience. So, in addition to tolerance democracy must guarantee education and experience. The wider the suffrage, the more people are required to exercise political and rational capacities, whatever their current level of competence.

Liberal theorists like J.S. Mill were not unmindful of the risks in calling for widespread individual involvement and participation. Mill suggested a variety of "hedges" against possible excesses of popular power, such as plural voting by the educated and other more respected segments of society, and only gradually exposing political institutions to citizens' demands. Nonetheless he believed that democracy, toleration, and individualism would finally lead to a better world, as human development was stimulated by participation in the economic and political marketplaces. According to this logic, as individuals pursued their self-interest (whether political, social, or economic), they would acquire greater rationality, permitting the restraints on complete participation to be eased. Tolerance is crucial to protect these developing human capacities of responsibility and judgment.

The later work of J.S. Mill implies the hypothesis that people would become less concerned with material necessities and more attuned to principles and ideals as this developmental process took place. This projected development permitted democrats to argue that class conflicts would not render a democracy unworkable. Thus, Mill meets the primary objection to democracy—mob rule that would destroy culture, property, and capital—by gradually extending political power to the population as it acquires sophistication through participation and education. As he claims in *On Liberty:*

> though individuals may not do the particular thing so well, on the average, as the officers of government, it is nevertheless desirable that it should be done by them, rather than by the government, as a means to their own mental education—a mode of strengthening their active faculties, exercising their judgment, and giving them a familiar knowledge of the subjects with which they are thus left to deal (p. 133).

Through the practice of democracy humans can develop political skill and judgment (but see Mansbridge, 1980).

Since in Mill's era the political tolerance required for the full development of these faculties did not exist, it had to be created. Mill believed that education and participation would generate greater understanding both of political norms and of other participants, pointing up the need for moderation and cooperation to build majorities. Thus, the influence of both education and participation would reduce intolerance.

However, certainly Mill, and De Tocqueville as well, were aware that the lower classes lacked some political competence; their full, and immediate participation would have the effect of increasing conflict and, in turn, intolerance. Initially, the working class would not recognize that they shared with the capitalists an interest in the development of industrial society. Thus, conflicts between the working class and the capitalists, especially if the working class came to power, may produce a partisan conflict that puts continued industrial growth at risk. These theorists hoped that, over time, the moderating influences of education and participation would negate the disruptive potential of mass political involvement.

Education and participation should create individuals with the ability to understand the interests of others and to conceive of the best interests of the entire society. This expectation can become an empirical question, readily amenable to empirical analysis. The hypothesis is that those with more education and who participate more should be personally more tolerant of disliked groups and more supportive of tolerance as a general principle. Moreover, these relationships should be strong enough to produce, sooner or later, a tolerant electorate, which would remain so even in circumstances where intolerance would be most tempting.

In summary, then, tolerance plays a major role in liberal democratic theory. Tolerance ensures the opportunity to express unpopular opinion without fear of reprisal. The precise limits of tolerance are unclear, although it is reasonable to assume that in a mature democracy these limits ought to be elastic. Gradually, mass education, an extended franchise, and increased participation in the political process will lead to a higher degree of tolerance. At present, given broader educational opportunities and reasonably free access to political participation, one might expect widespread tolerance in the United States. One might also expect variations in political tolerance to be strongly related to educational level and political involvement. A liberal program to abolish the remaining vestiges of intolerance would therefore expand both educational and participatory opportunities. However, even if opportunities for widespread participation currently exist, as liberals claim, it is clear that, with few exceptions, the mass public does not take fullest advantage of these opportunities, certainly not to the extent that Mill envisioned. Mill seemingly had day-to-day political involvement, not merely occasional acts of voting in mind. Although mass education has reached levels undreamed of in Mill's time, superficial participation limited to occasional voting may mitigate the benefits of education and retard the development of tolerance.

## Conservative Democratic Theory and Political Tolerance

The momentous events of the twentieth century—the rise of fascism and authoritarian regimes, the outbreak of World War II, and the use of "popular" regimes to sustain tyrannies—scarcely seemed to confirm the optimism of nineteenth century British liberalism. Moreover, these events gave credence to the new exponents of a "realistic," and factually based, science of politics: Mosca, Pareto, and, in the United States, Joseph Schumpeter.

Three major themes run through this new, conservative theory, although of course various thinkers reflect these themes differently. First, the science of politics studies political organizations and asserts that such organizations do not, or cannot, be run democratically, but rather become oligarchies. This conclusion is most important in the work of Mosca and Pareto. Large-scale western industrial societies require large bureaucracies. Representative government precludes widespread participation. Elites, who share expertise, information, and common interest, will always dominate organizations and make impossible the development of pure democracies.

Second, the scientific approach concludes that the proper focus of political scientists must be on democracy as it actually operates. Thus, democracy properly involves the control and replacement of competing elites. Since oligarchy will always predominate, democracy simply defined as rule of the people is not possible and democratic regimes must exist by counterposing elites against each other and forcing them to compete for public support. This redefinition is at the heart of Joseph Schumpeter's *Capitalism, Socialism and Democracy* (1950):

> democracy does not mean and cannot mean that the people actually rule in any obvious sense of the terms "people" and "rule." Democracy means only that the people have the opportunity of accepting or refusing the men who are to rule them. But since they might decide this in entirely undemocratic ways, we have had to narrow our definition by adding a further criterion identifying the definition method, viz., free competition among the would-be leaders for the vote of the electorate (pp. 284–285).

Third, some of these conservative theorists fear that the workers and lower classes in a democracy will be able to use their numbers to make excessive demands that the economy cannot meet or that overburden the political system. Indeed, the view that the lower orders are destructive and must be restrained by the enlightened orders has a long tradition in conservative thought (Halebsky, 1975).

In short, the optimistic expectations of liberal democrats were rejected. In the face of a world war and the development of totalitarian movements, a new concern for realism arose. Fascism, especially the Nazi overthrow of the Weimar Republic and the fall of the Spanish Republic, served to warn conservative democrats of the need to protect democracy, and made them realize that mass mobilization could be used by an authoritarian cadre to create a mass society under central control (Kornhauser, 1959).

In America, Walter Lippmann (1955) argued that public opinion was not, and could not be, sufficiently competent to provide guidance (particularly in foreign affairs) for political leaders because:

> In ordinary circumstances voters cannot be expected to transcend their particular, localized and self-regarding opinions. As well expect men laboring in the valley to see the land from the mountain top (p. 39).

This argument provides insight into the differences between what we have labeled the liberal and the conservative theories of democracy. One central distinction between these two views reflects the concept of personality, especially as it relates to politics.

J.S. Mill took the position, not shared by all liberal theorists, that men could develop a capacity for reason and intellectual growth under favorable conditions. With time, experience, and education most people would be able to develop the skills of citizenship. Mill was guarded in his optimism about how well and how rapidly this process would occur; hence his proposed restrictions of the franchise and plans for multiple voting. Nonetheless, he clearly believed that mankind was capable of improvement through political participation and education. In his analysis, the proper framework for evaluating mass electorates would be within a developmental context.

The conservative theory, by contrast, typically adopts a "trait" view of personality: certain enduring characteristics typify human actions and attitudes. The most widely known studies of this type are those on "the authoritarian personality" (Adorno et al., 1950), "tough-tendermindedness" (Eysenck, 1954), and "dogmatism" (Rokeach, 1960). Adults can be located along these dimensions, as authoritarian (or not), toughminded (or tenderhearted) or dogmatic (or not). These attributes are related to the behavior and attitudes of the individuals. The proper framework for evaluating mass electorates is within a descriptive context (i.e., differences in traits within a cross-sectional comparison). The expectation is that only massive generational changes over time would fundamentally alter any distributions of traits, since mature adults would not ordinarily change their personality types. This assumption leads to a focus on primary socialization, the creation of trait characteristics in early childhood. By contrast, the participatory or citizenship oriented liberal democratic theory is more concerned with secondary socialization, the acquisition of capacities in adulthood.

The conservative theory finds that anti-democratic and other undesirable traits, frequently labeled pathological, are correlated with social isolation. Because the lower classes are more likely to be isolated in various ways, they remain ill-equipped for citizenship while the middle and upper classes have successfully adapted to society.

Lipset (1960) noted, for example:

> Both evidence and theory suggest, however, that the lower strata are relatively more authoritarian, that (again, other things being equal) they will be more attached to an extremist movement than to a moderate and democratic one, and that, once recruited, they will not be alienated by its lack of democracy, while more educated and sophisticated supporters will tend to drop away (p. 92).

And:

> A number of elements contribute to authoritarian predispositions in lower class individuals. Low education, low participation in political or voluntary organizations of any type, little reading, isolated occupations, economic insecurity, and authoritarian family patterns are some of the most important (pp. 100–101).

Since in conservative theory traits tend to be enduring and fixed, the value placed on participation by J.S. Mill, and more recent liberal theorists like Pateman and Bachrach, seems to conflict with regime legitimacy and political stability. Mobilization of the lower classes would bring into politics those ill-equipped for citizenship. According to Elms (1976):

> The passive alienated and the uninterested should not be completely ignored, on the assumption that they won't bother anyone if they're left alone . . . But insisting that they vote will not lessen their hostility and ignorance, and by the time other efforts to improve the quality of their participation begin to take effect, our government may have suffered major wounds by these reluctant balloters (p. 25).

On these grounds, Schumpeter and others argue that democracy must limit its expectations of the mass citizenry to choices among competing elites. The professional politician has the responsibility to guide citizen choices and to create proper democratic behavior. Since the citizenry in general is not sophisticated or tolerant, and is unlikely to become so under conceivable circumstances, these theorists argue for "minimalist democracy."

Thus, conservative democratic theory does not *require* high levels of tolerance among the citizenry, particularly of extremist ideas and groups, such as communists and fascists. The mass public must tolerate a dissenting elite, but not necessarily *all* dissenting elites, nor is it necessary to tolerate a dissenting mass movement. The conservatives are more likely to set specific limits on tolerance, such as those Mayo noted, arguing that to enjoy civil liberties one must give allegiance to them. If one opposes democracy, one forfeits one's right to protection under its rules.

It was for these reasons that political scientists in the 1950s found some reasurrance in the fact that those who were alienated tended not to participate. Lipset (1960), Prothro and Grigg (1960), Berelson (1954), and Dahl (1961), all argued that the apathetic were more likely to be authoritarian and ignorant of the "rules of the game." The low levels of participation by these people thus seems fortuitous, because it is beneficial to the democratic character of the regime.

In summary, then, the conservative democratic theorists do not require broad tolerance, even in a relatively mature, stable democratic regime. They do not expect high levels of tolerance in the mass public; nor do they believe that democracy requires these high levels. Their theories require tolerance only for a dissenting, but loyal, elite that can resist the tendency of the governing elite to abuse its power.

## The Conservative Solution to Political Intolerance

Conservatives reject the possibility for dramatic changes in human nature that underlies the liberal solution. As a consequence, they do not believe education and participation can create a tolerant society. What we are calling conservative theory thus would argue for a link between education and understanding the norms of democracy (accepting the link between education and tolerance), but it would tend to reject any causal connection between participation and tolerance. Political participation will not transform human nature, but it simply reveals it.

Thus conservative theorists must search for the right level of political participation. There must be sufficient participation to legitimate the political regime and government policies, but excessive participation will involve those who do not understand or accept the political norms or the applications of civil liberties.

Empirically, the conservative approach would also lead us to expect some correlation between participation and education and increased political tolerance. However, these correlations reflect selective recruitment processes whereby the political leadership brings into greater activity those who subscribe to the creed of political tolerance. Participation does not cause tolerance; nor does education create a politically tolerant electorate. The strongest relationships should exist between political tolerance and measures of privilege. The most successful and competent segments of the community should be those who have demonstrated vision and discipline. Members of the higher strata should support the norms of political tolerance. Therefore such measures as occupational prestige, income, social class, and education should be positively correlated with measures of political tolerance. Concurrently, members of the privileged strata are also more likely to have psychological traits that sustain political tolerance: openness, flexibility, and a democratic personality structure. Conservative theorists thus expect tolerance to correlate with education, participation, class privilege, and personality characteristics. The crucial underlying causal process generating tolerance is, however, social class background and privilege, so that correlations between personality and participation on one hand, and tolerance on the other, are spurious and will disappear once social class is controlled.

The "solution" to intolerance, then, is to construct barriers to participation such that only those properly prepared will be able to participate meaningfully. These elites will then be free to govern with only minimal citizen control, although to maintain a democratic system there must be a reasonably free competing elite. Furthermore, since the conservatives' underlying assumptions about human nature are pessimistic, there is no expected developmental progression toward more meaningful mass participation.

## Federalist Democratic Theory and Political Tolerance

Each of the previous approaches—the classic liberal and the conservative—attempts to mitigate the threat posed by political intolerance with a variation of the same solution. The liberal version envisages a transformation of human nature. This "new citizen," through political participation and education, will be virtuous, setting aside the temptations of selfish interest in favor of common interests, and learning to tolerate opposing political views. Politics and conflict will continue, but within the constraints imposed by the commitment of the electorate to creeds of moderation and tolerance.

The conservative variant displays an aristocratic bias. *Universal* transformation of human nature is too much to expect. However, virtue *can* exist among professional politicians and among the more highly educated and more responsible segments of the public. So long as the political system relies on these "virtuous" groups, their commitment to the common good and to civil liberties will be sufficient to offset the selfish and intolerant instincts of the apathetic masses. Behavior motivated by ideals and by tolerance is possible, but only among the higher political strata—those trained to rule; for the remainder of society self-interest and intolerance are likely to prevail.

Both solutions reflect the fear of a tyrannical majority. If virtue is not inherent in humankind's political nature, then emerging majorities may be tempted not only selfishly to disregard the interests of others but also, intolerantly, to punish those who have opposed them. Both liberals and conservatives place confidence in the virtue of those with political power to resist such tyrannical majorities.

In short, both liberal and conservative theories subscribe to the following general views of democracy. In democracies, conflicting parties must have the right to engage in politics, within the bounds of what is legal and civil. Each party must be able to continue legal opposition after any particular determination of public policy. Opposition must be a legitimate activity. However, the nature of conflict is to divide, and the more serious the conflict the greater the division between the sides. Winners may wish to punish those who opposed them, while losers may seek revenge on those who defeated them. This is particularly true if the conflict is heavily weighted with moral or ideological content, as with racial or religious issues. Since such conflicts tend to inflame the participants, democracy must keep them within the limits of legitimate political procedures. The creed of political tolerance is one means to protect access for all participants. If everyone in the political system understood and respected civil liberties and tolerance, all parties to any conflict would know that even intense and sustained conflict did not justify punitive action. Only when the norms of tolerance withstand such temptation, will the right of opposition be sustained by the political culture of the society.

Both the liberal and conservative models attribute the norms of tolerance to a set of political actors and then rely on that group's sufficient authority and power to preserve the norms against threats. The conservative view located this virtue in political leaders, while the liberal position finds it among followers as well as leaders.

What we will call the "federal" (or constitutional) model, in contrast to both the liberal and conservative models, protects against intolerance without assuming that any group will be virtuous. Madison did not rely on the virtue of either citizens or elites. Indeed, while many of the federalists hoped the electorate would select the best candidates for office, they did not expect the leaders' virtue to protect against intolerance. Virtuous leaders would not always be at the helm. Madison (*Federalist* 51) asserted that the division of government into "distinct and separate departments" protects against oppression:

In a free government, the security for civil rights must be the same as for religious rights. It consists in the one case in the multiplicity of interests, and in the other, in the multiplicity of sects. The degree of security in both cases will depend on the number of interests and sects; and this may be presumed to depend on the extent of the country and the number of people comprehended under the same government (pp. 351–352).

Thus a natural diversity of sects and interests, aided by a constitutional order that counterposes these conflicting interests by diffusing power and *then* requiring majorities to enact policies, sets ambition (selfish interest) against ambition. These processes of conflict protect the regime and the norms of tolerance. The rules (the federal constitutional order) provide for numerous offices, each requiring separate election, thereby requiring sustained and numerous political victories to gain control of government. The elections are held at different times, in different localities, and with different constituencies; the regime is divided into levels (the federal system), and into relatively independent executive, legislative, and judicial branches. These rules give various interests a role in government, where they can use the norms of tolerance to protect themselves and their allies. Since power is divided, and likely to be so in the future, political opponents are protected by their political victories and by their value as allies in future conflicts. Self-interest encourages respect for today's opponents, since they may be tomorrow's allies. Thus, the norms of tolerance are protected not by a commitment to an ideal creed, to be applied against the temptation of self-interest, but by setting interest against interest.

In this model, participation need not be limited: the more numerous and diverse the involved interests, the greater the need for allies in political coalitions. The norm of tolerance becomes entrenched in a political system that sets self-interest against self-interest, and that gives partial, not complete, victories. In such a federalist system, no faction is likely to gain complete control of the government, and shifting political fortunes require the continual re-formation of political majorities.

The famous constitutional "auxiliary precautions" also provide an additional safeguard should the system of "checks and balances" fail. Special insulated institutions (the law, and ultimately the Supreme Court) may protect the norms of tolerance. These institutions do not normally engage in direct political conflict, but they can be asked to intervene by one side or the other if the constitutional order or civil liberties are threatened. In this limited sense, then, "virtue" does play a role. The auxiliary precautions are not fully democratic. The Supreme Court is neither elected nor directly subject to review by the democratic institutions of the political system. These institutions can guard the norms of tolerance and civil liberties, but only to the extent that it can gain support and acceptance from other branches of government.

The weakest link in the federal model's solution is its assumption that most controversy is supra-local. Certainly as conflict grows, participants are usually forced to moderate their views to deal effectively with those who are apathetic or opposed to them. But at the local level, there may not be sufficient protection for the rights of the minority, particularly on issues that do not generate national or regional attention. The auxiliary protection of some outside intervention by the courts or by interested outsiders (e.g. the A.C.L.U.) is most likely to be needed in just such situations.[4]

In summary, therefore, the federalist theory, a special case of liberal democratic theory, does not require a high degree of tolerance from either the mass electorate or the political leadership. It requires only diversity and the decentralization of political power. Of course, Madison was concerned with a tyranny of the majority that might destroy legitimate property rights. Today we are primarily concerned with the protection of extremist groups and ideologies, i.e., tolerance of the extremes by the center. However, Madison's theory still applies to the modern problem of tolerance. A federalist theory of tolerance requires only that the targets of whatever intolerance does exist should be diverse. In other words, although a significant portion of the mass public may be intolerant of some ideas or groups, citizen hostility ought not to concentrate on particular groups or ideas. When citizen hostility is dispersed, ordinary politics will moderate mass sentiments of intolerance, given the practical necessity to forge a majority on other issues. If intolerance is directed at many targets, the federal constitutional order will protect the civil liberties of all. The same logic applies to political elites, who need not adopt the norms of tolerance, so long as they are unable to reach agreement about whom to repress.

*The Federalist Solution to Political Intolerance*

The above discussion presents intolerance as an undifferentiated concept, almost as an expected feature of political life. However, in-

4. Yet when a national majority is united in an intolerant attitude toward a particular group, these auxiliary precautions may not be sufficient safeguards. The federal model attempts to inhibit the development of such majorities, particularly spontaneous popular movements, yet it does not provide certain guarantees. The federal system may be inadequate by itself in modern society, with rapid and ready communications and shared social and political values (recall that Madison saw the virtue in the size of the American Republic in guaranteeing heterogeneity of attitudes, interests and values).

tolerance may vary greatly in intensity or reach. The major danger is that the members of the majority may not only be intolerant, but may also agree on a single target for intolerance.

For the federalist solution to work, numerous interests must not easily agree on the targets of their intolerance. Diversity produces factions and conflict. Factions and conflict produce a multiplicity of these targets. As the conflict heightens, the distinctions among targets will usually be sustained. Then, the diversity of interests must be reconciled through the politics of moderation and compromise, and the tyranny of the majority is unlikely since the political processes would "check and balance" the various factions.

In its twentieth century application, federalist democratic theory assumes, or at least is not inconsistent with a good deal of political intolerance. But it also assumes that intolerance is target-specific and, in a diverse society, will be directed toward a wide range of target groups. The theory makes no assumptions about the individual attributes that will be associated with levels of political intolerance. With its emphasis on interests and faction, it does, however, seem to suggest that economic and social concerns would be major determinants of target group selection. That is, without taking the view that economics determines political action, Madison did recognize the powerful influence of occupational and economic interests in creating factions and interest groups. One might therefore expect that different factions would select different targets, and that therefore social class and economic variables will correlate with individuals' selection of target groups.

## Summary and Conclusions

Tolerance implies a willingness to permit the expression of those ideas or interests that one opposes; it thus presumes opposition. To allow expression of doctrines with which one agrees, or to which one is indifferent, does not manifest political tolerance. Therefore, any attempt to measure tolerance must first determine the presence of opposition. The next chapter reviews and assesses recent empirical studies on political tolerance from this theoretical perspective. Chapter 3 presents a measurement strategy which flows directly from our definition of tolerance.

The concept of tolerance is important in democratic theory, in its several variants: liberal, conservative, and federalist. Liberal democratic theory assigns a significant role to political tolerance, and although absolute tolerance is not required, considerable tolerance of unpopular opinion is. Tolerance is highly valued in liberal democracy, both on moral grounds, as a recognition of equal rights for all citizens, and on the pragmatic grounds that the free market of ideas is the best means toward the discovery of "truth." Consistent with the liberal idea of progress, liberal democracy assumes that tolerance will increase as education and the opportunities for widespread, meaningful participation in the political process increase. Thus tolerance should increase over time, since education clearly has increased, and more broadly distributed educational experiences should enhance the capacity for widespread political participation. For individuals, liberal theories predict that both level of education and of political participation will be the principal correlates of political tolerance.

Conservative democratic theories, by contrast, assign a smaller role to political tolerance. Although they allow for progress among an elite class, these theories assume that the average citizen cannot surmount a limited capacity to govern. Furthermore, many citizens have intolerant impulses that they may unleash if given the opportunity. Because such action would destroy democracy, the best solution is to train an elite to govern and protect a democratic regime from the undemocratic masses. Thus in conservative theory, tolerance of unpopular opinion is not expected of the mass public, and tolerance of dangerous opinion is not necessarily valued. At the aggregate level, conservative theorists do not necessarily expect tolerance to increase over time, even as levels of education increase. It is social privilege—the appropriate class background and training for leadership—that ought to produce "reasonable tolerance," not merely increased levels of participation or of education. At the individual level, any relationship between political participation and tolerance should be spurious, a result of class background and personality, not of the direct effects of participation *per se*.

Federalist democratic theory expects political tolerance to be the result of diversity and of constitutional arrangements, not of progress, education, or even class background. Although tolerance is important in federalist theory, mainly on prudential grounds, high levels of tolerance of unpopular opinion are not expected of either the political leaders or the citizenry. Democratic protection from the intolerant acts of both citizens and leaders comes from diversity and from decentralized or shared power. The heterogeneous electorate has different and widely varying targets of intolerance, and is thus unable to agree about which unpopular groups or opinions to repress. Furthermore, it may sometimes be necessary to treat as allies groups against which one may have a tendency to direct one's intolerance. The necessity for building coalitions prevents total *attacks* against any group or interest. For society as a whole, then, federalist theory expects that intolerance rather than tolerance will be the norm, but that the targets of intolerance will be widely distributed. For individuals, the expectation is that demographic variables will not correlate with tolerance, although since interests are defined mainly along demographic lines, these factors may correlate with target group selection. That is, different socio-economic groups will undoubtedly select different targets for intolerance.

Our analysis will shed some light on the empirical plausibility of applying these three theories of democracy to contemporary American society. Although the empirical analysis that follows contains numerous shortcomings, it allows a crude test of the plausibility of the differing assumptions about political tolerance that are implied by these theories. Tentative conclusions will be offered about the validity of each theory, at least regarding the treatment of political tolerance. Thus we examine such issues as the aggregate distribution of target groups within the society as a whole, and within various demographic groups; the aggregate distributions of tolerance and intolerance; and individual level correlates and determinants of tolerance. Among the latter, sets of sociological, psychological, and political variables that theoretically ought to affect tolerance are examined. We begin, however, with a detailed examination of previous empirical efforts.

# Political Tolerance and American Politics: The Empirical Literature

Because tolerance is a theoretically important concept in democratic regimes, it has been the subject of numerous empirical studies in the generation since the development of survey research. These studies, insofar as they deal with the United States, have tried to determine the extent to which Americans support the principles of tolerance and to assess the condition of American democracy itself. This literature has been central to the development of empirical democratic theory, since tolerance can be studied empirically and is also clearly connected to theories of democracy, no matter how problematic that connection might be. In coming to grips with this literature, then, it is important to keep separate the empirical issues regarding public beliefs about tolerance and the more difficult claims regarding the connections between tolerance and democracy. As we shall see, this literature reveals a temptation to use empirical findings to judge the quality of American politics without considering the theoretical problems that such judgments involve.

We can point to six important studies of tolerance in America spanning the past two and one-half decades: Stouffer's (1955) study of attitudes toward communists; the Prothro-Grigg (1960) study of political tolerance; McClosky's (1964) study of support for democratic norms; Lawrence's (1976) study of relationships between political tolerance and attitudes toward dissenters; Davis's (1975) study testing Stouffer's predictions about the effects of generation, age, and education on tolerance toward communists and atheists; and the Nunn et al. (1978) extensive replication of Stouffer's study. In addition, a number of other studies pursue the implications of these major works or explore the problem of tolerance from a less political perspective.

The six studies are especially worthy of attention because they draw some important conclusions about the way democracy in America actually operates. Because their conclusions are based upon empirical findings, close attention should be given to the way they were executed and to the evidence on which their conclusions rest. In a sense, these studies represent a single tradition of research, since all incorporate in one way or another Stouffer's original assumptions. Hence, common problems of conceptualization and measurement occur. Furthermore, all presume that political tolerance is good, and that any significant deviation in the society from an absolute standard of tolerance is undesirable. We have already noted that this view is problematic, yet nearly all these studies assume that intolerant attitudes threaten the very existence of democracy. Since many citizens have been found to hold such attitudes, these researchers are forced to conclude either that democracy is in jeopardy or that some other factor preserves the system in the face of this threat. Such conclusions follow more from the original assumptions concerning democracy than from the empirical findings, and in this sense they are not fully justified by these findings.

As noted earlier, it is important to keep these empirical and normative domains separate, since it is very easy to confound them. We know that public beliefs about dissent and opposition are important in any regime that presumes to be democratic. We can treat these beliefs seriously through careful measurement of concepts and relationships, which are the principal objectives of any empirical analysis. Disciplined speculation about the theoretical meaning of these relationships is important, though necessarily difficult. The precise relationship between tolerant norms and democratic politics cannot be settled easily by an empirical analysis, particularly one that uses individuals as units of analysis. In any case, such a judgment will depend on our prior understanding of democracy and must vary to some extent depending on practical circumstances. In reviewing these studies, then, we shall try to keep separate these problems of evidence and inference.

## Communism, Conformity, and Civil Liberties

As we have already noted, the earliest systematic study of political tolerance in the United States was Stouffer's (1955) analysis of public attitudes toward communism and communists, titled *Communism, Conformity, and Civil Liberties*. Based on a large national survey conducted in 1954, the study measured public attitudes toward communism and the extent to which Americans were prepared to extend procedural rights to communists and suspected communists. It also examined attitudes toward two other groups on the left, atheists and socialists. Though Stouffer purported to study tolerance of "non-conformity," all but four of the fifteen items used to measure tolerance used communists or suspected communists as points of reference.[1] Stouffer's conclusions, therefore, bear more closely on tolerance of communists than on tolerance more broadly understood.

Nevertheless, his findings were important and, to many, disturbing. Substantial majorities said that an admitted communist should not be permitted to speak publicly, or to teach in high schools or colleges, or, indeed, to work as a clerk in a store (Stouffer, 1955: Chapter 2). Majorities also agreed that communists should have their citizenship revoked, that books written by communists should be taken out of public libraries, that the government should have the authority to tap personal telephone conversations to acquire evidence against communists, and that admitted communists should be thrown in jail. These attitudes softened considerably when the same questions were posed about socialists, atheists, and those merely suspected of being communists. However, large numbers of citizens responded intolerantly to these targets as well. These results must be interpreted against the background of the McCarthy period, but they did undermine the assumption asserted by some political scientists that there exists a consensus in the society around procedural norms that guarantees all groups access to political institutions. In short, Stouffer's findings indicated that a majority of American citizens did not accept the doctrine of the "free market-place of ideas."

In addition to mapping these public attitudes, Stouffer also attempted to identify factors most closely associated with tolerance and intolerance. The two most important were education and perceptions of threat from dissenting groups. Education, in particular, was strongly related to his measure of tolerance; the higher the level of education, the greater the tolerance. Education, he argued (Chapter 4), exposes citizens to a greater range of opinions and gives them the ability to evaluate information. Hence, to the extent that intolerance reflects fear of the unknown and conclusions drawn from false information, education works to form a more tolerant outlook. Looking to the future, Stouffer suggested that tolerant norms would eventually become more common

1. The items used to construct the cumulative scale of "willingness to tolerate non-conformists" are listed in Appendix C to *Communism, Conformity, and Civil Liberties.* Of the fifteen items used to construct the scale, eleven referred to communists or suspected communists. The other four referred to atheists and those advocating government ownership of "railroads and big industries." See Appendix C, pp. 262–269, as well as Stouffer's discussion of the scale in the text, pp. 49–54.

in American society as more and more citizens pursued advanced education. Speculations aside, the conclusion that education influences tolerance has become the most durable generalization in this whole area of inquiry, and has been replicated in virtually every subsequent study of tolerance (see Prothro and Grigg, 1960; Jackman, 1972; Nunn et al., 1978: Chapter 4).[2]

A second important variable was the degree to which individuals felt communism to be an internal danger to the security of the nation. As expected, those who did not see communism as a major domestic threat were much more likely to be tolerant than those who did see it as a threat. This suggested that citizens were prepared to trade-off tolerance against other political values, and that levels of tolerance at a given time depend upon contextual factors, such as the perceived threat posed by opposition groups (which is presumably related in some way to objective conditions). Given the politics of that period, then, it is not surprising that levels of tolerance of communists were quite low.[3]

Stouffer also discovered several other variables that were related to tolerance of non-conformity (as he understood it). Women, for example, tended to be less tolerant than men, even when controls were introduced, one at a time, for education, occupation, place of residence, and religion and religiosity. Stouffer was thus unable to explain fully these consistent differences between men and women. Religiosity was also related to tolerance, as those who attended church regularly were less tolerant than those who did not. People living in cities tended to be more tolerant than those living in rural areas, and those living outside the South were much more tolerant than southerners. In addition, younger citizens were generally more tolerant than older ones. Finally, Stouffer suggested, though he could not prove it, that personality type is related to tolerance of non-conformity. Those who were optimistic about the future tended to be more tolerant than those who were pessimistic, and those who were tolerant of ambiguity tended to be more tolerant of political non-conformists than those who understood events and people in terms of rigid categories (pp. 94–101).[4]

Perhaps Stouffer's most important finding, from the standpoint of democratic theory, was that political elites tended to be more tolerant

2. For a dissenting view on this relationship, see Jackman (1978), who found little relationship between education and support for school integration policies. However, support for such policies is not the same thing as tolerance or support for the rules of democratic procedure, so this finding is only marginally relevant here. The reader is also directed to the further discussion of education and tolerance in Chapter 5.

3. The relationship between threat and tolerance is discussed further in Chapter 7.

4. All of these findings are reviewed in relation to our own data in Chapters 5 and 6.

on the average than a national cross-section of non-elites. By nearly every measure, political influentials were more likely than rank-and-file citizens to recognize the procedural claims of these dissenting groups. From this finding Stouffer concluded that elites are in a unique position to educate the public about the value of tolerant norms and that in the future support for civil liberties would depend upon such efforts. At the same time, this implied that the functioning of a democratic system may depend more on the acceptance of the "rules of the game" among elites than among citizens at large, since the latter do not participate in the day-to-day life of politics.

Stouffer did not pursue this argument, but we can see that his findings fit nicely with the view of democracy developed by Schumpeter and others (see our Chapter 1). If ordinary citizens are less respectful of the "rules of the game" than political elites, their participation in the day-to-day activities of government may be undesirable. Viewed this way, the threat to democratic stability in the United States, and in other democracies as well, comes not from elites bent on increasing their power, but from ordinary citizens who do not understand the procedural requirements of democracy. Leaving aside the normative merits of this theory, it now appears that too much has been made of Stouffer's empirical findings regarding differences between masses and elites. Jackman's (1972) reanalysis of Stouffer's data shows that the differences between masses and elites in these samples reflected, almost entirely, differences in educational levels. That is, elites were more tolerant, on the average, because they tended to be more highly educated. Jackman's analysis thus suggested that there is nothing in elite status that, in and of itself, causes one to be more tolerant.[5]

Stouffer's conclusions about tolerance in the United States, however, were much more optimistic than his empirical findings at first glance seemed to warrant. He suggested that tolerant norms in the society would inevitably grow stronger as time passed. The reasons for this optimism were summed up in his conclusion to *Communism, Conformity, and Civil Liberties*.

> Great social, economic, and technological forces are operating slowly and imperceptibly on the side of spreading tolerance. The rising level of education and the accompanying decline in authoritarian child-

5. St. Peter et al. (1977) have criticized Jackman's reinterpretation of Stouffer's data on methodological grounds, claiming that the original differences found by Stouffer between mass and elite samples cannot be fully explained in terms of demographic differences between the two samples. After reinterpreting the data again, they claim that the evidence still supports the existence of a tolerant elite stratum. See, in turn, Jackman's (1977) response to these critics.

rearing practices increase independence of thought and respect for others whose ideas are different. The increasing geographical movement of people has a similar consequence, as well as the vicarious experiences supplied by the magic of our ever more powerful media of communications (p. 236).

Despite his alarming findings, then, Stouffer concluded that the intolerance of the early 1950s would gradually abate in the face of social and economic change.

Stouffer's study remains impressive for the care and thoroughness with which it explores the problem of political tolerance. Many of its conclusions have become "conventional wisdom" about American politics and have influenced subsequent studies of public attitudes on civil liberties. In its own way, this study remains a model for the way in which empirical research can address important political and social issues. Yet, because Stouffer's conclusions have been so influential and because his conceptualization of tolerance and his methodology for measuring it have been adopted by so many other investigators, it is important to reconsider his analysis critically. Stouffer acknowledged at several points that he was not studying tolerance as a general attitude but rather tolerance toward the particular groups mentioned in his questionnaire. For example, he says at one point:

> Let us continually keep in mind the fact that we are not here measuring tolerance, in general. Rather, we are measuring willingness to grant certain rights to people whose views might be disapproved, such as the right to speak, the right to hold certain kinds of jobs, etc. The kinds of people used as test cases are Socialists, atheists, Communists, and people whose loyalty has been criticized but who avow they were never Communists. We are not measuring willingness to tolerate other kinds of people whose views may be disliked (p. 111).

This caveat was certainly warranted. Nevertheless, his warning seems to have been generally ignored and many people interpreted his conclusions as bearing on tolerance as a general phenomenon. It is well to remember, however, that Stouffer claimed that he was studying "tolerance of non-conformity," a more general attribute than the quotation above suggests.

The consequences of this confusion are significant. The groups mentioned in Stouffer's questionnaire—communists, socialists, and atheists—are all leftist. It might be assumed, therefore, that it would have been easier for respondents on the left to be tolerant of these groups than it would have been for respondents on the right. This suggests that Stouffer's methodology makes it easy to confound tolerance with respondents' political beliefs on other matters. That is to say, the responses to his questions probably reflected citizens' attitudes toward communists, socialists, and atheists as much as their commitment to tolerant political norms. We do not know what the results would have been if Stouffer had asked respondents about comparable groups on the right, such as the Ku Klux Klan or the American Nazi Party. We might speculate that he would have found even higher levels of intolerance had he done so, since those tolerant of communists, atheists, and socialists might have been intolerant of targets on the right. Thus, it is important to remember Stouffer's own warning that his findings bear only on tolerance of these groups on the left.

We cannot say how this particular focus affected the relationships he reported between tolerance and the various explanatory factors cited above. It is possible, and perhaps quite likely, that perceptions of those groups included in his questionnaire varied with precisely those factors used to explain differences in tolerance, such as education, age, sex, place of residence, or personality. If perceptions of these groups differed systematically with any or all of these factors, then the differences Stouffer reported might have resulted from different perceptions of the targets than from real differences in tolerance. For example, Stouffer reported that tolerance varies directly with the level of education. But it is at least possible that the more highly educated respondents were less sensitive than those with less education to potential threats posed by communists, socialists, and atheists. At the heart of this matter is the proper measurement of tolerance. If intolerance presupposes an objection to a group or to an idea, the investigator must test respondents in terms of groups or ideas that they actually oppose. Since what is objectionable will vary from respondent to respondent, tolerance cannot be measured by responses to a narrow range of political groups. To the extent, therefore, that Stouffer's findings purport to explain tolerance as a general attribute, they are of uncertain validity.

These observations also apply to Stouffer's prediction that tolerant political norms would gain wider acceptance in the future. He based his prediction, in part, on his empirical findings, in particular on the relationship between tolerance and education. Stouffer's view of social and political change implies that traditional attachments to locale, ethnic group, family, and religion give way to attachments to more inclusive institutions and to more rational and universal values, a process abetted to some extent by education. As American society changes in this fashion, one might expect it to become more tolerant of communists, atheists, and socialists, since these groups are themselves identified with this process. On this point, Stouffer was correct, as recent research has shown (Erskine and Siegel, 1975; Nunn et al., 1978: Chapter 3). But he erred, perhaps, in assuming that tolerance in a society can be tracked by monitoring its treatment of these particular groups, since there are other potentially important targets of intolerance. It is quite possible that political change yields new targets of intolerance on both the left and the right. In any event, it is not necessarily true that a society tolerant of communists, socialists, and atheists will also tolerate dissenting opinion in general. The notion of a "tolerant" society is highly problematic, since such a society will sometimes find it difficult to tolerate groups that challenge its central assumption of complete procedural fairness.

These problems of conceptualization, measurement, and inference that arise in Stouffer's study should be kept in mind when evaluating the other works on tolerance and when evaluating our own analysis. Since Stouffer's methods were widely adopted in subsequent studies, some of these criticisms will reappear below. The main point, however, is that Stouffer's study, along with those that later adopted his methods, are primarily concerned with "intolerance of the left" and thus do not permit us to draw inferences about tolerance or intolerance in relation to the entire political spectrum. If there is any significant contribution to be made to this literature, it will lie in the correction of this weakness.

## Tolerance and the Democratic Creed

Stouffer tried to assess the extent to which Americans were prepared to extend procedural liberties to unpopular political groups. In subsequent studies, Prothro and Grigg (1960) and McClosky (1964) formulated the problem differently. They tried to discover if a consensus existed in the United States around the general procedural norms of democracy and minority rights, and whether citizens were prepared to apply these abstract principles to specific situations involving unpopular groups or individuals. They sought to test a central proposition of modern democratic theory: that a popular consensus around procedural norms is required for democratic systems to survive. Their investigations thus addressed three related, though theoretically separable, questions: (1) whether a consensus around abstract procedural norms existed in the United States, (2) whether citizens were prepared to apply these abstract norms to concrete situations in which controversial political groups or ideas were involved, and (3) whether in fact both a consensus around the abstract norms and some degree of consistency between these norms and actual practice are required to sustain a democratic polity.

This formulation involved several difficulties. First, the authors were obliged to spell out those fundamental principles around which a democratic consensus was supposed to exist, a problem that has frustrated a generation of theorists. For Prothro and Grigg, and McClosky, these principles consisted of those procedural rules by which people are permitted to persuade others and by which they gain access to political influence. Next, they had to develop valid and reliable statements of these principles, both in the abstract and in the concrete, so that respondents could be questioned about them. In addition, they assumed that agreement on the abstract principles is substantially meaningless unless citizens are prepared to apply these principles consistently to practical situations. In their formulations, then, consensus requires substantial consistency between abstract principles and actual behavior, a requirement on which few theorists have insisted. Finally, they presumed that this procedure represented a valid test of the proposition that stable democratic systems require a consensus around procedural norms. As we shall see, each of these steps involves difficulties that, when accumulated, undermine the authors' final conclusions.

The Prothro-Grigg study used samples from two cities—Ann Arbor, Michigan, and Tallahassee, Florida. The authors initially presented respondents with a series of statements designed to express in abstract form the "fundamental" principles of democracy, majority rule, and minority rights. For example, respondents were asked if they agreed that "democracy is the best form of government" or that "public officials should be chosen by majority vote" or that "the minority should be free to criticize majority decisions." These were followed by a series of statements describing specific situations to which respondents were given the opportunity to apply these abstract principles. Among such statements were these: "If a communist were legally elected mayor of this city, the people should not allow him to take office"; "If a person wanted to make a speech in this city against churches and religion, he should be allowed to speak"; "A communist should not be allowed to run for mayor of this city." As the authors put it, "these specific propositions are designed to embody the principles of majority rule and minority rights in such a clear fashion that a 'correct' or 'democratic' response can be deduced from endorsement of the general principles" (p. 283).

As expected, they found a general consensus on the abstract principles, but this consensus broke down on the specific applications of the norms, especially when applied to communists. On each of the abstract statements, over 90 percent of the respondents supported the democratic principle. However, with respect to the specific applications, the authors found very little consensus among their respondents. On seven of the ten items designed to incorporate the abstract principles in specific situations, fewer than 75 percent of the respondents provided the "democratic" response. In addition, only 44 percent would allow a communist to speak in their city and only 42 percent would allow a communist to run for mayor of their city. Only 21 percent disagreed with the statement that "In a city referendum deciding on tax-supported undertakings, only taxpayers should be allowed to vote." The authors also examined the relationship between education and responses to these statements, and found, like Stouffer, that support for "democratic" principles increased with the level of education. All told, their findings substantiated Stouffer's conclusion that there was an alarming lack of support for democratic procedural norms in the mass public, especially when these norms were formulated in terms of practical situations.

Despite their findings, Prothro and Grigg did not conclude their study pessimistically. Since the United States is a functioning democracy, they suggested, a general commitment to tolerant norms need not be a condition for a stable democracy:

> Discussions of consensus tend to overlook the functional nature of apathy for the democratic system. No one is surprised to hear that what people say they believe and what they actually do are not actually the same. We usually assume that verbal positions represent a higher level—a more "democratic" stance—than non-verbal behavior. But something close to the opposite may also be true: many people express undemocratic principles in response to questioning but are too apathetic to act on their undemocratic opinions in concrete situations (p. 293).

The system itself may appear tolerant even as its citizens express intolerant beliefs. In their view, then, the American system is tolerant in practice though not in spirit.

Though this conclusion is plausible, their explanation for it is unsatisfactory. It is perhaps true that liberal democracies are based upon a kind of "negative" consensus by which citizens agree to pursue private ends at the expense of public ones. But it is difficult to explain something as fundamental as democratic stability in terms of apathy. The authors do not explain, for example, why people are more reluctant to act on undemocratic beliefs than on democratic beliefs. The effects of apathy would seem to cut both ways. If people are too apathetic to violate democratic norms, perhaps they are also too apathetic to defend them. Moreover, to accept this explanation would be to abandon the study of public beliefs, since these beliefs have no influence on behavior. Apparently, it does not matter if people are tolerant or intolerant, if they are too apathetic to act upon their beliefs.

In addition, Prothro and Grigg failed to demonstrate that citizens do not act on their "undemocratic" opinions. They merely combined their assumption that the United States is a stable democracy with their empirical findings that many people hold undemocratic opinions and concluded that a consensus around democratic principles is not necessary to sustain a stable democracy. This step, in turn, required an alternative explanation for democratic stability, which was found in the felicitous consequences of apathy. Neither conclusion was justified by their empirical results, since there was no independent evidence to show that citizens actually were apathetic, nor were the authors' criteria for judging the United States to be a democratic polity presented.

Since these criteria, whatever they might be, are independent of the empirical findings, the question of whether a consensus is required to sustain a democratic system was settled in advance of the empirical analysis. The authors simply assumed that the United States is a democratic polity, whether a consensus happened to exist or not. By this reasoning, the issue is settled by definition, since the criteria by which a system is judged to be democratic are independent of the question of consensus. Hence, democratic systems do not require consensus, and the empirical findings reported in the study were not necessary to reach the conclusion. Finally, we are left with the empirical finding that large numbers of citizens are intolerant because they do not apply the abstract principles of democracy consistently to concrete situations. To assess this conclusion fairly, we need to take a closer look at their study's design.

The first question is whether it is reasonable to expect citizens to apply abstract principles to actual practice in a logically consistent manner. Prothro and Grigg assume that, to be fully democratic, citizens must be able and willing to do so, a requirement that few democratic theorists have thought necessary. The most obvious problem with this formulation is that it is often difficult to achieve logical consistency between principles and practice because the requirements of different principles sometimes conflict in practical situations. At a very general level, for example, the principle of majority rule is often in conflict with the principle of minority rights, a problem that Madison (1961) recognized in *Federalist* 10 when he argued, in defense of the Constitution, that "To secure the public good, and private rights against the danger of such a (majority) faction, and at the same time to preserve the spirit and the form of popular government, is then the great object to which our enquiries are directed'' (p. 61).

It is difficult to settle such conflicts formally or logically because the values are expressed differently in different situations. Hence, it is often necessary in practical situations to trade-off political values. Political processes are designed precisely to allow for such bargaining among values. As a consequence, citizens may believe in the general principles of democracy, majority rule, and minority rights, as Prothro and Grigg formulated them, without believing that they must be applied absolutely in every circumstance; they are general standards of action, not hard and fast rules. The authors formulated an exessively abstract version of democracy, one that is perhaps impossible to implement fully because it imposes unreasonable burdens on citizens. In a sense, this formulation obscures the fact that the "fundamental principles of democracy" are in constant tension and that one of the objectives of democratic systems is to maintain some balance among them.

In addition, the logical connections asserted between the abstract principles of democracy and their practical applications are disputable. As already noted, Prothro and Grigg assumed that citizens should be free to criticize majority decisions and to persuade others to accept their beliefs. They found it contradictory, for example, that large numbers of respondents did not agree that an admitted communist should be free to make a speech in their city. But respondents need not have accepted the authors' assumptions. If respondents believed that communists themselves do not accept these abstract principles, not an unreasonable belief, they may have been justified on purely logical grounds in drawing the practical conclusion they did (see the discussion of this point in Brown and Taylor, 1973: 35–36).

If this was the case, as it almost certainly was for many, then the authors were not justified in drawing the conclusion that citizens accept the abstract principles of democracy but do not apply them in practice. Many respondents may have simply believed that the defense of "democratic" principles requires some degree of intolerance toward groups that challenge those fundamental principles. To accept such a view raises the possibility that tolerance, in an absolute sense, may not be a fundamental principle of democracy. This, in turn, challenges the very presumption from which Prothro and Grigg began their investigation. It is certainly more difficult to study tolerance after accepting the legitimacy of this view, because it renders tolerance somewhat problematic as a central value in democratic systems.

These observations bear on the general understanding of democracy informing this study. Two other criticisms bear on narrower empirical questions. There is, first, the problem that the descriptions of specific situations in their questionnaire did not adequately test the abstract principles of democracy. At issue here is the validity of their questionnaire items. For example, one of the practical situations presented to respondents was the following: "In a city referendum deciding on tax-supported undertakings, only tax-payers should be allowed to vote." This statement does not raise the issue of majority rule so much as the issue of what will define the political community which a majority will govern. Such restrictions on participation have been commonplace in the United States and, though one may argue on abstract grounds that such restrictions are undemocratic, this must be done in the face of compelling historical opinion that they were not. Since the standards by which we judge institutions to be "democratic" or "undemocratic" change over time, there are bound to be disagreements over the proper application of these terms. There seems to be no *a priori* reason to settle such disagreements in terms of the standards set forth by Prothro and Grigg.

A similar objection applies to another practical situation Prothro and Grigg presented to respondents: "In a city referendum, only people who are well-informed about the problem being voted on should be allowed to vote." Presumably, one should disagree with this statement, though fully 51 percent of those questioned in their study agreed with it. Like the situation cited above, however, this one brings into play values other than majority rule. In this case, the value of full popular participation conflicts with that of a well-informed citizenry, both deemed essential to democracy. In practice, these values have conflicted in battles over literacy requirements and the expansion of the suffrage. Given such conflicts, it is not surprising that respondents should have been divided on the question. In both situations, Prothro and Grigg tried to solve these conflicts in terms of one definition of democracy, which is by no means beyond dispute, and which therefore respondents need not have accepted. Thus, the authors' conclusion that many respondents subscribed to undemocratic values was perhaps unwarranted.[6] In addition, their results might have been even more

6. The particular items chosen for discussion here do not exhaust the list of questions presented to respondents in the Prothro-Grigg study. They used ten different items to portray the concrete situations to which respondents could apply the abstract principles of democracy. The two items just discussed dealing with city referenda are open to the criticism of bringing into play competing democratic values, as are three additional items dealing with the political rights of communists. This criticism does not apply with such force to the remaining five items, which are by and large reasonable measures of the

alarming—in their own terms—had they used a broader range of political groups as points of reference against which to measure support for democratic principles (as the authors understood these principles). As in Stouffer's study, most of the groups specifically mentioned were leftist. Among the five items used to measure tolerance of minority views, one referred to a person making a speech against churches and religion, one to a person speaking in favor of government ownership of industry, two to a communist either making a speech or running for office, and one to a Negro running for mayor. Thus, four of the five items make reference to groups on the left and none makes reference to comparable groups on the right. Had right-wing groups been mentioned, the levels of tolerance Prothro and Grigg found might have been much lower, since those hostile to the right would have been given a chance to express their intolerance. In a sense, then, their method may have led them to overestimate the level of tolerance in American society, though they did not recognize this problem because they were concerned largely with the consistency between abstract beliefs and a few specific applications of them.

In a related study, McClosky (1964) compared political influentials and rank-and-file citizens in levels of support for the abstract principles of democracy and their willingness to apply these principles to specific situations. He was thus concerned with a problem Stouffer had initially raised: the difference in levels of tolerance between elites and nonelites. However, in focusing on the consistency between abstract principles and specific applications, McClosky formulated the problem similarly to Prothro and Grigg. He expected to find empirical support for the following propositions:

> That the American electorate is often divided on "fundamental" democratic values and procedural "rules of the game" and that its understanding of politics and of political ideas is in any event too rudimentary at present to speak of ideological "consensus" among its members.
>
> That . . . the electorate exhibits greater support for general abstract statements of democratic belief than for their specific applications.
>
> That the constituent ideas of American democratic ideology are principally held by the more "articulate" segments of the population, including the political influentials; and that people in these ranks will exhibit a more meaningful and far reaching consensus on democratic and constitutional values than will the general population.
>
> That whatever increases the level of political articulateness—ed-

---

tolerance principle. Thus, only half of their items are suspect on the grounds set forth in the text.

ucation, S.E.S., urban residence, intellectuality, political activity, etc.—strengthens consensus and support for American political ideology and institutions (p. 362).

To test these propositions, McClosky used data from national surveys of elites and the general electorate conducted in 1956 and 1958. Like Stouffer, he found elites much more sympathetic to statements expressing support for the rules of democratic procedure, or for the "rules of the game," as he called them. In addition, elites were more likely than the general electorate to support the application of the general principles of free speech and opinion to specific situations. In short, he found substantial support for his initial hypotheses. He therefore concluded that "a large proportion of the electorate has failed to grasp certain of the underlying ideas and principles on which the American political system rests" (p. 365).

Many of the criticisms raised earlier in relation to the theory of democracy underlying the Prothro-Grigg study might be reiterated here. It is worth repeating that this theory did not originate with these writers, but had already been elaborated in detail by such writers as Berelson and his associates (1954), Dahl (1956; 1961), and Key (1961). McClosky and Prothro and Grigg, however, helped to lay an empirical foundation for the theory.

McClosky, attempting to measure support for the "American democratic ideology," tried to explain the meaning of the term:

> Although scholars or Supreme Court justices might argue over fine points of interpretation, they would uniformly recognize as elements of American democratic ideology such concepts as consent, accountability, limited or constitutional government, representation, majority rights, the principle of political opposition, freedom of thought, speech, press, and assembly, equality of opportunity, religious toleration, equality before the law, the rights of juridical defense, and individual self-determination over a broad range of personal affairs. How widely such elements of American liberal democracy are approved, by whom and with what measure of understanding, is another question . . . But that they form an integrated body of ideas which has become part of the American inheritance seems scarcely open to debate (p. 363).

Few would dispute his claim that such values are at the center of the American democratic creed. However, the interpretations of these values in practical situations have always been matters of dispute, among elites and non-elites alike. McClosky's procedure implies that there are rules by which these abstract values can be translated into practice and that these rules are not controversial. We have already discussed the problems with this assumption, but it may be useful to raise them again.

McClosky used three sets of items to measure the concept of tolerance. Two sets consisted of abstract statements expressing support for the "rules of the game," and for free speech and opinion. The third set consisted of statements specifically applying the principles of free speech and opinion. Since the conclusions depended heavily on the presumed validity of these items, it is important to see how they hold up.

Consider the following statements which were posed to respondents to measure their support for the "rules of the game":

> If congressional committees stuck strictly to the rules and gave every witness his rights, they would never succeed in exposing the many dangerous subversives they have turned up.
>
> I don't mind a politician's methods if he manages to get the right things done.
>
> Politicians have to cut a few corners if they are going to get anywhere.
>
> Very few politicians have clean records, so why get excited about the mudslinging that sometimes goes on?
>
> It is all right to get around the law if you don't actually break it.

These items, especially the first two, reflect the concerns with procedural rights and with the relationships between political means and ends raised by the issues of domestic communism in the 1950s. Presumably, one would have to disagree with all of these statements to express full support for the "rules of the game." But the responses to these statements are difficult to interpret because the statements themselves are somewhat ambiguous. They bring into play several issues not easily resolved in terms of the abstract values of democracy.

The first item poses a factual question and only implicitly invokes a procedural value. It may be true that congressional committees would not have turned up as many subversives as they did if they had followed neutral procedural rules. Respondents may have recognized this, though they need not have approved of it. In addition, the very notion of "subversive" is ambiguous and open to various interpretations and misinterpretations.

The next four items do not express fundamental principles either, but deal with situations that are really matters of degree. Respondents had to answer several questions for themselves before proceeding to answer McClosky's questions, such as (taking the items in the order listed) what methods are contemplated? what corners are being cut? what type of mudslinging is going on? and how far must one maneuver to get around the law? The procedure assumes these matters can be settled by a form of democratic logic taking the abstract principles of democracy and applying them routinely. In practice, solutions are rarely so cut and dried. There are, of course, culturally accepted responses to such items, and perhaps many respondents dutifully gave them. But considering this, the items may test whether respondents knew what these responses are and whether they were prepared to give them to the interviewers. One might suspect also that the more "articulate" respondents were more likely to understand these cultural expectations.

With respect to freedom of speech and opinion, he found that elites and the general electorate agreed on the abstract principles, but that elites tended to be more supportive of their specific applications. His findings on this point were thus consistent with Stouffer's. It is somewhat more difficult to interpret McClosky's results, however, because the specific applications in this questionnaire tended to be nearly as ambiguous as his statements of the abstract principles.

Among the nine items used to represent specific situations, only one mentioned a specific political group, in this case, communists. Most posed questions of dubious relationship to free speech or procedural rights, as we commonly understand them. For example, the statement that "A book that contains wrong political views cannot be a good book and does not deserve to be published" raises at least three questions—whether there can be "wrong" political views, whether a book that contains such views can be a good book, and whether such a book deserves to be published. Responses to this question are subject to numerous interpretations.

The same is true of the following statement: "If a person is convicted of a crime by illegal evidence, he should be set free and the evidence thrown out of court." Apparently one should agree with this to support the application of basic procedural rights. Yet this is a problem that has long vexed judges and constitutional scholars. Until 1962, four years after these surveys were completed, many states permitted tainted evidence to be introduced in criminal trials. In that year, the United States Supreme Court settled the question constitutionally in the case of *Mapp* v. *Ohio* by imposing the federal "exclusionary rule" upon the states, thus barring the introduction of tainted evidence in state criminal proceedings. The decision was carried in the face of a vigorous dissent by Justices Harlan, Frankfurter, and Whittaker, and it continues to be a matter of controversy in the courts. In a sense, the political process settled this issue in a manner consistent with Mc-Closky's formulation. But this had to be established through political argument and conflict. In this way, definitions of the fundamental principles of democracy, as scholars understand them, become matters of political controversy and, hence, they are often part and parcel of the political process itself. It is not surprising, therefore, that citizens should not unanimously endorse some of these principles.

To a significant degree, then, the difficulties with McClosky's study, as with the Prothro-Grigg study, stem from the emphasis on consistency between abstract principles and their specific application. In the nature of things, any real situation is bound to bring into play competing values. Thus, there is always going to be some tension between abstract principles and both the extent to which they are applied and, just as important, the extent to which one believes they *should* be carried out in practice. So long as one insists on consistency, narrowly conceived, as a standard for democratic practice, the beliefs and practices of citizens are bound to fall short of the standard. In treating the problem in this way, the authors assumed that the concepts in question—democracy, majority rule, minority rights—are not controversial, even though the results of their studies indicated the opposite.

The confusion thus stems from a mistaken emphasis on the importance of consistency and from the questionable view that the correct responses to the specific items can be derived logically from a single set of abstract principles. Obviously, the more abstractly these principles are formulated, the more tenuous will their connection be with practical circumstances. Instead of focusing narrowly on the consistency between principles and practice, it may be more appropriate to consider the extent to which the acceptance of the abstract principles of tolerance "cause," or allow us to predict, responses to concrete situations without judging these responses as democratic or undemocratic.[7]

Like Stouffer's work, these two studies were original in design and influential in relation to later work on tolerance. It should be kept in mind that these studies were carried out more than two decades ago, so that problems that seem clear to us now could only have been dimly

7. Both Prothro and Grigg, and McClosky, failed to examine the individual level relationship between support for the abstract principles of democracy and the specific applications. They merely noted the differences in percentage "democratic" or "tolerant" on the abstract and specific items, and found higher levels on the former than on the latter. If they had used more appropriate measures of the "specific applications," their thesis could have been more accurately tested by using some kind of correlational analysis. On this general problem, see also Jackman (1978).

perceived when they were written. We have gone over them carefully because they are important and because there have been few subsequent works which actually succeeded in improving upon them. Most of the recent work on the subject has merely refined their empirical findings and theoretical formulations. As the above discussion should make clear, however, we need to develop alternative conceptualizations and measures of tolerance before we can hope to improve upon their efforts.

## Changing Levels of Tolerance, 1954–1978

The Stouffer, Prothro-Grigg, and McClosky studies were carried out and written during the peak of the cold war, when the denial of procedural rights to communists and related groups was a major concern of civil libertarians. Since then, the dimensions of political conflict have grown more complex, and challenges to the political consensus have come from many sources, including civil rights activists, feminists, opponents of the war in Vietnam, and radicals and reactionaries of various persuasions. As the potential targets of intolerance have proliferated, it is no longer appropriate to consider tolerance solely in terms of the treatment afforded communists and associated groups. The ferment of the 1960s and 1970s may have created a more tolerant environment for dissent by broadening the range of political opinion in the society. For these reasons, the conclusions of these earlier studies must be reconsidered and updated.

The question of whether tolerance has in fact increased since Stouffer conducted his study in 1954 has been addressed in several recent studies. Davis (1975) attempted to test Stouffer's prediction that tolerance would increase as levels of education in the society increased and as the average age of the population declined. Drawing upon a survey conducted in 1972 by the National Opinion Research Center which repeated several of Stouffer's items, he found a significant increase in levels of tolerance. He attributed some of this to higher levels of education and some to cohort replacement, but at the same time he found significantly higher levels of tolerance in 1972 among all cohort and educational groups. Thus, the bulk of the change apparently reflected general trends in society that strengthened tolerant political norms. What these trends were he did not spell out in much detail, though he suggested that they involved a "general movement" toward more liberal positions on various non-economic issues, such as race relations, women's rights, sexual practices, and so forth. In a related piece of research, Cutler and Kaufman (1975) supported this conclusion, finding increased levels of tolerance among all age cohorts between 1954 and 1972, though the changes were most pronounced among the young. Apparently, then, these changes resulted from a changed "climate of opinion" in the society as a whole.

Similarly, Nunn, Crockett, and Williams (1978) measured changes in levels of tolerance in a 1973 survey, which also repeated the Stouffer items. Like Davis and others, they found a considerable increase in levels of tolerance between 1954 and the early 1970s. Since they used Stouffer's questions, they were able to measure quite precisely the changes in levels of tolerance for communists, atheists, and socialists. For example, they found an increase of 14 percent in support for a socialist's right to speak, an increase of 20 percent in support for a socialist's right to teach, and a 24 percent increase in those classified as "more tolerant" on an overall tolerance scale (see Nunn et al., 1978: Chapter 3). Thus, they concluded that while only 31 percent of the public could be classified as tolerant in 1954, fully 55 percent could be so classified in 1973 (p. 51). These results parallel those reported by Erskine and Seigel (1975), who relied upon NORC surveys. According to Nunn and his associates, "the most important finding from our efforts to track trends in American tolerance is that citizens who are most supportive of civil liberties have emerged as the majority in our society—and they are not a 'silent majority' " (p. 2).

The research on this question thus yields a consensus that levels of tolerance in the United States have increased significantly in the past generation. These changes apparently reflect broad political forces that created a more comfortable climate for political dissent. Nunn and his associates go so far as to conclude that "Given the substantial increase in public support for democratic principles, the risk of demagogic take-over or the undermining of civil liberties is now less than it once was" (p. 159). This conclusion goes well beyond their empirical findings that there is now greater tolerance for communists, socialists, and atheists and argues that tolerant norms are now more widely accepted and that support for democratic principles has increased as well.

As we have noted, these generalizations assume that tolerance for these particular groups is equivalent to tolerance as a more general belief. Hence, these conclusions are true only if the assumption underlying them is true. In the next chapter we examine the empirical validity of this assumption. In the meantime, we leave it an open question whether Americans are now more tolerant than they were a generation ago. Though Americans may now be more tolerant of communists, atheists, and socialists, it does not necessarily follow that they are fully tolerant of those dissenting groups on the left and on the right that emerged during the 1960s and 1970s.

## Alternative Strategies for Measuring Tolerance

Our survey of these studies has focused on the problem of devising valid and reliable measures of political tolerance. If measurement strategies are flawed, then so will be the conclusions based upon these strategies. Others have recognized this problem and have formulated their own answers to it. In a recent article, Lawrence (1976) reconsidered the measurement of tolerance and, in so doing, refined the conclusions of these earlier studies. He was concerned with the relationship between the manner in which people evaluate dissenting acts and dissenting groups and their willingness to tolerate these acts and groups. He suspected, correctly, that tolerance depends heavily on how respondents evaluate dissenters and their acts. Hence, to measure tolerance, one must first find some way to take these evaluations into account.

In Lawrence's study, respondents were asked three sets of questions: first, if they believed that various general modes of protest (circulating a petition, criticizing a government decision, holding a peaceful demonstration and blocking a government building) should be permitted; next, how they evaluated two controversial political groups (radical students and black militants) and two controversial political views (legalization of marijuana and government action to prohibit race discrimination in housing). Finally, he presented respondents with hypothetical situations, in which political groups were promoting controversial issues by means of various modes of protest, to find out if they would apply their general norms about the modes of protest to the specific situations irrespective of their views about the groups or the issues. Failure to do so would indicate intolerance. Lawrence hypothesized that the willingness to tolerate protest would depend on the respondents' evaluations of those protesting.

His results by and large confirmed the hypothesis. He found a somewhat higher level of tolerance in 1971 than Stouffer's study suggested, though the items Lawrence used were not strictly comparable to Stouffer's. A majority of respondents would permit all of the general modes of protest, except the one with the most potential for violence (blocking a government building). In addition, there was considerable consistency between evaluations of the general modes of protest and their application to specific situations. However, this consistency varied depending on the issues and the groups involved in the protests. As expected, inconsistencies between the general evaluations and the specific applications were accounted for in large part by evaluations of the groups and issues in question. When people refused to apply their general evaluations to specific situations, it was frequently because they strongly disapproved of those protesting. In addition, Lawrence found that the well educated were somewhat more likely than the less educated to disregard their negative evaluations of groups in deciding whether to permit the acts of protest, thus reconfirming the traditional relationship between education and tolerance.

This study's importance lies in demonstrating that tolerance of protest in general can be easily confounded with evaluations of the groups and issues involved in specific acts of protest. The real test of tolerance is what people will do when such evaluations are clearly negative. In the earlier studies, especially Stouffer's, it was assumed that attitudes toward communists and related groups were negative and that levels of tolerance of these groups fully measured the level of tolerance in the society as a whole. Lawrence attempted to control for these evaluations. In so doing, he showed that for many people, tolerance is not accepted as an abstract creed, the rules of which are applicable on a neutral basis to all groups. Instead, judgments about whether protest should be permitted are made in reference to specific groups or issues. Moreover, Lawrence treated the problem of consistency between general principles and specific applications much more practically than McClosky or Prothro and Grigg. In this study, the general norms involved evaluations of fairly specific acts of protest; they did not refer to general values such as majority rule and minority rights. His specific applications, then, involved situations in which acts of protest were connected with controversial groups. This narrowed considerably the gap between norm and application, and thus made the inferences required to impute consistency or inconsistency between the two less problematic.

As observed above, the importance of Lawrence's study lies in its demonstration that willingness to extend procedural claims to a group depends heavily on one's political evaluations of that group. In a sense, therefore, Lawrence's principal conclusion points to the limitations of his own study. If this generalization is true, as we believe it is, then one cannot fully measure tolerance in terms of consistency between evaluations of general acts of protest and the willingness of citizens to apply these evaluations to acts committed by a narrow range of political groups. Given the generalization, responses will depend heavily on the groups selected as points of reference. Lawrence's groups—black militants and radical students—represent a narrow range of the ideological spectrum. Thus, the extent to which respondents were judged as tolerant probably depended on their evaluations of these two groups. As a consequence, the tolerance of those who made positive evaluations of black militants and student radicals was not as severely tested as was the tolerance of those who evaluated the groups negatively. This does not challenge Lawrence's generalization, but only his application of it.

Herson and Hofstetter (1975) also recognized this problem of content-bias. Their solution was to ask each respondent to evaluate two groups, one from the extreme right (the KKK) and one from the extreme left (communists). Their sample consisted of some 400 Ohio residents, who were presented with a list of questions measuring levels of tolerance for each group. The list included statements about free speech, running for office, and teaching at a university. They then created a scale of tolerance-intolerance for both the Klan and the communists, and divided the sample into four groups, based on scores on these two scales: those respondents tolerant of both the left-wing and right-wing groups (38 percent); those tolerance of the right but not the left (23 percent); those tolerant of the left but not the right (11 percent); and finally those tolerant of neither extreme (28 percent). They therefore found lower levels of tolerance than either Davis or Nunn and his associates because (no doubt) they selected target groups from both ends of the ideological spectrum.

Thus, both Lawrence and Herson and Hofstetter improved on the previous work in the area. Lawrence recognized that attitude toward the target group is an important determinant of tolerance, while Herson and Hofstetter included a group from each ideological extreme in their study. The latter researchers did not, however, discern respondents' attitudes toward the Klan or the communists, other than to ask whether they would tolerate the group in question. Certainly, there were some respondents for whom neither the Klan nor the communists were particularly salient, probably because they did not see these groups as a personal or a political threat. These respondents may well have been more concerned with other groups on the right or left, or perhaps even the center.

Though these two approaches were clear improvements over those used in the earlier studies, they still do not allow us to reach conclusions about tolerance that are untainted by the range of groups selected by the researcher. Because tolerance presumes opposition or disagreement, the concept must be measured in relation to groups that respondents actually oppose. Once opposition (or disagreement) is held constant or controlled for all individuals studied, we can then proceed to measure how tolerant they are. Thus, none of the approaches considered above allows us to measure tolerance fully.

## Attitudes and Behavior

The studies reviewed in this chapter deal with political tolerance as an attitude or a set of attitudes, not as behavior. Although the general relationship between attitudes and behaviors is not well understood, systematic investigation into the topic has recently intensified. The early conclusions were generally pessimistic, and as recently as 1969, Wicker concluded that in only a small minority of cases did attitudes and behavior correlate even at the .30 level. In most cases, the correlation was smaller or even nonexistent. More recent efforts, however, have pointed up methodological shortcomings in the earlier studies and have clarified the conditions which maximize the attitude-behavior relationship (Fishbein and Ajzen, 1975; Schwartz and Tessler, 1972; and Oskamp, 1977). We cannot provide a detailed presentation of these criticisms and conditions here, since our own efforts add little to the ongoing debate about the relation between attitude and behavior. We wish only to point out the general difficulties in discussing behavior while studying attitudes.

Two studies of particular relevance to the attitude-behavior linkage in the study of political tolerance include Prothro and Grigg (1960) and LaPiere (1934). Prothro and Grigg found that although 42 percent of their Tallahassee sample agreed that a Negro should not be allowed to run for mayor of their city, a few months before the survey was conducted, a Black did in fact campaign for mayor without any actions designed to prevent his candidacy. LaPiere found that when he traveled the country with a Chinese couple, they were refused service at only one of 250 establishments. When he later surveyed these establishments, of the 128 replies, 118 said they would refuse to serve members of the Chinese race. In both instances, these studies suggest that many respondents will express intolerant attitudes yet engage in tolerant behaviors. Some scholars would undoubtedly therefore dismiss the study of tolerance as a set of attitudes as irrelevant since it is behavior that is most important to the functioning of the political system and the maintenance of a democratic regime.

These studies have been criticized, however, as misleading because the verbal statements and the behavioral situations involve different "situational thresholds" (Campbell, 1963). In the LaPiere study, for example, face to face discrimination is more difficult than abstract discrimination in answering a letter. Thus the two acts fall at different points along the "discrimination" or "tolerance" dimension, and one is clearly "easier" than the other. As a result, the apparent inconsistency is nothing more than the result of different discrimination thresholds. As a final note on the matter, Calder and Ross (1973) review the recent literature and conclude that attitudes and behavior are generally related at a reasonably strong level.

Although not directly related to the study of political tolerance, we might note in passing the studies conducted by Stanley Milgram (1963). These studies are well known and will not be summarized here, but we do wish to point out that Milgram's subjects were generally quite willing to inflict considerable harm onto other people for whom they had no apparent antipathy or intolerance. A loose interpretation might suggest that these subjects were behaviorally intolerant without being attitudinally intolerant. The situation was structured in such a way that intolerant behavior was "easy" since the pressure of an authority figure provided a very low situational threshold. No doubt if Milgram's subjects had been queried, before the experiment began, about the "stooges" they shocked, they would have expressed little or no intolerance toward either that person or his social and ethnic characteristics. (See Milgram's studies for the details of his experiments.) We note this to suggest that while there are undoubtedly discrepancies between tolerant attitudes and tolerant behaviors, it is not necessarily the case that the attitudes will be more intolerant than the behaviors. Depending on the situation and on the "situational threshold" associated with each attitude and behavior, the slippage can run in either direction.

In our own study, there is little that we can contribute to an understanding of the relationship between attitudes of tolerance and behaviors. Although we hope to offer an improved conceptualization and measurement strategy for the study of tolerant attitudes, we do so within the mainstream of research on political tolerance. We ask our respondents about their attitudes and about their behavioral intentions, but in this analysis we cannot examine the degree to which, or the conditions under which, these intentions are likely to translate into action. We nevertheless believe that our efforts to examine tolerant and intolerant attitudes are important for at least two overarching reasons. First, even though attitudes and behavioral predispositions do not automatically translate into behavior, they do set the stage by creating a range of potential behaviors and by making some behaviors more likely than others. Oskamp (1977) has isolated eight factors which affect the degree of consistency between attitudes and behavior in general, and no doubt these factors apply to tolerance as well. We shall not detail these factors here, but merely note that there are many sets of conditions under which intolerant attitudes will translate in an almost one-to-one fashion into intolerant behaviors. Thus an understanding of attitudinal tolerance is crucial to an understanding of behavioral tolerance.

The second reason it is important to understand attitudinal tolerance is that attitudes form an important component of political culture and of the norms of democracy. In many respects, the study of political culture and of democratic norms is the study of political attitudes, not behaviors; it involves an examination of the states of mind which underlie political traditions and political institutions. Even in the absense of overt intolerant actions at a particular point in time, a regime or a citizenry which is characterized by intolerant attitudes should not be described as fully tolerant. If intolerant impulses underlie seemingly tolerant behavior, it is probably only a matter of time and circumstance before this impulse will surface. To illustrate the problem, if an overwhelmingly intolerant population has in some way eliminated the targets of their intolerance, then after that point in time, that population may appear to be very tolerant behaviorally. If we understand the history of the situation, we would conclude that should circumstances change (i.e., the target group reassert itself), this population would again manifest its intolerant attitudes through behavior. It is for these reasons that actual episodes of intolerant behavior on the part of a citizenry are likely to be rare during certain historical periods and hence it is the study of the underlying attitudes that becomes most important.

## Implications for the Study of Tolerance

What have we learned from these studies of tolerance? The following conclusions seem to us the most important:

1. Many empirical studies of tolerance begin from particular definitions of democracy or from particular views of what is required of citizens in democratic systems. The danger here is that the investigator may draw conclusions that are determined as much by the original assumptions as by the empirical results. Indeed, the very measures of tolerance the investigator uses are likely to be influenced by his or her assumptions about democracy. Thus, the McClosky and Prothro and Grigg studies began with a view of democracy holding that citizens should accept the abstract principles of tolerance and should be prepared to apply these principles in controversial situations. Citizens who did not measure up to this standard were deemed intolerant. The authors then proceeded to redefine democracy in order to find sources

of democratic stability in places other than in citizen support for democratic values. Though this conclusion may be generally true, it was heavily determined by the standard of democracy from which these studies originated. That is, citizens were judged as intolerant, in part, because of the expectations they were required to meet.

2. As a corollary, the investigator should at least temporarily suspend judgment on the desirability or undesirability of tolerance in democratic regimes. It need not be assumed at the outset that tolerance is desirable in all conceivable circumstances or that tolerance is a fundamental principle of democracy that most citizens must endorse before a regime qualifies as democratic. This assumption complicates matters by linking tolerance with the conditions of democracy. Though some degree of tolerance may be one of the conditions of democracy, this approach can lead to the conclusion that complete tolerance is the fundamental condition of democracy. This then locates the very definition of democracy in public attitudes on an important but limited subject, thus subordinating the role of democratic institutions. It is more appropriate, we think, to begin the study of tolerance with clear specifications of the meaning of the concept and of the ways in which it should be measured. The empirical results thus generated may then have important implications for our understanding of democracy. It is important, in any event, to remember that the theoretical connections between tolerance and democracy cannot be fully settled through empirical analysis.

3. Tolerance cannot be measured using a narrow range of political groups or ideas as points of reference. This approach tends to confuse tolerance with respondents' evaluations of particular groups on the questionnaire.[8] Neither can tolerance be measured in terms of the respondents' willingness to endorse highly abstract principles. Since such abstract statements tend to be disconnected from actual political groups or situations, responses to them tell us little about how respondents might be prepared to act. Tolerance refers to the willingness of citizens to apply procedural rules (within some general limits) on a neutral basis to those groups they oppose, so long as those groups themselves do not violate constitutional guarantees. Given this, it is more appropriate to use some kind of self-anchoring measure that allows respondents

8. This critique of the Stouffer items runs parallel to the critique levelled years ago against the scales used by Adorno and his associates in *The Authoritarian Personality* (1950). Critics argued, with considerable validity, that the scales only measured authoritarianism of the right and did not bring into play authoritarianism of the left or the center. For a complete presentation, see the articles collected in Christie and Jahoda (1954).

themselves to choose the groups they most strongly oppose. Then they might be asked about what steps, if any, they are prepared to take against these groups. Such a strategy would avoid the difficulties involved in posing abstract statements to respondents and, at the same time, it would control for different evaluations of potential targets by making certain that respondents are asked about groups to which they are strongly opposed.

4. Stouffer's method of measuring tolerance with reference to communists, socialists, and atheists is inadequate and, to a large extent, time-bound. It is inadequate because, for reasons just mentioned, it does not fully capture the meaning of tolerance. It is time-bound because it presumes that these particular groups are the only important targets of intolerance in the society. This may have been more or less true in 1954, and Stouffer's conclusions may have been appropriate for the purposes of his research, but it is certainly not true now. Attempts to monitor changing levels of tolerance with this procedure are thus inappropriate and produce misleading conclusions.

5. These considerations, while important in their own right, also raise other questions about the understanding of tolerance and its sources that stem from this earlier tradition of research. If we are correct that tolerance has been incorrectly conceived and measured, it is also likely that other widely accepted generalizations in the area are incorrect. For example, Stouffer and others found that education was the most important source of a tolerant outlook. Given what has already been said, it is possible that this relationship, as well as others, was an artifact of the procedures used to measure tolerance.

These conclusions will be kept in mind as we proceed with our own analysis of tolerance in the United States. Since the tradition of empirical research on tolerance is enlightening and persuasive in many respects, we have examined its assumptions in detail in order to demonstrate its limitations. Our first step in reformulating the problem will be to develop and justify a self-anchoring measure of political tolerance that more fully captures the meaning of the concept as we understand it. In the succeeding chapters, then, we outline our approach and proceed to our analysis of tolerance in America.

# A Profile of Political Tolerance in the 1970s: Implications of a Different Approach

**3**

Having stated serious objections to previous research on tolerance, we must show that these objections have real consequences and that they are more than just conceptual quibbles. In this chapter, therefore, we examine the empirical consequences of Stouffer's approach to measuring tolerance. We then show that another approach, more consistent with our understanding of the concept, yields different results and different interpretations of the role of tolerance in American politics. Throughout this chapter, special attention is given to the validity of these measurement procedures, and the chapter concludes with a discussion of a theoretical framework which guides the analysis presented in subsequent chapters.

## Changing Levels of Political Tolerance: The Stouffer Items

Stouffer, of course, in 1954, found very high levels of intolerance directed at atheists, communists, and socialists. Given the political context of the period, which was dominated by the issues of domestic and international communism, such results were certainly not surprising. However, as noted in Chapter 2, more recent studies (Nunn et al., 1978; Davis, 1975) have relied on Stouffer's questions and have found much smaller proportions of intolerant respondents. Comparing the 1950s responses to those of the 1970s, these studies report an apparent across-the-board increase in the level of political tolerance in American society.

In Table 3-1 we present the proportion of tolerant responses to each of the Stouffer items given in his original survey and in a 1977 NORC survey. As is apparent, none of the items in the 1954 survey gen-

**Table 3-1**          **Changing Levels of Tolerance for Atheists and Communists, 1954–1977: Percent Giving the Tolerant Response to Each Question**

| Question | 1954 Stouffer | 1977 NORC | Increase |
|---|---|---|---|
| Should an atheist be allowed to speak? | 37 | 63 | 26 |
| Should an atheist be allowed to teach? | 12 | 39 | 27 |
| Should a book written by an atheist be removed from the library? | 35 | 60 | 25 |
| Should a communist be allowed to speak? | 27 | 57 | 30 |
| Should a communist be allowed to teach? | 6 | 41 | 35 |
| Should a book written by a communist be removed from the library? | 27 | 57 | 30 |
| Average: | 24 | 53 | 29 |

The Stouffer data are taken from his book (1955: Chapter 2) and the 1977 NORC data are taken from the codebook of the General Social Science Survey of that year. The exact wordings of these questions are presented later in this chapter.

erated anything close to a majority of tolerant responses: the average for the six items is 24 percent. In 1977, however, a majority of respondents gave the tolerant response on four of the six items, all except the "teaching" questions. Between 1954 and 1977 the proportion of tolerant responses increased substantially, from 25 to 35 percentage points, on each of the six items. The average for each of the six items in the 1977 survey was 53 percent, an increase of 29 percent from 1954.

Several writers (Davis, 1975; Nunn et al., 1978) have tried to explain these changes, citing cohort replacement, the expansion of educational opportunities, the communications revolution, the reform politics of the 1960s, and the "Watergate" episode as factors contributing to the more tolerant political climate of the 1970s. Though these interpretations are necessarily speculative, these writers agree that the dangers of a wholesale assault on civil liberties are now much less than they were a generation ago.

Nunn and his colleagues have even gone beyond these modest conclusions. They assert that there has been a "dramatic increase in public support for democratic principles" (p. 158), a conclusion they reach by assuming an identity between tolerance and democratic principles. In addition, they suggest that on the basis of these empirical results scholars can begin to recast their understanding of democratic theory, as defined by earlier researchers, whose studies began with the "classical" theory of democracy (a major assumption of which was that nearly all citizens would accept the creed of tolerance in a form similar to that laid down by John Stuart Mill in *On Liberty*). When citizens failed to measure up to this standard, researchers tried to recast their understanding of democracy, seeking to find sources of democratic stability in other places, such as in institutions or in elite values. Now that more recent studies have reported that levels of tolerance have greatly increased, Nunn and his associates suggest (p. 159) that we can begin to resurrect the classical theory.

Clearly, a great deal has been made of these findings. What *should* be made of them? Recalling the critique, developed in the previous chapter, of Stouffer's procedures as content-biased, it is appropriate at this point to examine the validity of this critique and to re-examine the validity of these recent findings. We do so first by re-analyzing the original Stouffer data, comparing them to the responses to the same items on the 1974 NORC General Social Survey; we then present an alternative measurement strategy and compare the results obtained by Stouffer's method with those obtained using our strategy.

We have analyzed three "procedural" questions from the 1954 Stouffer data and these same questions from another NORC General Social Survey conducted in 1974. These questions examine attitudes on giving a public speech, teaching in a college, and allowing a book in a library— asked about each of three groups—communists, socialists, and atheists. (The precise question wordings are listed shortly.) This gives nine questions for analysis, all of which were asked in identical fashion in both 1954 and 1974.

For purposes of analysis, we posited a six-factor model to explain respondents' answers to these nine questions. We expected that the answers to each question would depend on two sets of factors: (1) the nature of the act in question, i.e., how difficult it is to be tolerant of that act; and (2) each respondent's attitude toward the group in question. Since each of the nine questions links a specific act to a specific group, respondents' answers to these questions will be influenced both by their degree of tolerance (their attitudes toward the three acts of giving a speech, teaching, and allowing a book in the library) and by their attitudes toward the three groups, which of course varies considerably from respondent to respondent. In this analysis, we hope to distinguish between attitudes of tolerance (act factors) and attitudes toward the groups (group factors). To the extent that Stouffer's items merely reflect the latter, they are invalid measures of political tolerance. If a person is truly tolerant, he or she should be prepared to tolerate the (legal) act without respect to the group involved.

Figure 3-1 presents the results of our attempt to fit this six-factor model to the two data sets simultaneously. The two data sets were fit

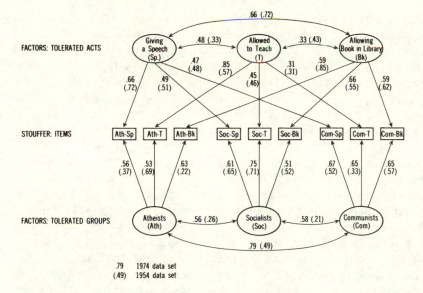

Fig. 3-1. Six-Factor Model of Tolerance Data, 1954 and 1974

to this model through the use of maximum likelihood estimation techniques. Although the details of the estimation procedures and the statistical techniques are relatively complex and difficult for the average reader to follow, the emphasis here will be on the substantive interpretation and implications of the results. The interested reader is referred to Appendix 8-A for more details about the techniques used here and in Chapter 8.[1] The results of the analysis are summarized in

1. We used the SIFASP model, which allows us to fit a single model to two data sets simultaneously. See Joreskog, 1969, 1970, and 1973. This analysis program estimates the correlations called *epistemic correlations*, the square roots of the more conventional reliability coefficients between the unmeasured factors, or constructs, and the measures. The correlations tell us how good each item is as a "measure" of the hypothesized underlying factor, and are analogous to factor loadings in ordinary factor analysis. For example, in Figure 3-1, the epistemic correlation between the question about whether atheists ought to be allowed to give a speech and the underlying act factor, giving a speech, was .72 in 1954 and .66 in 1974; the epistemic correlation between the same item and the underlying factor, attitude toward atheists, was .37 in 1954 and .56 in 1974. Thus we see that response to the question was a function of both attitude toward atheists and attitude toward, or tolerance of, the act of giving a speech in 1974. The program also estimates the correlations called *structural parameters* among the unmeasured factors. For example, in Figure 3-1, the correlation between the unmeasured factors, attitude toward atheists and attitude toward socialists, was .26 in 1954, but .56 in 1974. Thus respondents made a finer distinction between atheists and socialists in 1954 than they did in 1974. Similarly, the correlation between attitude toward, or tolerance of, the acts

Figure 3-1. The six-factor model fits the data quite well.[2] Looking at the coefficients in the model, several points are immediately clear. First, there has been little change over time in the correlations among the procedural or "act" factors. A person generally tolerant on the "speech" questions in 1954 was very likely to be tolerant on the "book" questions as well. Responses to these same questions were also closely related in 1974 (the correlations between the two were .72 in 1954 and .66 in 1974). On the other hand, the degree of predictability from the "speech" or "book" questions to the "teaching" question was quite low in 1954 and remained low in 1974. An examination of the percentages in Table 3-1 demonstrates that the reason for this finding is that teaching is perceived by most respondents as "harder" to tolerate than speaking or allowing a book in the library. This is true in 1954 and it is still true as late as 1977. Tolerance clearly depends on the act to be tolerated, at least in part, and one must obtain a sample of acts in order to measure the degree of political tolerance.

A second important point is that the extent to which responses on each question are a function of tolerance of the three acts remains unchanged between the two time points. The average epistemic correlation between the act factors and the nine questions is the same in 1974 as it was in 1954 (.56). Clearly tolerance as measured by these questions has changed, since there were more "tolerant" responses in 1974. But if these questions are relatively pure measures of tolerance, then attitudes toward these acts should have changed as well. More respondents should give tolerant answers to the Stouffer questions

---

of giving a speech and of allowing them to teach, was .33 in 1954 and .48 in 1974. These structural parameters thus relate unmeasured variables one to another. The computational details are complicated, but it must be kept in mind that all of these estimates— epistemic correlations and structural parameters—are derived from the empirical correlations among the nine Stouffer items, noted in Figure 3-1.

In estimating the same model from two data sets simultaneously, we have assumed a constant factor structure across populations, while allowing the parameters to vary freely. That is, we assumed that the same factors, correlated in the same ways, fit both sets of data individually, although we assumed that the exact values for the epistemic correlations and the structural correlations could differ between the two data sets. The goodness-of-fit analysis suggests that the same model does indeed fit both data sets well. (See Appendix 8-A.)

2. The chi-square divided by degrees of freedom is 3.28 and the average residuals are very small, indicating a good fit to the data. For the goodness of fit chi-square, the higher the value of chi-square, the greater the deviations between predicted correlations and the actual values. Thus the greater the chi-square, the worse the fit between model and data. Since the N's are so large (the 1954 data contain over 4,000 cases) any model with more than one degree of freedom will be significantly different from the data at the .01 level. The smaller the chi-square to degrees of freedom ratio, the better the model fits the data. The ratios in Table 3-2 are quite satisfactory.

because they feel that speaking, teaching, and allowing books in the library are important aspects of tolerance to be defended. Yet, answers to the Stouffer questions in 1974 were no more affected by respondents' attitudes toward these acts than was the case in 1954. But the marginal responses on these questions have changed considerably (Table 3-1). What, then, has changed?

The results in Table 3-2 provide an answer. Most importantly, the degree to which the group factors predict answers to the nine questions increased considerably between 1954 and 1974. The average epistemic correlation between the group factors and the responses to the nine items was .51 in 1954, but increased to .62 in 1974. Thus, attitudes toward the three groups now have a more powerful influence on respondents' answers to these nine questions than they had in 1954. As we suggest later, attitudes toward these three groups are currently less negative than they were in 1954 and, as a consequence, the answers to these questions reflect greater "tolerance." Of more immediate concern, however, is the fact that the Stouffer items evoke even more group-specific responses in the 1970s than they did in the 1950s. In other words, the level of tolerance exhibited on these questions depends more than ever on the specific groups asked about.[3] Another point worth noting is that the correlations among the group factors have also

**Table 3-2        Summary Statistics for Figure 3-1**

|  |  |
|---|---|
| Chi Square, Goodness of Fit = 78.82 | |
| Degrees of Freedom = 24 | |
| Chi Square/Degrees of Freedom = 3.28 | |

| | |
|---|---|
| Average Residual: | 1954 Stouffer = .008 |
| | 1974 NORC    = .013 |
| Averages of Structural Correlations Among Group Factors: | 1954 Stouffer = .32 |
| | 1974 NORC    = .64 |
| Averages of Epistemic Correlations Between Group Factors and Items: | 1954 Stouffer = .51 |
| | 1974 NORC    = .62 |
| Averages of Epistemic Correlations Between Items and Act Factors: | 1954 Stouffer = .56 |
| | 1974 NORC    = .56 |
| Averages of Structural Correlations Among Act Factors: | 1954 Stouffer = .49 |
| | 1974 NORC    = .49 |

3. In fact, in 1954, the answers to the Stouffer questions were determined more by attitude toward the act than by attitude toward the group (.56 versus .51); by 1974, these answers were determined less by attitude toward the act than by attitude toward the group (.56 versus .62). See Table 3-2. We conclude that these questions were thus less valid measures of tolerance in 1974 than they were in 1954.

increased considerably, from an average of .32 in 1954 to .64 in 1974, indicating that there were closer relationships in 1974 than in 1954 among the levels of "tolerance" for each of the three target groups. In other words, the degree of "tolerance" for communists is now more closely related to that for atheists (and socialists) than it was in 1954. This suggests further that the distinctions among these three groups are now less salient than they were in the 1950s. Apparently, then, in the 1950s the issue of domestic communism was sufficiently important that citizens were able to distinguish clearly among communists, socialists, and atheists and to "tolerate" the latter (socialists and atheists) more than the former (communists). With the decline in the salience of the communist issue in the 1970s, the public tends to lump these groups together, and, importantly, to "tolerate" all of them.[4] We tentatively conclude, then, that levels of tolerance per se *may* not have changed very much since the 1950s, since we find considerable stability in attitudes toward the three procedures or acts listed in Figure 3-1. On the other hand, the salience and visibility of the three groups have changed considerably, so that citizens are now more "tolerant" of them than they once were. However, this does not imply that there is now a greater commitment to tolerant norms than in the 1950s, but only that citizens in the aggregate are now more tolerant of these particular groups. It seems clear that there are currently no political groups that are as widely distrusted as communists were in the 1950s. Instead, there are now numerous political groups about which people may hold strong feelings but no one group monopolizes attention as the communists did a generation ago. If we could designate such groups, we could measure more validly the current level of tolerance and compare it with the levels that Stouffer found in the 1950s. According to the results in Figure 3-1, we might expect the responses to questions relating such salient political groups to various procedural acts will produce a substantially lower level of tolerance than that suggested by current replications of the Stouffer items.

## A Content-Controlled Measure of Political Tolerance

Our problem, then, is that tolerance can only be measured with reference to groups that people strongly dislike, but these groups are bound to vary from person to person. Smith may be hostile to com-

---

4. It may well be the case that societies will generally be more tolerant when unpopular groups are equally non-salient than when these groups are unequally salient. The latter condition may allow a clearer focus for the expression of intolerant impulses or predispositions. This point is developed further in the next chapter.

munists while Jones may be hostile to the Ku Klux Klan, while each may approve of or be indifferent toward the group the other dislikes. If we tried to measure tolerance strictly with reference to communists, it is very likely that Smith would appear to be more intolerant than Jones, who might in fact be equally intolerant but of a different target. The solution to this problem is to find a procedure to enable us to measure Smith's tolerance with reference to communists and Jones's with reference to the Ku Klux Klan. Such an approach would minimize the influence of the "group" factors.

To obtain such a measure, we developed and tested a self-anchoring procedure in which respondents themselves were allowed to select the group or groups they most strongly opposed. Each respondent was presented with a list of extremist groups, ranging from communists and socialists on the left to fascists, the John Birch Society, and the Ku Klux Klan on the right. We also included several other groups on this list, such as atheists, pro-abortionists, and anti-abortionists, which may represent positions that are independent of the left-right dimension. (See Appendix 3-A for the exact question wording and the specific groups listed.) Respondents were then asked to identify the group they liked the *least,* from this list or to name the group, if not on the list. Next they were presented with a series of statements in an agree-disagree format that elicited their views about a range of peaceful activities in which members of that group might participate or about steps the government might take against that group. These statements were as follows:

(1) Members of the —––— should be banned from being President of the United States.

(2) Members of the —––— should be allowed to teach in public schools.

(3) The —––— should be outlawed.

(4) Members of the —––— should be allowed to make a speech in this city.

(5) The —––— should have their phones tapped by our government.

(6) The —––— should be allowed to hold public rallies in our city.

(7) I would be willing to invite a member of the —––— into my home for dinner.

(8) I would be upset if a member of the —––— moved in next door to me.

(9) I would be pleased if my daughter or son dated a member of the —––—.

These statements were read as they appear above, with the blanks filled in with the name of the group each respondent selected. After these questions were posed, respondents were asked to choose a *second* group that they did not like.[5]

It should be emphasized that the activities referred to in these questions—such as running for office, teaching in the public schools, holding a rally, and making a public speech—are all peaceful in nature and otherwise perfectly legal and constitutional. Since tolerance refers to the willingness to permit the peaceful expression of ideas that one rejects, it was necessary to measure it in connection with activities that are legal and constitutional. Whatever the reputations of the various groups selected, respondents were asked to evaluate them in connection with a series of otherwise legitimate activities. Respondents were never asked to approve or to disapprove of violent or illegal activities.[6]

We used this content-controlled procedure to avoid contaminating the tolerance-intolerance dimension with the contents of respondents' political beliefs. If we had merely asked all respondents whether communists should be allowed to hold public office, for example, their responses would depend not only on their degree of tolerance but also on their feelings toward communism. The advantage of our procedure is that it creates a situation in which the evaluation of each respondent toward the group in question is held more or less constant. Although it is possible that respondents could still differ considerably in how much they dislike their least-liked group, evidence to be presented shortly indicates that almost all respondents harbored considerable dislike for their selected group. Our strategy generates "content-controlled" responses and allows us to put general procedural norms into a specific context without completely predetermining the context. This method prevents respondents from expressing agreement with general norms that they fail to apply to specific groups. Clearly, our measures are not "content-free" since there *is* a context and a specific group toward which each respondent is asked to react. We therefore call it a "content-controlled" measure to emphasize that we are controlling

5. The first six items on the list are political in content, whereas the last three items describe hypothetical social situations. For this reason, these six items formed the basis of our scale of political tolerance, which will be discussed in detail in Chapter 5. The three social items will not be analyzed until Chapter 8 but they are listed here and in the tables which follow for easy comparison with the six political items.

6. It will become evident in Chapter 7, however, that most of the respondents did not put our questions into this legal, constitutional context. They tended to respond to these groups in terms of violence or other illegal activities. They responded less in terms of constitutional and legal rights of these groups than in terms of how these groups infringe upon the constitutional and legal rights of other citizens.

for the contents of group beliefs by allowing respondents to select functionally equivalent groups. Hence, we may view the groups selected by different respondents as having an equivalent meaning for all of them, even though they may select different groups.

The traditional method presents respondents with a set of items specifying either communists or atheists as points of reference. These items were developed by Stouffer (and used by NORC in its recent surveys) to measure tolerance for nonconformity. Some of these items were:

(1) There are always some people whose ideas are considered bad or dangerous by other people. For instance, somebody who is against all churches and religion . . . If such a person wanted to make a speech in your city against churches and religion, should he be allowed to speak, or not?

(2) Should such a person be allowed to teach in a college or university, or not?

(3) If some people in your community suggested that a book he wrote against churches and religion should be taken out of your public library, would you favor removing this book, or not?

(4) Now, I should like to ask you some questions about a man who admits he is a Communist. Suppose this admitted Communist wanted to make a speech in your community. Should he be allowed to speak, or not?

(5) Suppose he is teaching in a college. Should he be fired, or not?

(6) Suppose he wrote a book which is in your public library. Somebody in your community suggests that the book should be removed from the library. Would you favor removing it, or not?

By our standards, these questions are not content-controlled, since they measure tolerance with reference to groups selected by the investigators. We would expect that these items really measure attitudes toward communists and atheists rather than tolerance. Since we have presented both the Stouffer questions and ours to separate samples, we can readily measure the influence of different measurement strategies.

## The Twin Cities Samples

These sets of questions were administered to two independent random samples in Minneapolis and St. Paul, Minnesota, during the spring and summer of 1976. One sample received the "content-controlled" tolerance questions while the other sample got the old Stouffer items. Two independent random samples of size 300 were selected from the Twin Cities' directories, which include listings of all adults residing in Minneapolis and St. Paul. Interviews were completed with 200 persons using the Stouffer items and with 198 persons using the new questions.[7] The demographic characteristics of these two samples closely approximated those of the Twin Cities population (Sullivan, Piereson, and Marcus, 1978). These samples were representative of the larger population and very similar to one another. Any differences in levels of tolerance between these two samples may therefore be attributed to the different measures of tolerance that were administered to each.

The top part of Table 3-3 presents the proportions of tolerant responses for the least-liked and second least-liked groups for the sample that was administered the content-controlled questions. The corresponding percentages for the Stouffer items in the second sample are presented in the bottom part of the table. As expected, the Stouffer items produce substantially higher percentages of tolerant responses than do the content-controlled items. In every case, the Stouffer questions produced tolerant majorities, ranging from 62 percent tolerant on the question dealing with a communist teacher to 80 percent tolerant on the question dealing with a library book written by an atheist. With respect to the content-controlled questions, however, there is much more variation in the pattern of responses, but the proportions of tolerant responses are well below a majority on nearly all of these questions. The percentage of tolerant responses ranges from 26 percent on the teaching question to 70 percent on the speech and wiretapping questions (omitting the last three items, which deal with social tolerance). These questions produce some interesting results. For example, only a third of our respondents were willing to say that their least-liked group should not be outlawed and only about one-fourth would allow members of their least-liked group to teach in public schools. In addition, only about one-half of these respondents were willing to allow this group to hold public rallies in their city.[8] There is little doubt that

7. Interviewers were trained during a one-day workshop and subsequent individual training sessions. Weekly meetings were held after the interviewing began to discuss problems and to standardize responses to them. The interviewers were hired by placing a job description with the University Employment Service at the University of Minnesota. Approximately 15 interviewers were used, some of them undergraduates, some graduate students, and some non-students. We uncovered no data problems related to interviewers.

8. Since our questions are five-point agree-disagree items, the percentage tolerant reflects those who agree or agree strongly (or disagree, depending upon the *direction* of the statement).

**Table 3-3.**   **Levels of Tolerance for Content-Controlled Questions and for Stouffer Questions, Twin Cities Split Samples**

| A. *Content-Controlled* | Percent Tolerant, Least-Liked Group | Percent Tolerant, Second Least-Liked Group |
|---|---|---|
| Members of the ——— should be banned from being President of the U.S. | 28% | 32% |
| Members of the ——— should be allowed to teach in public schools. | 26 | 30 |
| The ——— should be outlawed. | 33 | 43 |
| Members of the ——— should be allowed to make a speech in this city. | 70 | 67 |
| The ——— should have their phones tapped by our government. | 70 | 70 |
| The ——— should be allowed to hold public rallies in our city. | 57 | 51 |
| I would be willing to invite a member of the ——— into my home for dinner. | 31 | 33 |
| I would be upset if a member of the ——— moved in next door to me. | 34 | 36 |
| I would be pleased if my daughter or son dated a member of the ———. | 4 | 4 |

| B. *Stouffer* | Percent Tolerant |
|---|---|
| Should an atheist be allowed to speak? | 78% |
| Should an atheist be allowed to teach? | 63 |
| Should a book written by an atheist be removed from the library? | 80 |
| Should a communist be allowed to speak? | 71 |
| Should a communist be allowed to teach? | 62 |
| Should a book written by a communist be removed from the library? | 79 |

See the text for the exact wording. For Part A, N = 198 and for Part B, N = 200.

the content-controlled items generate more intolerant responses than the Stouffer items because they permit respondents to select from a much wider range of groups. People who would permit communists or atheists a full range of civil liberties may be unwilling to allow extremist groups on the right these same liberties. This is, in any event, a likely explanation for these patterns.

It should be noted, however, that there are some differences between these two sets of questions. For example, the Stouffer set does not include items dealing with the right to run for office, or with outlawing groups, questions appearing among the content-controlled items. In addition, the content-controlled items are presented in an agree-disagree format while the Stouffer items are presented in a yes-no format. Thus, our format allows respondents to state the strength of their agreement or disagreement with a particular question. Nevertheless, these slight differences in format do not account for the differences in levels of tolerance these sets of questions produced. The high levels of intolerance the content-controlled items reflect raise some questions about the claims, cited above, about the strengthening of tolerant norms in American politics over the past twenty-five years. At a minimum, these results suggest that though tolerance of communists and atheists has increased over the years, tolerance as a more universal attitude may not have changed much at all. During a period when domestic communism was a very salient issue, communists and those perceived to be in league with them provided a visible target for intolerance. As this issue declined in importance, tolerance for these groups apparently increased, while at the same time, other groups were emerging to take their place as potential targets of intolerance. It is difficult to prove this interpretation conclusively, since it rests upon some untested (and untestable) assumptions about the range of visible targets that existed in the 1950s. However, the case is plausible and it is consistent with our findings.

The figures in Table 3-4 present the results of a national survey conducted for us by NORC in the spring of 1978. Though we did not have the resources to conduct two national samples to repeat the question wording experiment (nor did we deem it necessary to do so), we did present our content-controlled questions, as well as four of the Stouffer items, to a single national sample of respondents. We used the results from NORC's 1977 General Social Survey to compute the percentages for the two remaining Stouffer items (see Table 3-4). In general, the patterns presented here are similar to those presented above: the Stouffer items generated higher levels of tolerance than did the content-controlled items. In the national sample, 19 percent were

**Table 3-4**          **Levels of Tolerance for Content-Controlled and for Stouffer Questions, 1978 NORC National Survey**

| A. *Content-Controlled* | Percent Tolerant Least-Liked Group |
|---|---|
| Members of the ——— should be banned from being President of the U.S. | 16% |
| Members of the ——— should be allowed to teach in public schools. | 19 |
| The ——— should be outlawed. | 29 |
| Members of the ——— should be allowed to make a speech in this city. | 50 |
| The ——— should have their phones tapped by our government. | 59 |
| The ——— should be allowed to hold public rallies in our city. | 34 |
| I would be willing to invite a member of the ——— into my home for dinner. | 18 |
| I would be upset if a member of the ——— moved in next door to me. | 37 |
| I would be pleased if my daughter or son dated a member of the ———. | 4 |

| B. *Stouffer* | |
|---|---|
| Should an atheist be allowed to speak? | 65% |
| Should an atheist be allowed to teach?[a] | 40 |
| Should a book written by an atheist be removed from the library? | 62 |
| Should a communist be allowed to speak? | 63 |
| Should a communist be allowed to teach? | 40 |
| Should a book written by a communist be removed from the library? | 64 |

See the text for exact question wording. N = 1509
[a] Question not asked in the 1978 survey. Figures are from the 1977 NORC General Social Survey.

tolerant on the content-controlled teaching question, while on the corresponding Stouffer item, 40 percent were. Similarly, 50 percent were tolerant using the content-controlled question about free speech, while 65 and 63 percent were tolerant using the two Stouffer items dealing with speech. The results from the national and the local surveys thus yield the same conclusion: the Stouffer measures produce higher levels of tolerance than do the content-controlled questions. In addition, the results from the latter items do not generally support the claim made by several writers that levels of tolerance among American citizens are now very high relative to the 1950s.[9]

9. Lest we overstate our case, we must point out that overall tolerance may have increased somewhat over the last 20 years, though not nearly so much as the Stouffer measures suggest. For example, as noted in Table 3-1, in 1954 Stouffer found that

Another point corroborating this interpretation is that respondents become slightly more tolerant when asked about their second least-liked group (see Table 3-3A). This is true of the first three items listed in the table, which are the ones with the smallest proportions of tolerant responses. To be sure, these differences are quite small, and on at least three of the nine items the pattern does not hold. Yet this does suggest that respondents become more tolerant when they are asked about groups toward which they feel less hostile. One may assume, therefore, that the reason the Stouffer items produce higher levels of tolerance is that many current respondents do not feel particularly hostile toward communists and atheists.

This point can be examined in more detail in terms of the data in Table 3-5. After respondents in the Twin Cities survey had selected

**Table 3-5**      **Semantic Differential Items for Both the Content-Controlled and the Stouffer Measures: Twin Cities Samples**

| Adjectives | Mean Score[a] Least-Liked Group | Mean Score Second Least-Liked Group | Mean Score for Communists | Mean Score for Atheists |
|---|---|---|---|---|
| important-unimportant | 4.55 | 4.29 | 4.33 | 4.48 |
| honest-dishonest | 5.27 | 5.20 | 4.77 | 3.74 |
| good-bad | 6.14 | 6.09 | 5.41 | 4.61 |
| predictable-unpredictable | 4.96 | 4.66 | 4.71 | 4.65 |
| safe-dangerous[b] | 6.11 | 5.80 | 5.38 | 4.63 |
| strong-weak | 3.62 | 3.48 | 3.63 | 3.92 |
| democratic-undemocratic | 6.38 | 6.24 | 6.07 | 4.81 |

[a] These means are based on semantic differential scales ranging from 1 to 7. The higher the mean, the closer the average perception was to the second of the adjective pairs. For example, the mean of 6.14 for good-bad reflects the fact that almost every respondent perceived their least-favorite group as bad, while the mean of 6.11 on safe-dangerous means almost all of them perceived this group as dangerous (rather than safe).

[b] This adjective pair was reversed on the questionnaire. In the table, its scoring is presented to be consistent with the other adjective pairs. In all cases, the higher the score, the more toward the "bad" end of the continuum.

37 percent thought atheists should be allowed to give a speech, and 27 percent would extend this same right to communists. As noted in Table 3-4, however, in 1978, 50 percent were prepared to allow their least-liked group to make a speech in their city. Similarly, in 1954, 12 percent thought an atheist should be allowed to teach, while 6 percent would extend this right to communists. By 1978, 19 percent were prepared to extend this right to their least-liked group. The latter increase is not very large, and in any event, not nearly so large as the figures in Table 3-1 would suggest. A large proportion of the apparent increase in tolerance undoubtedly reflects the content-bias of the Stouffer questions.

their "least-liked" group, they were asked to evaluate that group in terms of the seven pairs of adjectives listed in the table. This procedure was repeated for their "second least-liked" group. In the sample presented with the Stouffer items, each respondent was asked to evaluate both communists and atheists on the same seven pairs of adjectives. These responses allow us to compare the aggregate evaluations of "least-liked" groups with evaluations of communists and atheists; thus we can test the assumption that the latter two groups are equivalent to the former.

The pattern of mean scores presented in Table 3-5 demonstrates that the target groups respondents selected are evaluated more negatively than are communists or atheists. The pairs with the most extreme scores for the "least-liked" groups are "good-bad," "democratic-undemocratic," and "safe-dangerous." The other items all have means in the middle three categories of 3, 4, or 5 (the scales range from 1 to 7). The respondents' least-preferred groups are perceived as uniformly bad, undemocratic, and dangerous; and this is generally true of the second "least-liked" groups as well, though these scores are, as expected, somewhat less extreme. A different picture emerges, however, in connection with the Stouffer items. The scores for communists and atheists are less extreme and tend to cluster in the middle categories of the scales. When the means for the "least-liked" groups are compared to those for communists and atheists, they are uniformly more positive or desirable. Thus, atheists and communists are less important, less dishonest, less bad, less unpredictable, less dangerous, less strong, and less undemocratic than the least-preferred groups. Although the magnitude of these differences is not always large, it is the consistent pattern that is most important.

These results lead to three conclusions. First, regardless of what may have been appropriate in the 1950s, the use of communists and atheists as points of reference against which to measure tolerance is no longer appropriate. Citizens are now able to point to other political groups toward which they feel more hostility and which they regard as more threatening. The Stouffer measures, when used to make comparisons across time, are bound to lead to a confusion between changing evaluations of communists and atheists and changing levels of tolerance. For theoretical and practical reasons, then, our content-controlled measure is the more appropriate strategy for measuring tolerance. Second, the scores on the adjective pairs clearly indicate that almost all respondents selected target groups toward which they feel very hostile. The standard deviations for the good-bad, safe-dangerous, and democratic-undemocratic adjective pairs for least-liked groups are very small (data not shown). This relates to our earlier point, that although respondents could still vary considerably in their degree of dislike toward their individual target groups, they generally do not. Perceptions are uniform and negative. This was, of course, the objective of the measurement procedure, since tolerance can only be measured validly in relation to such perceptions.

Third, it appears that the U.S. public should continue to be described as attitudinally intolerant rather than tolerant. In spite of recent data to the contrary, there does not appear to have been a marked increase in political tolerance during the last two decades. These results have probably arisen because of a more limited understanding of political tolerance coupled with an apparently flawed measurement procedure. This, of course, demonstrates the extent to which issues of conceptualization, measurement, and substance are interrelated and the degree to which they must each be given careful attention so that carelessness in one sphere does not lead the researcher astray in all three. Our point, then, is that we need to re-evaluate previous conceptions of tolerance, the resulting measurement operations used in previous research, and the substantive findings and interpretations to which they led. Here we have concluded that previous conceptualizations of political tolerance have often ignored a key element—the element of a serious objection to the target group, shared equally by all respondents. Failure to establish whether the target group is equally objectionable has produced content-biased measures of political tolerance, and as a consequence, recent conclusions that the U.S. public is now a bastion of tolerance are off the mark and should be re-evaluated.

### The Content-Controlled Measure: The Problem of Validity

The results reported earlier support many of our criticisms of the traditional measures of tolerance and, in addition, have led to some surprising conclusions about the levels of tolerance in American society in the 1970s. But it is one thing to criticize the old measures and another to prove the validity of our own approach. It is therefore appropriate to consider more directly the validity of our "content-controlled" measure. Since this measure assumes that it is necessary to control for the contents of respondents' political beliefs, it seemed appropriate to test its validity by examining an important substantive point—the degree to which people select target groups in a manner consistent with their ideological outlooks. If the measure is valid, people at different points along the ideological continuum should select target groups some distance from their own position. If, for example, liberals are as likely as conservatives to select left-wing groups as targets, the assumption underlying our measure is wrong, and the Stouffer measures might serve as well as, or better, than ours.

To test this assumption, the target groups were arrayed according to the ideological positions of the respondents who selected them. Ideology was measured by a seven-point liberal-conservative scale on which respondents were asked to place themselves. Scores ranged from 1 (very liberal) to 7 (very conservative), with 4 the mid-point. We also used a scale of domestic liberalism and conservatism based on four questions dealing with the role of the federal government in the issues of job security, health insurance, school integration, and fair employment practices.[10] This scale ranged from 4 (very liberal on all four issues) to 28 (very conservative on all four issues), with 16 the mid-point.

In Figures 3-2 through 3-5, the mean scores on these two scales are presented for respondents who picked each of the various groups as their least or second least-liked group. In Figure 3-2, for example, the respondents who selected the John Birch Society as their least-liked group had a mean self-placement score of 3.38, nearer the liberal end of the scale; those who selected socialists had a mean score of 4.47, nearer the conservative end of the scale. As is evident from this figure,

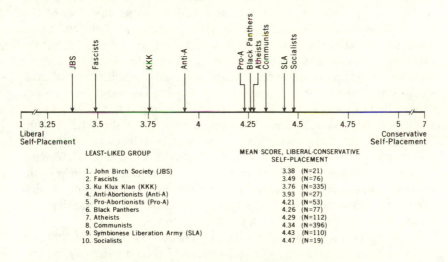

| LEAST-LIKED GROUP | MEAN SCORE, LIBERAL-CONSERVATIVE SELF-PLACEMENT | |
|---|---|---|
| 1. John Birch Society (JBS) | 3.38 | (N=21) |
| 2. Fascists | 3.49 | (N=76) |
| 3. Ku Klux Klan (KKK) | 3.76 | (N=335) |
| 4. Anti-Abortionists (Anti-A) | 3.93 | (N=27) |
| 5. Pro-Abortionists (Pro-A) | 4.21 | (N=53) |
| 6. Black Panthers | 4.26 | (N=77) |
| 7. Atheists | 4.29 | (N=112) |
| 8. Communists | 4.34 | (N=396) |
| 9. Symbionese Liberation Army (SLA) | 4.43 | (N=110) |
| 10. Socialists | 4.47 | (N=19) |

**Fig. 3-2. Liberal-Conservative Self-placement by Least-Liked Group**

10. See Chapter 7 for a discussion of these items and the resulting scale. In Chapter 7 we examine the substantive nature of these findings. Validity is the only concern here.

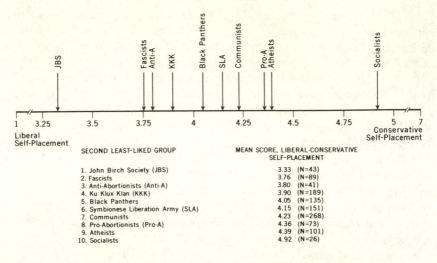

SECOND LEAST-LIKED GROUP          MEAN SCORE, LIBERAL-CONSERVATIVE
                                        SELF-PLACEMENT

|  | | |
|---|---|---|
| 1. John Birch Society (JBS) | 3.33 | (N=43) |
| 2. Fascists | 3.76 | (N=89) |
| 3. Anti-Abortionists (Anti-A) | 3.80 | (N=41) |
| 4. Ku Klux Klan (KKK) | 3.90 | (N=189) |
| 5. Black Panthers | 4.05 | (N=135) |
| 6. Symbionese Liberation Army (SLA) | 4.15 | (N=151) |
| 7. Communists | 4.23 | (N=268) |
| 8. Pro-Abortionists (Pro-A) | 4.36 | (N=73) |
| 9. Atheists | 4.39 | (N=101) |
| 10. Socialists | 4.92 | (N=26) |

**Fig. 3-3. Liberal-Conservative Self-placement by Second Least-Liked Group**

the groups are ordered roughly as one would expect them to be if liberals generally disliked right-wing groups while conservatives disliked left-wing groups. Four groups of respondents had mean scores toward the liberal end of the scale: those who selected the John Birch Society, fascists, the KKK, and anti-abortionists as their least-liked group. On the other hand, six groups had mean scores toward the conservative end of the scale: those who selected socialists, the SLA, communists, atheists, the Black Panthers, and pro-abortionists. We make no claim that the precise ordering among left-wing (or among right-wing) groups is significant. Although many scholars would consider communists to be "more" left-wing than socialists, we do not expect that respondents who select the former group as their target should be more conservative than those who select the latter group. We only expect that conservatives will usually select one of the five left-wing groups whereas liberals will select one of the three right-wing groups. The validity of our measurement does not depend on respondents in a mass sample making the finer distinction. No doubt, which particular right-wing group is picked by a self-defined liberal depends on all sorts of random and idiosyncratic factors.

Those respondents who selected the groups listed in the Stouffer items had mean scores between 4.29 and 4.47 (see Figure 3-2), clearly on the conservative side. In other words, conservatives tend to select these particular groups as targets. It may be inferred, then, that the Stouffer measures posed a more difficult test for conservatives than for liberals.

This pattern remains the same for respondents' second "least-liked" group. The same four groups on the right are selected by liberals and the same six groups on the left are selected by conservatives. Though there is some shifting in the order of the groups on either side of the mid-point, the general clusterings remain the same. Some shifting of this sort was expected because of the small number of respondents selecting some of the groups (for example, the John Birch Society and socialists) and because the combinations of respondents selecting different groups were bound to change between the first and second choices. More importantly, however, we expected liberals to be more likely than conservatives to select right-wing groups on both the first and second rounds, and this turned out to be the case.

Turning to the second measure of ideology, based on responses to the domestic issue questions, we find roughly the same pattern (Figure 3-4). As noted, the scores range from 4 to 28, with 16 the mid-point. The respondents who selected four left-wing groups (the SLA, Black Panthers, communists, and atheists) had mean scores nearer the conservative end of the scale. Two clusters of respondents had mean scores at the neutral point of the scale—those selecting pro-abortionists and anti-abortionists as targets. Finally, four groupings had mean scores nearer the liberal end of the scale—those selecting the Birch Society, the KKK, fascists, and socialists. The only departure from the pattern in all of these figures thus involved those selecting socialists as a target group: socialists are more often selected by domestic liberals than by

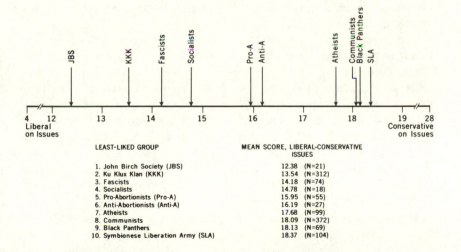

| LEAST-LIKED GROUP | MEAN SCORE, LIBERAL-CONSERVATIVE ISSUES | |
|---|---|---|
| 1. John Birch Society (JBS) | 12.38 | (N=21) |
| 2. Ku Klux Klan (KKK) | 13.54 | (N=312) |
| 3. Fascists | 14.18 | (N=74) |
| 4. Socialists | 14.78 | (N=18) |
| 5. Pro-Abortionists (Pro-A) | 15.95 | (N=55) |
| 6. Anti-Abortionists (Anti-A) | 16.19 | (N=27) |
| 7. Atheists | 17.68 | (N=99) |
| 8. Communists | 18.09 | (N=372) |
| 9. Black Panthers | 18.13 | (N=69) |
| 10. Symbionese Liberation Army (SLA) | 18.37 | (N=104) |

**Fig. 3-4. Liberal-Conservative Location on Issues by Least-Liked Group**

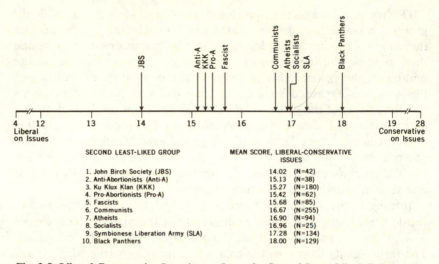

Fig. 3-5. Liberal-Conservative Location on Issues by Second Least-Liked Group

domestic conservatives. However, this undoubtedly reflects the small number of respondents involved (N = 18) rather than any systematic tendency of those on the left to dislike socialists.

The anomaly is not repeated, however, in Figure 3-5, in which the issue scale is arrayed by the second "least-liked" group. Here, the socialists tend to be selected by those nearer the conservative end of the spectrum. As before, the left-wing groups tend to be chosen by conservatives on domestic issues, while the right-wing groups are chosen by those who are more liberal.

These patterns demonstrate, as expected, that respondents tend to select target groups some distance away from their own political position. Another way to test the validity of the measure is to examine what we have called (for want of a better term) "crossovers," respondents who selected one left-wing and one right-wing group as their two least-liked groups. Given our previous findings, we expect those close to the center of the left-right dimension to be most likely to "crossover," to select a group from the left on one round and a group from the right on the second. Those who are closer to the extremes should tend to select two groups from the same (opposite to their own) extreme.

The results of this analysis are in Table 3-6. Among those most liberal on the scale, 40 percent selected two right-wing groups, despite the fact that there were only three groups on the questionnaire that could be clearly labeled as right-wing. There is then a sharp and consistent

Table 3-6          **Liberal-Conservative Self-Placement and Target Groups Picked
(1978 NORC)**

| Groups Picked Are: | Liberal | | | | | Conservative | |
|---|---|---|---|---|---|---|---|
| | 1 | 2 | 3 | 4 | 5 | 6 | 7 |
| Both Left Wing | 11% | 16% | 20% | 35% | 38% | 47% | 53% |
| One Left and One Center[a] | 0 | 6 | 9 | 14 | 10 | 12 | 6 |
| One Left and One Right | 40 | 49 | 53 | 41 | 42 | 38 | 29 |
| One Right and One Center | 9 | 9 | 5 | 6 | 5 | 2 | 12 |
| Both Right Wing | 40 | 18 | 13 | 4 | 4 | 1 | 0 |
| N = | 35 | 109 | 136 | 428 | 224 | 144 | 17 |

In this and subsequent tables, columns may not total 100% because of rounding.
[a] The two abortion groups were defined as centrist groups. No respondents selected both abortion groups as their two least-liked groups.

decline in the percentages selecting two such groups as we move across the scale from left to right. At the extreme right pole of the scale, no respondents are found who selected two right-wing groups as targets.

On the other hand, fully half of those who labeled themselves conservatives selected two left-wing groups, while only about one in ten of the liberals did so. With respect to the "crossovers," those respondents nearer the middle of the scale were in fact more likely to select one left-wing and one right-wing group. Moving from left to right along the scale, 40 percent of the most liberal respondents "crossed-over," and this percentage rises to 53 percent for those in the third category (slightly liberal) after which point it decreases steadily as we move further to the right. It is likely that more liberals than conservatives "crossed-over" because there were five left-wing but only three right-wing groups listed on our questionnaire, increasing the likelihood that left-wing groups would be chosen. Nevertheless the ideological pattern remains clear.

We have presented these patterns in considerable detail to make certain that the assumptions underlying our measure of tolerance have empirical validity. By and large, our assumptions seem warranted. We demonstrate that respondents did not select target groups randomly or capriciously but were guided by their own political views. This indicates, in turn, that the groups respondents selected are valid points of reference against which tolerance may be measured. At the same time, these patterns indicate that the traditional measures of tolerance, specifying a narrow range of groups to which people were asked to respond, produce misleading results. While we have also presented respondents with a definite list of political groups, these groups were selected from the entire range of the political spectrum.[11] Hence, though some respondents, left to their own imaginations, might have designated a group not on our list, nearly all were certain to find at least one group on this list to which they were strongly opposed. Given the reasonable limits of any survey design, this is all we could expect.

## A Framework for the Analysis of Political Tolerance

Matters of theory and conceptualization, measurement strategy, and substantive conclusions are bound inextricably throughout the research process. In this chapter we have sought to demonstrate this fundamental point, one generally accepted by social scientists yet often ignored in the actual research process. It seems clear that in order to make any significant progress in understanding political tolerance, all of these matters must be reconsidered and thought through from the beginning. Stouffer faced squarely many of these issues, but most subsequent empirical work on political tolerance has failed to do so. The apparent results are mistaken research strategies which have spawned misleading findings and interpretations.

In our effort to begin at the beginning, we have reconsidered a number of important and fundamental questions. By way of review and of preview, we shall go over them briefly here:

1. *What is political tolerance?* How does one recognize it, and how do researchers know when it is absent? In Chapter 1 we answered this question with the claim that political tolerance exists when respondents allow the full legal rights of citizenship to groups they themselves dislike. We put forward the explicit claim that political tolerance does not exist when there is no real objection, and that intolerance exists whenever respondents object strongly to a group or its ideas, *and* refuse that group the rights of participation in the political process. Implicit in this understanding of political tolerance is the notion that violence or other activities outside the legal framework of a mature democracy

11. As noted in Figure 3-2, the three groups included in the Stouffer items fall between 4.29 and 4.47 on the scale, a range of 0.18 on a seven-point scale; our total array of groups fall between 3.38 and 4.47, a range of 1.09. In Figure 3-3, the Stouffer groups have a range of 0.69 while ours have a range of 1.59. The greatest difference between the two methods may be apparent in Figure 3-5, where the Stouffer items have a range of 0.29 while our measure has a range of 3.98, on a 24-point scale. (Recall that these are all group means, so the range refers to mean differences among these groups of respondents selecting particular target groups.) Moreover, respondents were given the option of selecting a group not on the list. (Some 2% of the national sample, as noted above, did so).

need not be allowed, nor does tolerance come into play in relation to these activities.

2. *How tolerant is the U.S. public?* The generally accepted answer to this question is that although the public was intolerant in the 1950s, it is now generally quite tolerant. The relevant literature was reviewed in Chapter 2. Earlier in this chapter, however, we argued that although attitudes toward communists, socialists, and atheists are now more favorable, there has been little if any change in tolerance, more generally understood. Our analysis of Stouffer's 1954 data and NORC's 1974 data supports this conclusion, as does the analysis of data collected using the content-controlled strategy.

3. *If the public is generally intolerant, what are the targets of this attitudinal intolerance? How do respondents select one set of targets over another?* Answers to these questions are important both in understanding the individual psychology of intolerance, and in determining the broader political implications of intolerance and its targets. These questions are addressed more fully in Chapter 4. Here it is sufficient to note that the targets of intolerance in the U.S. are diverse and cover the ideological spectrum from extreme left to extreme right. The implications of this selection pattern differ from those of the 1950s pattern, which focussed on a small number of left-wing targets. In the more recent pattern, there is less agreement about the targets of repression, a phenomenon we label "pluralistic intolerance." (See Chapter 4.)

The pattern of target group selection is important but does not clarify the decisional calculations involved in target group selection. We have already provided one important clue in this chapter, *viz.*, that it is largely ideological. Individuals apparently perceive politics, at least in part, in terms of a left-right continuum. They place themselves somewhere along this continuum, and also locate most major political groups somewhere along it. They then select their target groups from among those groups that are farthest from their own position. This assumption has not been tested rigorously, but the data are consistent with it. There is a strong tendency for liberals to select right-wing targets, and for conservatives to select left-wing targets. Furthermore, the moderates (those individuals closest to the center of the continuum) are very likely to select one right-wing and one left-wing target, since both left and right-wing extremes are distant from their own ideological position.

In the next chapter, we examine other variables which play a significant role in target group selection. Although political ideology plays the most important part in this process, it does not completely determine it. Since different social and demographic groups in American society often adhere to different political ideologies, these social variables themselves play a role in the process.

Another motivation for this analysis is our view that the traditional measures are content-biased. Since the left-wing content of the traditional measures provides an "easier" test of tolerance for people on the left, then perhaps those variables traditionally identified as "causes" of tolerance are only spuriously related to it. Since we conceptualize a two-step decision-making process—first selecting a target group, then deciding how much (or how little) to tolerate that group—it is plausible that these "causes" of tolerance identified earlier affect the first step in the process, but not the second. For example, education may affect target-group selection but not the degree of tolerance toward that target group. Other factors come into play during the second stage of the decisional process. In the next chapter, therefore, the role in target group selection played by social variables such as education, age, religion, region and others are examined. Subsequently, Chapter 5 examines their importance in the second step, the decision of how much to tolerate target groups.

4. *Once a target is selected, how do individuals decide to tolerate, or refuse to tolerate, that group?* Of course, there are matters of degree involved — the real question that respondents face is "how tolerant ought I to be of this group?" Here we identify the major sets of variables involved in that decision-making process, and we examine them in subsequent chapters, generally proceeding from the more distal and remote variables to those that relate directly to tolerance. In Chapter 5 we examine the social sources of tolerance. This includes the broad demographic and subcultural factors that shape the contours of one's experience. Chapter 6 presents the personality factors that influence how one interprets these experiences, including self-esteem, dogmatism, faith in people, and other variables which influence personal security. Chapter 7 explores the political variables and processes that influence tolerance. We include in that discussion perceptual and cognitive processes which are general in nature but specifically political in content, such as perceptions of threat posed by target groups.

It is this general progression—from the more remote variables which shape the conditions of experience, to the more personal mechanisms involved in interpreting this experience, and finally to the more directly political aspects of experience—that guides the analysis in the coming chapters. It is more convenient in the *present* context, however, to reverse the order and discuss the more proximal variables first.

In deciding how tolerant or intolerant to be toward a target, there are several obvious considerations. The first and foremost is probably perceptions of threat posed by the group. In most cases, respondents might be expected to be tolerant of a target group no matter how much they object to it, provided it does not pose any serious threat to them or their values. Thus respondent X may object violently to the American Nazi Party, yet tolerate it because of the perception (accurate or not) that this group has no power in American politics, and has no opportunity to seize power in the future. Respondent X may also believe that the Nazis are harmless enough, and will not cause anyone in the U.S. any significant harm. Respondent Y, however, may have suffered at the hands of the Nazis and believe that, although they are not an immediate threat, there is some likelihood that they will obtain power in the future; further, the respondent believes that they *are* a serious current threat to various elements of the Jewish community. We might expect respondent Y to be less tolerant than respondent X, even though they both harbor strong objections to the Nazis. This is explored in Chapter 7.

Another consideration that guides decisions about tolerance is the respondents' commitment to the norms of democracy—their belief in abstract principles such as free speech, equality under the law, and other such generalizations designed to serve as guides to behavior. Respondents who have a firm belief in these abstract norms may find it more difficult to violate them than those who either do not believe in them, or who agree vaguely but hold no strong feelings one way or the other. Respondents first make a judgment about the degree of threat their target group represents, and then they "examine their consciences" to see whether the threat is strong enough to override their concern for democratic principles. Some respondents who have equal perceptions of threat will differ in their judgments about how far to tolerate an extremist group because of their unequal commitment to these norms. Other respondents who basically agree in their commitment to these norms will differ in their judgments of tolerance because they hold different interpretations of the norms in practical situations. Some will merely note that the norms themselves require tolerance even of threatening groups; others will conclude that the target group itself is a serious threat to the norms, and thus, if they are to defend the norms, they must not tolerate the group. The merits of these two points of view aside, these factors affect respondents' decisions to give a tolerant or an intolerant set of answers to our questions. This is also explored further in Chapter 7.

Perceived threat and commitment to the norms of democracy are examples of two of the more direct "causes" of tolerance. They are perhaps the first things that respondents consider when they are asked various questions about tolerance. The responses to several open-ended questions, reported in Chapter 7, support this supposition. There are other factors entering into the decision that respondents cannot be expected to articulate, although they may play an important role. Foremost among these is undoubtedly the respondents' differing personalities. Foremost among the personality characteristics involved in this process is the respondents' sense of inner security. In Chapter 6 we examine the variables which influence this sense of security, including self-esteem, self-actualization, and others.

In making a decision about tolerance, respondents most certainly do not ask themselves whether they are personally secure. Yet such factors affect the decision-making process, either by creating a separate decisional calculus for different types of respondents, or by magnifying some respondents' sensitivity to external threats. In the former circumstance, affect may be so strong that some merely give an intolerant set of responses without considering the question of threat, or without tempering this judgment because of a consideration for democratic norms. For other respondents, affect does not interfere, and cognitive judgments are based on the types of considerations outlined above. In the latter circumstance, all respondents use basically the same decisional calculus, but insecure respondents experience a heightened sense of threat and thus arrive at consistently less tolerant responses than more secure individuals. The details of these processes are presented in Chapters 6 and 8.

Considering factors even more distal than cognitions and personality, there is a large set of social variables that undoubtedly affect the decisions to tolerate or not to tolerate. These social and demographic variables influence decisions about tolerance either by having a direct impact on the degree of tolerance, or by setting the stage for different decisional processes by different types of respondents. For example, education may directly influence levels of tolerance, other things being equal, by creating a more open environment that is less suspicious of unpopular groups and their ideas. These more distal factors are covered in depth in Chapter 5.

The relative importance of these three sets of variables—social, psychological, and political—is assessed in the multivariate analysis presented in Chapter 8. Chapters 5–7 present a detailed description of each of the sets of variables and the ways in which they appear to affect levels of tolerance. The "causal" impact of each set of variables on the two stage process described above—selecting a target, and then determining whether to tolerate it—is assessed in Chapters 8 and 9 below. It is well to remember, however, that in this analysis we are not interested in casual relationships alone, but also in those descriptive characteristics of the population that have political or theoretical implications. Some of these implications will become apparent in the next chapter when we discuss the first stage of the process—the choice of target groups in the American electorate and among various subgroups in the electorate.

## APPENDIX 3-A

INSTRUCTIONS TO INTERVIEWER: HAND THE RESPONDENT OUR HANDOUT A, THE "LIST OF GROUPS IN POLITICS." THEN SAY:

> I am giving you a list of groups in politics. As I read the list please follow along: socialists, fascists, communists, ku klux klan, John Birch Society, black panthers, symbionese liberation army, atheists, pro-abortionists, and anti-abortionists. Which of these groups do you like the least? If there is some group that you like even less than the groups listed here, please tell me the name of that group. (NOTE TO INTERVIEWER: IF THEY HAVE TROUBLE MAKING UP THEIR MIND, ENCOURAGE THEM TO THINK, JUST GENERALLY, WHICH GROUP IS THE MOST UNPLEASANT, IN THEIR OPINION. IF THEY REALLY CAN'T DECIDE, MARK THAT OPINION BELOW.)

\_\_ respondent can't decide; doesn't know
\_\_ respondent dislikes group not listed here (fill in name of group below)

_____

\_\_ socialists
\_\_ fascists
\_\_ communists
\_\_ ku klux klan
\_\_ john birch society
\_\_ black panthers
\_\_ symbionese liberation army
\_\_ atheists
\_\_ pro-abortionists
\_\_ anti-abortionists (pro-lifers)

# Pluralistic Intolerance:
# The Distribution of Target Groups
# in American Society

4

In the previous chapter, we demonstrated that although there has been a significant change in the public's perception of communists, socialists, and atheists during the last two and one-half decades, the level of intolerance among the mass public has probably changed very little. Before the skeptic interjects evidence of significant change in the legal and political structure, seeming to reflect a more tolerant regime in the 1970s, let us consider three mitigating factors, each of which can diminish the impact of attitudinal intolerance on political structures: the intensity and salience of tolerance and intolerance; the number and diversity of target groups selected by the public; and the extent to which the cleavages created by the presence of diverse targets are cross-cutting. We consider each of these in turn.

The salience and intensity of tolerance is a central issue. If the majority exhibits intolerant attitudes but fails to act on them, whereas the tolerant minority feels very strongly that tolerant norms should be protected (as through activities by, for example, the A.C.L.U.), then a tolerant regime may be sustained. The concept of an uninformed, intolerant, but apathetic majority is central in the work of McClosky (1964) reviewed earlier. An informed, tolerant, and participatory set of "carriers of the creed" is sufficient, in this view, to preserve an open, tolerant political system. If this is true, then the political structures of the U.S. may have recently become more tolerant in spite of the apparently high level of attitudinal intolerance.

Second, if most people agree on a single target, repression of that group is facilitated. If, however, people are generally intolerant toward different groups, repression is more problematic. The lack of agreement about targets may provide some protection for unpopular groups. We label this diversity of targets "pluralistic intolerance." It is discussed more fully below.

A third mitigating factor is the extent to which cleavages created by the presence of diverse target groups are cross-cutting. If, for example, people in the upper class selected a left-wing target while people in the lower classes selected a right-wing target, then the level of conflict in the society is likely to be great. Whichever group gains control of the state is likely to repress the other. If, however, some upper class people select left-wing but others select right-wing targets, and the lower classes are similarly divided, then conflict is muted and repression of any particular group becomes more difficult to arrange. In this chapter, we consider the extent to which these three factors—intensity, pluralistic intolerance, and cross-cutting cleavages—moderate the collective intolerance of a society composed of relatively intolerant individuals.

As noted in the conclusion to the previous chapter, we also address the question of target-group selection in this chapter. Since tolerance and intolerance reflect a two-step process, the first being the selection of a target group, and the second being the decision of how much to tolerate that target, we need to examine both steps in some detail. After exploring the problems of intensity and of pluralistic intolerance, we present the distribution of target groups within various subgroups and subcultures in American politics, hoping to gain insight into the target group selection process. The reader should recall, through all of this analysis, that the selection of target groups is an inherently political process, affected primarily by the ideology of the respondent and of the target group.

## The Problem of Intensity

The figures in Table 3-4 indicate that there are two questions on which a bare majority of the respondents could be characterized as tolerant. Nevertheless, perhaps those who are tolerant feel strongly about their tolerance while those who are intolerant care less. The 34 percent of respondents who agree that their least-liked group should be allowed to hold public rallies in their city may be intense advocates of the rights of free speech and assembly, whereas those who disagree may be more casual in their opposition. Thus the intense minority may protect democracy from the apathetic majority.

The results in Table 4-1 disprove this possibility. On eight of the nine items, the percentage strongly intolerant is much greater than the percentage strongly tolerant. The ratio of intolerance to tolerance ranges

Table 4-1      **Strength of Tolerance and Intolerance for Content-Controlled Questions, 1978 NORC National Survey**

| Item: | Strongly Intolerant[a] | Strongly Tolerant[a] | Ratio |
|---|---|---|---|
| President | 48% | 4% | 12.0 |
| Teach | 30 | 3 | 10.0 |
| Outlawed | 22 | 4 | 5.5 |
| Speech | 11 | 4 | 2.8 |
| Phone Tapped | 5 | 14 | 0.4 |
| Rallies | 12 | 2 | 6.0 |
| Dinner | 31 | 1 | 31.0 |
| Next Door | 17 | 4 | 4.3 |
| Dated | 39 | 1 | 39.0 |

[a] Percent strongly agreeing or strongly disagreeing with the statements listed in Table 3-4.

from 39 to 2.8, except on the phone tap question, which shows more intense tolerance than intolerance. But, minimally, almost three times as many respondents are strongly intolerant than strongly tolerant. Although strong feelings do not automatically translate into strong actions, these data suggest that those who are intolerant feel more intensely than those who would protect the norms of tolerance and civil liberties. Thus the first of these mitigating circumstances does not exist. To the extent that intensity plays a role in expressing or restraining intolerance, it does not protect unpopular minorities. Those who would promote a more tolerant regime must look elsewhere for protection.

## Pluralistic Intolerance

As we have noted, many theorists have discussed the problem of tolerance with reference to the "tyranny of the majority." Emphasis has been placed on the need for widespread support for "democratic norms" or for "the rules of the game." One could argue, however, that some intolerance will exist in nearly any circumstance. If a majority singles out one particular target for "special attention" then the problem of intolerance in a democratic society is much more serious than if the targets are widely scattered. A necessary condition of a tyrannical majority is that it must agree on a target.

Theoretically, societies could differ along a continuum ranging from those societies in which a majority agrees on one particular target group as "least-liked" to those which exhibit a complete lack of consensus, with virtually every member of the society selecting a different target group as their "least-liked." Of course, in practical terms, most societies would be somewhere between these extremes, and of course, most societies would differ across time in the extent to which target group selection is concentrated on one or a small number of groups. These differing levels of agreement on target groups would undoubtedly have different political consequences, especially with respect to the degree of repressive action taken within a society.

During the 1950s, the United States was undoubtedly a society characterized by considerable consensus in target group selection. The Communist Party and its suspected sympathizers were subjected to significant repression, and there seemed to be a great deal of support for such actions among large segments of the political leadership as well as the mass public. It appears that a very high percentage of citizens would have selected communists as their least-liked group, although one cannot, of course, estimate any precise figure.

The political fragmentation and the proliferation of extremist groups in American politics since the 1950s has undoubtedly resulted in a greater degree of diversity in target group selection. If this is the case, such a situation is less likely to result in repressive action, even if the mass public is roughly as intolerant *as individuals* as they were in the 1950s.[1] We examine this by presenting the targets selected in the national sample. To the extent that these targets are diverse rather than concentrated, this will increase the likelihood of a tolerant regime. We also examine target selection within various demographic and political groups, both to explore the action potential within such homogeneous subgroups, and to examine the degree to which such cleavages are cross-cutting.

## The Distribution of Target Groups

The figures in Table 4-2 present the distributions of target groups selected in the national sample. It is clear that the respondents scattered their choices among a variety of groups and did not focus on any particular group or groups. The most frequently selected groups were

1. To be clear about our point: even though respondents disagree about their least-liked groups, a consensus could still be generated against one particular group, provided a sizable percentage of the electorate had strongly negative feelings about it. Thus among those respondents who most strongly dislike the Ku Klux Klan, if most of them also harbor strong negative feelings toward the communists, they would certainly be capable of joining with those respondents who most strongly dislike the communists. Our only point is that, the more diverse the targets are, the more unlikely it is that such an unholy coalition will arise.

**Table 4-2**          **Targets of Intolerance (1978 NORC Survey)**

|  | Least-Liked Group[a] | Second Least-Liked Group[a] |
|---|---|---|
| Socialists | 1% | 2% |
| Communists | 29 | 19 |
| Atheists | 8 | 7 |
| Symbionese Liberation Army | 8 | 10 |
| Black Panthers | 6 | 10 |
| Pro-abortionists | 4 | 5 |
| Anti-abortionists | 2 | 3 |
| John Birch Society | 1 | 3 |
| Ku Klux Klan | 24 | 14 |
| Fascists | 5 | 6 |
| Other Group | 2 | 1 |
| Don't Know | 10 | 19 |

N = 1509
[a] Percentage of national survey selecting each group.

communists (29 percent) and the Ku Klux Klan (24 percent), but neither group was selected by anything close to a majority of respondents. Aside from these two groups, no other group was selected by as many as ten percent of the respondents (that is, as the least-preferred group). In addition, a sizable proportion of respondents (fully one in ten) could not even identify any group as their least-liked or their second least-liked (one in five). It may be difficult to arouse such people because they lack clear targets for any intolerance they may have. Another group of respondents selected groups not provided on our list. Their targets were likewise diverse.[2]

The American political system is in many respects decentralized, with multiple points of access to power and multiple levels of political action occuring simultaneously. Furthermore, many efforts to suppress unpopular groups and ideas occur at the local level. The fact that we have shown a great deal of diversity at the national level does not preclude the possibility that a more powerful potential for repression exists locally. It may merely be the case that local majorities are different and cancel one another out when aggregated nationally. For

2. Among those selected were Weathermen, Moonies, consumer advocates, Holy Roller Baptists, liberals, pacifists, labor unions, homosexuals, the Palestinian Liberation Army, the Black September Movement, ban handgun groups, Blacks, poor white trash, Anita Bryant's group, the mafia, policemen, politicians, capitalists, Jane Fonda's group, and Hell's Angels. It is difficult to know exactly what some of these respondents had in mind when making their selections.

example, one community may agree that the group to suppress is the communists, while another agrees that it is the fascists or Nazis. In the aggregate it appears that there is little consensus, when in fact there are a series of local consensus situations. To explore this possibility, we examined the distribution of target groups at different levels.

After the nation, the largest meaningful aggregation is the region. There are distinct regional cultures in the United States (Sharkansky, 1970), and it is plausible that regional prejudices differ and that regional majorities agree on targets for intolerance. In Table 4-3, using nine regions of the country, we present the regional breakdowns of the targets of intolerance.[3] There are few major differences in regional patterns; the differences between the highest and the lowest percentage in each row is between 4 and 12 percent. The largest difference is for the atheists—only 1 percent of the New Englanders but 13 percent of the people in the East South Central United States select atheists as their least-liked group. Even this is not a terribly large range, and the inter-region similarities are very great. The largest percentage in the table is 33 percent, and the two largest percentages in each column are for the communists and the Ku Klux Klan, one left-wing and one right-wing group. Thus the diversity and disagreement that characterize the nation also characterize the major regions of the nation, and there is little if any intra-region consensus.

Admittedly, the use of region to examine local communities is not a good test of the local intolerance thesis. Consequently, we report the distribution of target groups for the Twin Cities survey. The first column of Table 4-4 contains the relevant data, and again the diversity of targets is clear. Although there are some differences from the national survey, they are neither extensive nor important for our thesis. The Twin Cities survey has a much higher percentage selecting the Symbionese Liberation Army, but that survey was completed two years before the national survey when the SLA was considerably more salient. Other than that, no percentage in Table 4-4, column one is more than 5 percent different from the corresponding percentage in column one of Table 4-2, the national sample. Clearly, St. Paul and Minneapolis are not representative of the universe of cities in the United States, but this analysis gives no reason to expect that the diversity that characterizes the nation and the various regions somehow disappears at the local level.

In a society increasingly homogenized by the influences of the mass media and by more centralized government, laws, and rules, the skeptic

3. For a listing of states within regions, refer to the *Statistical Abstracts* (any edition), published by the U.S. Bureau of the Census.

**Table 4-3    Targets of Intolerance by Region (1978 NORC Survey)**

| Groups | New England | Middle Atlantic | East North Central | West North Central | South Atlantic | East South Central | West South Central | Mountain | Pacific |
|---|---|---|---|---|---|---|---|---|---|
| Socialists | 0% | 2% | 2% | 1% | 1% | 3% | 0% | 2% | 2% |
| Communists | 24 | 26 | 30 | 29 | 31 | 33 | 30 | 30 | 31 |
| Atheists | 1 | 6 | 8 | 10 | 11 | 13 | 11 | 8 | 3 |
| Symbionese Liberation Army | 13 | 8 | 6 | 9 | 6 | 5 | 12 | 8 | 9 |
| Black Panthers | 7 | 8 | 7 | 4 | 4 | 5 | 2 | 8 | 5 |
| Pro-abortionists | 7 | 1 | 5 | 9 | 3 | 1 | 6 | 5 | 4 |
| Anti-abortionists | 5 | 3 | 2 | 2 | 1 | 0 | 1 | 2 | 2 |
| John Birch Society | 5 | 1 | 1 | 1 | 1 | 1 | 1 | 3 | 1 |
| Ku Klux Klan | 20 | 29 | 20 | 19 | 25 | 24 | 24 | 20 | 27 |
| Fascists | 4 | 8 | 6 | 3 | 5 | 1 | 3 | 2 | 5 |
| Other Group | 3 | 1 | 3 | 1 | 1 | 1 | 1 | 2 | 3 |
| Don't Know | 11 | 8 | 9 | 11 | 13 | 11 | 8 | 10 | 8 |
| N = | 75 | 270 | 330 | 105 | 280 | 75 | 111 | 60 | 195 |

**Table 4-4**              **Targets of Intolerance, Twin Cities Survey (1976)**

| Groups | Twin Cities Survey 1976 |
|---|---|
| Socialists | 1% |
| Communists | 25 |
| Atheists | 5 |
| Symbionese Liberation Army | 17 |
| Black Panthers | 5 |
| Pro-abortionists | 5 |
| Anti-abortionists | 3 |
| John Birch Society | 3 |
| Ku Klux Klan | 29 |
| Fascists | 3 |
| Other Group | 1 |
| Don't Know | 5 |
| N = | 198 |

might argue that one should not expect wide regional and community disparities in target group selection. The relevant criterion is not shared locale, but shared interests and experiences, and the only genuinely relevant political communities rest on shared characteristics such as religion, education, race, and so on.[4]

To explore the possibility of a majority agreeing on a single target, we examined various combinations of groups our respondents chose. To simplify the presentation, the groups have been placed in six categories: (1) communists and socialists, (2) atheists, (3) New Left groups, (4) radical right groups, (5) pro-abortionists, and (6) anti-abortionists.

Comparing the target groups respondents selected as "least-liked" and "second least-liked," we explore the possibility that a majority coalition will agree on a particular target. If, for example, all those who

4. A starting place, neither an examination of particular communities nor of purely demographic categories, is to examine size of the city where the respondents live. We divided the national sample into nine different types of cities and locales, ranging from cities of over 250,000 to people who live on the open range. There are very few notable patterns and respondents from most locations are very similar. The only divergent group are those in cities of over 250,000, where many fewer select the communists or atheists (17 and 4 percent vs. averages of 34 and 9 percent in the other eight groups), and where a higher percentage select the Ku Klux Klan (38 percent vs. an average of 20 percent elsewhere). With this exception, the other eight community types have similar patterns, and the pattern is internally heterogeneous. Even in the large cities, there is no consensus on target groups; it is merely that the pattern of dissensus differs from the other cities.

chose communists as their "least-liked" group selected socialists as their second target (and vice versa), there would be some basis for cooperation among these different respondents. This kind of clustering along the left-right dimension could provide a basis for mobilization against a number of groups at one end of the ideological spectrum.

Assessing this possibility, the figures (Table 4-5) clearly show that the ideology of the target group does not provide the *sole* basis for respondents' choices. Individuals who selected one group from among the cluster of groups on the left do not necessarily select their second group from the same cluster. For example, among those who selected one of Stouffer's original groups—communists, socialists, or atheists— as their first choice, only 28 percent selected another group from this cluster as their second choice. On the other hand, fully 38 percent of those who picked a target from the extreme right as their "least-liked" group selected one from Stouffer's list as their second "least-liked" group. As the figures indicate, these patterns are diverse, with sizable proportions picking two left-wing groups, two right-wing groups, one of each, and various combinations of these groups with one of the two abortion groups.[5]

These patterns are summarized in Table 4-6 where the three Stouffer groups are combined with the New Left groups to create a cluster of left-wing groups. The largest proportion of respondents (42 percent) selected one right-wing and one left-wing group; the next largest (34 percent) selected two left-wing groups. Only seven percent of the sample selected two right-wing groups as targets, suggesting that many liberal respondents also chose targets on the left. In any case, many respondents did not focus their hostility on one end of the political spectrum; rather, they tended to diffuse it toward both extremes. As noted, over four times as many respondents (34 percent to 7 percent) selected two left-wing groups as opposed to two right-wing groups, perhaps because they could choose from five left-wing groups but from only three right-wing groups.

To summarize, respondents have numerous potential targets of intolerance. While some groups are more unpopular than others, no group comes close to being selected by a majority of respondents. Moreover, when respondents are allowed to select more than one group, their combinations of choices often cut across ideological lines. Hence, respondents do not appear to select clusters of groups defined purely in ideological terms. Thus, though (as noted earlier) there continue to be

---

5. It is interesting that none of the more than 1500 respondents selected both the pro- and the anti-abortion groups as their two "least-liked" groups.

**Table 4-5**   **Respondents' Least-Liked Group, by Their Second Least-Liked Group (1978 NORC)**

|  | Respondent's Least-Liked Group is: | | | |
|---|---|---|---|---|
| Respondent's Second Least-Liked Group Is: | Socialists, Communists, or Atheists | New Left (Black Panthers, Symbionese Liberation Army) | Radical Right (John Birch Society, Ku Klux Klan, Fascists) | Abortion (Anti- or Pro-abortionists) |
| Socialists, Communists or Atheists | 28% | 39% | 38% | 61% |
| New Left (Black Panthers, Symbionese Liberation Army) | 27 | 20 | 29 | 15 |
| Radical Right (John Birch Society, Ku Klux Klan, Fascists) | 34 | 32 | 20 | 24 |
| Abortion (Anti- or Pro-abortionists) | 10 | 9 | 12 | 0 |
| N = | 509 | 191 | 400 | 80 |

**Table 4-6**          **Distribution of Least-Liked Groups (1978 NORC)**

|  |  |
|---|---|
| Respondent's Least-Liked Groups are: | |
| Both Left-Wing | 34% |
| One Left, One Center[a] | 11 |
| One Left, One Right | 42 |
| One Right, One Center | 6 |
| Both Right-Wing | 7 |

N = 1176
The "center" groups consist of the two abortion groups.

high levels of intolerance in society, this intolerance is directed at disparate combinations of target groups ("pluralistic intolerance").

### Social and Political Bases of Target Group Selection

Thus, in 1978, the choices of target groups were widely dispersed and there was no clear majority consensus around such choices. We suggest that this kind of fragmentation may work against the high levels of intolerance reported earlier through a process similar to that described by Madison in *Federalist* 10 and by numerous subsequent writers. (See Chapter 1.)

However, this does not take the question far enough. It may still be possible, even with the patterns outlined above, for well defined minorities in the electorate to agree generally on potential targets of intolerance. For example, most Catholics might select proponents of abortion, blacks might select racists, fundamentalists might select atheists, and so on. Such consensus within groups could be translated into political action at either the national or (more likely) the local level. This could occur when there are no countervailing pressures against such action or where groups are willing to "log roll" with others to gain enough support for action. Hence, it is important to look at the social and political bases of target group selection.

Another important reason to examine these demographic variables is that tolerance is sometimes said to relate to such factors as education, religion, and place of residence. Given the traditional tolerance measures, which specify communists, socialists, and atheists as targets, we may ask whether these explanatory factors are related only to the target groups selected. In other words, the groups found to be most tolerant in the earlier studies (the better educated, urban residents,

Jews, and religiously unaffiliated) may simply have been less hostile to the groups specified in the tolerance measures.

The first variable we examine is education. Of course, the more and the less educated are not organized groups in society, but education has been mentioned as the major factor contributing to higher levels of tolerance. Tables 4-7 and 4-8 present the distributions of targets (for "least-liked" and second "least-liked" groups) by levels of education, and show that respondents at different levels of education tend to select different targets. The data (Table 4-7) reveal that those with low and medium levels of education are more likely to select one of the three groups mentioned in the Stouffer items than are those at the highest level. Almost one-half of those at the lowest level pick one of these as their "least-liked" group, compared with a third of those at the highest level. On the other hand, almost half of the highly educated respondents selected groups from the extreme right, while only a little more than a fourth of those at the lowest level of education picked a right-wing group.

This pattern is repeated for the second "least-liked" groups (Table 4-8). One might have expected the pattern to be weakened to some degree here, since those at the highest level of education have disproportionately selected one of the right-wing groups on their first choice, thus leaving fewer of these groups to select the second time. However, the relationship remains the same. In fact, when we compare the per-

**Table 4-7        Least-Liked Group by Level of Education (1978 NORC)**

|  | Education | | |
|---|---|---|---|
| Groups | Low (Grade School) | Medium (High School) | High (Some College) |
| Communists and Socialists | 41% | 38% | 26% |
| Atheists | 7 | 11 | 6 |
| New Left Groups (Black Panthers, Symbionese Liberation Army) | 13 | 13 | 17 |
| Radical Right Groups (Fascists, Ku Klux Klan, John Birch Society) | 29 | 28 | 43 |
| Pro-abortionists | 8 | 6 | 3 |
| Anti-abortionists | 1 | 2 | 2 |
| Others | 1 | 2 | 3 |
| N = | 150 | 698 | 507 |

Table 4-8          **Second Least-Liked Group, by Level of Education (1978 NORC)**

| | Education | | |
|---|---|---|---|
| Groups | Low (Grade School) | Medium (High School) | High (Some College) |
| Communists and Socialists | 28% | 28% | 23% |
| Atheists | 11 | 12 | 5 |
| New Left Groups (Black Panthers, Symbionese Liberation Army) | 30 | 26 | 25 |
| Radical Right Groups (Fascists, Ku Klux Klan, John Birch Society) | 21 | 22 | 37 |
| Pro-abortionists | 9 | 8 | 3 |
| Anti-abortionists | 2 | 3 | 4 |
| Others | 0 | 1 | 3 |
| N = | 118 | 631 | 469 |

centage of each education group selecting one of the three Stouffer groups on either the first or the second round, we find that 87 percent and 89 percent of those at the two lowest levels selected communists, socialists, or atheists as targets compared to 61 percent of those at the highest level. Conversely, the corresponding percentages for the three right-wing groups are 50, 50, and 81 percent respectively.

There is thus a very clear relationship here: the most highly educated respondents differ considerably from the rest of the sample. The most poorly educated groups selected left-wing targets and the highly educated groups picked right-wing targets. It may be inferred, then, that the original Stouffer study, as well as those studies that repeated his items in the 1970s, have a built-in class bias because they have tried to measure tolerance in connection with groups most disliked by those at the lower end of the educational ladder. The reputed relationship between tolerance and education may thus be an artifact of the measurement strategy, a possibility we explore in greater detail in the following chapters.

Even with this clustering within educational levels, there is still a significant dispersion among the target groups selected. One does not find a majority of any educational group agreeing on a "least-liked" group, even when several groups are collapsed into single categories. Thus, while there is a tendency for the more highly educated to look to the right-wing for targets and for the less educated to look to the left, this does not mean that there is sufficient agreement on individual targets within each level, to easily mobilize that group.

To explore the possibility that it is not simply education that affects respondents' selection of target groups, but more broadly, social status, we repeated the analysis of Table 4-7 using income levels and subjective social class (a question asking the respondents to identify themselves as lower class, working class, middle class, or upper class). If the relevant factor is class structure, these different social status variables should have more or less the same impact on target group selection. However, the results in Table 4-9 show clearly that income and subjective social class have a very different impact than education. While those with low education are more likely than those with high education to select left-wing targets, the low income and lower class identifiers are more likely than the higher income and higher class group to select right-wing targets. Status appears to have an opposite impact from education on target-group selection. For example, among those who identify with the lower classes, fully 45 percent select right-wing targets; among those who identify with the upper classes, only 27 percent do so.

These findings suggest a distinction between education on the one hand, and the social class structure (as measured by income and subjective social class) on the other. Education and class do not combine to produce a powerful impact, but work in opposite directions, to some extent muting the overall importance of social class in the selection of target groups.[6] Thus, in terms of our earlier distinction between superimposed and reinforcing cleavages, education and social class clearly crosscut one another. As these variables are two that are most likely to be superimposed, this is powerful evidence that "pluralistic intolerance" may mitigate the effects of individual intolerance.

Race is a potentially severe cleavage in America. Racial differences

6. The opposing processes will be discussed at length in Chapter 8. Briefly, one plausible explanation, that younger respondents have higher educational levels but are not yet represented at higher income levels, producing a spurious set of differences in the impacts of education and income on target group selection, is dispelled in Chapter 8. Even controlling for age, education and social class have opposite impacts on the ideological nature of target group selection. It is sufficient for now to speculate that education produces liberalism on social issues and greater tolerance of the more traditional left-wing targets: communists and socialists. On the other hand, it may be that the overt violence of right-wing groups such as the Ku Klux Klan, along with their virulent persecution of minority groups, leads the well educated to weigh threats to minority groups more heavily than the threats to the economic system socialists and communists pose. Education seems to produce sympathy for the underdog and for minority groups, but,

in attitudes are among the most significant generated by social background characteristics (Erikson and Luttbeg, 1973: Chapter 6; Hamilton, 1972). Table 4-10 presents the relationship between race and target groups selected, and shows large racial differences. Fully 77 percent of the Black respondents selected groups on the radical right, while only 27 percent of the White respondents did so. Conversely, 48 percent of the Whites selected communists, socialists, or atheists, while this was true of only 15 percent of the Blacks. Thus, Whites tend to be more diverse and pluralistic in their choices, and they are much more likely to select groups on the left. Blacks, on the the other hand, generally agree on their targets, which are on the right. It should be said, however, that the overwhelming proportion of Black choices involved the Ku Klux Klan, and it is therefore not surprising that these choices cluster on the extreme right.

Although Blacks overwhelmingly select right-wing targets, they constitute only a small proportion of all those who select such targets. Of the approximately 400 respondents who select right-wingers as their least-liked group, over 70 percent are Whites. Thus even though Blacks form a potentially cohesive group against the right wing, the diversity among those who dislike the right wing may, once again, moderate the organized expression of such attitudes.

The tendency of Blacks to select target groups from the extreme right conflicts with the general pattern, discussed above, in which those with less education tend to select groups from the left; Blacks, on the average, are not as highly educated as Whites, suggesting that the relationship between education and the ideology of the target groups selected is stronger among Whites than among Blacks (cf. Tables 4-7 and 4-8). The percentages in Table 4-7 were therefore re-computed for Whites only; these figures are presented in Table 4-11. This procedure increases the educational differences, primarily by increasing the proportions of these in the two lower categories selecting communists, socialists, or atheists as targets. Among Whites only, 59 and 55 percent (respectively) of the low and medium education respondents selected one of these groups, while only 34 percent of the most highly educated respondents did so. The comparable figures for groups on the radical right were 15, 20, and 39 percent, respectively, among these at the low, medium, and high levels of education. Among Blacks, on the other

on the other hand, a high income, regardless of education, may lead one to be protective of that wealth and to fear groups on the left who would redistribute it.

**Table 4-9    Least-Liked Group, by Subjective Class and Income (1978 NORC)**

| | Subjective Class | | | | Income Categories | | |
| --- | --- | --- | --- | --- | --- | --- | --- |
| Groups | Lower Class | Working Class | Middle Class | Upper Class | Under $6,000 | $6,000–20,000 | Over $20,000 |
| Communists and Socialists | 29% | 35% | 34% | 36% | 31% | 36% | 29% |
| Atheists | 6 | 9 | 9 | 9 | 8 | 8 | 10 |
| New Left Groups | 12 | 13 | 17 | 18 | 11 | 14 | 20 |
| Radical Right | 45 | 36 | 31 | 27 | 41 | 33 | 33 |
| Pro-abortionists | 6 | 4 | 5 | 3 | 6 | 5 | 3 |
| Anti-abortionists | 2 | 2 | 2 | 3 | 1 | 2 | 3 |
| Other | 0 | 1 | 2 | 3 | 1 | 2 | 2 |
| N = | 51 | 563 | 684 | 33 | 270 | 644 | 362 |

**Table 4-10**            **"Least-Liked" Group, By Race (1978 NORC)**

|  | Race | |
|---|---|---|
| Groups | White | Black |
| Communists and Socialists | 38% | 11% |
| Atheists | 10 | 4 |
| New Left | 16 | 3 |
| Radical Right | 27 | 77 |
| Pro-abortionists | 5 | 2 |
| Anti-abortionists | 2 | 2 |
| Other | 2 | 1 |
| N = | 1065 | 149 |

There are no significant racial differences in second least-liked group. After Blacks select the Klan, then their choices are similar to the Whites.

**Table 4-11**            **Least-Liked Group, by Education, Whites Only (1978 NORC)**

|  | Education | | |
|---|---|---|---|
| Groups | Low (Grade School) | Medium (High School) | High (Some College) |
| Communists and Socialists | 50% | 43% | 28% |
| Atheists | 9 | 12 | 6 |
| New Left Groups | 16 | 15 | 18 |
| Radical Right Groups | 15 | 20 | 39 |
| Pro-Abortionists | 9 | 6 | 2 |
| Anti-abortionists | 2 | 2 | 2 |
| Other | 0 | 2 | 3 |
| N = | 117 | 599 | 452 |

hand, there were virtually no differences by education (data not shown); an overwhelming majority of Blacks at all education levels selected groups on the far right, primarily the Ku Klux Klan. There is thus some potential for agreement on the targets of intolerance among Blacks and more highly educated Whites. (A similar control for race, relating income to target group selection, works in the opposite direction; it reduces the relationship between income and least-liked group, even among Whites.)

Another potentially important cleavage centers around religion. Religious conflicts have always carried with them great potential for intolerance, because of the "appeals to heaven" usually made in such disputes. In fact, as noted, the terms "tolerance" and "intolerance" initially developed out of religious disputes. Given the importance most individuals attach to their religious affiliations, it is reasonable to expect persons of different persuasions to select different target groups. The figures from our national survey bearing on this question are presented in Table 4-12. As is clear from the table, the profiles for Catholics and Protestants are virtually identical, but they differ considerably from those of Jews and persons who claimed no religious affiliation.[7] Thus 47 and 42 percent of the Protestants and Catholics (respectively) selected one of the three Stouffer groups, while only 16 and 19 percent of Jews and the unaffiliated did so. And, as one might expect, these patterns are reversed in connection with groups on the extreme right. Indeed, majorities in each of the latter two groups selected targets from the radical right. Although these majorities are not as large as in the case of Blacks, there is a consensus among these groups that there is a danger on the right. Jews, as expected, are very concerned about Nazis and fascists, though a good proportion also select the Ku Klux Klan as a target. Again, these particular results are not surprising, and reflect the concern that Jewish organizations have shown in the past

**Table 4-12          Least-Liked Group, by Religion (1978 NORC)**

| Groups | Protestant | Catholic | Jewish | Other Religions | No Religion |
|---|---|---|---|---|---|
| Communists and Socialists | 35% | 37% | 13% | 40% | 17% |
| Atheists | 12 | 5 | 3 | 0 | 2 |
| New Left Groups (Black Panthers, SLA) | 15 | 16 | 11 | 10 | 15 |
| Radical Right Groups (Fascists, Klan, Birch Society) | 32 | 31 | 51 | 40 | 56 |
| Pro-abortionists | 4 | 8 | 5 | 5 | 0 |
| Anti-abortionists | 2 | 2 | 8 | 0 | 4 |
| Other | 1 | 1 | 8 | 5 | 6 |
| N = | 851 | 357 | 37 | 20 | 97 |

7. Those who profess a religion other than Protestant, Catholic, or Jewish differ from everyone else in their target group selection, but since there are only 20 of them, we hesitate to draw any conclusions from this fact.

about right-wing groups (see, for example, Forster and Epstein, 1964). The combination of religious fundamentalism and anti-semitism of groups on the extreme right probably accounts in large part for their selections by both Jews and non-religious respondents. It is, of course, difficult to speak of non-religious persons as a coherent social group because they are unorganized, without clear means to identify one another, which distinguishes them from Jews, Catholics, or Protestants.[8]

Men and women may select different target groups, and in Table 4-13 we present data on this question. The only significant difference apparently results from religiosity, the tendency for more women than men to find religion salient to their political concerns, manifested here in the fact that 21 percent of women select atheists or abortion groups as least-liked, while only 10 percent of men do so. Certainly, it is reasonable to infer the importance of religiosity here, since abortion is clearly related to religious issues. We return to this discussion of sex and religiosity in the next chapter, in somewhat greater detail, and present additional evidence consistent with this inference.

The final demographic variable we examine is age: there may be generational trends that influence target selection. There are in fact some significant differences between the younger and older cohorts in the sample. Dividing the sample approximately at the mean, we find that the younger respondents are 12 percent more likely than the older respondents to select right-wing targets, 10 percent less likely to select communists or socialists, and about equally likely to select atheists or New Left groups. This bolsters the argument, made earlier, that the Stouffer tolerance questions, focusing only on communists, socialists, and atheists, are less appropriate for measuring tolerance in the 1970s than they were in the 1950s because these groups are less salient now. This is especially true of younger respondents, who generally select radical right groups as least-liked. Clearly, the right wing is replacing the traditional left wing as the favorite extremist target. There does not, however, appear to be much potential for mobilization among the younger generation, as its targets are as diverse as those of its elders.

Mobilization of intolerance may reflect not only shared group or

8. When we divide the Protestants in the sample into their various denominations (data not shown), we find very few significant differences among them and a continued diversity of targets within each denomination. There are only two exceptions: the Lutherans (N = 91) are more likely than other Protestants to select left-wing groups (76 percent) and less likely to select right-wing groups; and the Presbyterians (N = 66) are more likely to pick the radical right (42 percent) than other Protestants.

**Table 4-13          Least-Liked Group, by Sex and Age (1978 NORC)**

| Groups | Sex | | Age[a] | |
|---|---|---|---|---|
| | Male | Female | Younger | Older |
| Communists and Socialists | 36% | 32% | 29% | 39% |
| Atheists | 6 | 11 | 8 | 9 |
| New Left Groups (Black Panthers, SLA) | 18 | 12 | 14 | 16 |
| Radical Right Groups (Fascists, Klan, Birch Society) | 33 | 34 | 39 | 27 |
| Pro-abortionists | 2 | 7 | 4 | 6 |
| Anti-abortionists | 2 | 3 | 3 | 2 |
| Other | 3 | 1 | 2 | 2 |
| N = | 583 | 640 | 699 | 663 |

[a] Age was dichotomized approximately at the mean (40 years was the cutting point).

demographic characteristics, but also the political characteristics of the citizens. Political action can occur quite apart from groups based upon shared demographic characteristics, and likewise the potential for repressive political action may exist on an entirely different basis. One such basis can be partisanship. If there are strong partisan differences in target group selection, then the potential for repression would always be great in spite of the apparent diversity of targets in the society at large. The groups subject to repression would shift as the electoral fortunes of different parties waxed and waned. Although such an outcome seems more likely in a party system dominated by ideological cleavages, one might expect that even in the United States the pattern of target group selection would differ considerably between Democrats and Republicans.

It is clear from Table 4-14A that although there is some disagreement between Democrats and Republicans, there is also considerable dissensus within each group. The Independents resemble the Democrats, and with them are more likely to select the radical right, and less likely to select the left-wing groups, than are Republicans. Not unexpectedly, there is little agreement among partisans about the targets of intolerance because party labels in the American system do not mean very much. Partisans are an extremely diverse lot.

A second set of possibilities revolve around distinctions between political activists and those who are politically passive. If the activists

**Table 4-14    Target Group Selection by Party Identification and Political Activism (1978 NORC)**

| Groups: | A. Party | | | B. Interest | | | C. Talk | | D. Participation | |
| --- | --- | --- | --- | --- | --- | --- | --- | --- | --- | --- |
| | Democrat | Independent | Republican | Low | Medium | High | Low | High | Low | High |
| Communists and Socialists | 33% | 31% | 40% | 33% | 34% | 37% | 36% | 32% | 37% | 28% |
| Atheists | 7 | 10 | 10 | 9 | 10 | 6 | 8 | 9 | 7 | 12 |
| New Left Groups | 13 | 15 | 19 | 14 | 15 | 15 | 15 | 14 | 16 | 13 |
| Radical Right Groups | 38 | 35 | 24 | 36 | 31 | 36 | 31 | 37 | 32 | 39 |
| Pro-abortionists | 5 | 4 | 5 | 3 | 5 | 5 | 6 | 2 | 5 | 3 |
| Anti-abortionists | 2 | 2 | 2 | 2 | 2 | 2 | 2 | 2 | 2 | 3 |
| Other | 1 | 3 | 1 | 2 | 2 | 1 | 1 | 3 | 2 | 2 |
| N = | 565 | 444 | 280 | 252 | 742 | 366 | 885 | 474 | 1001 | 345 |

The categories above are defined as follows: political interest (low = hardly interested at all in politics; medium = somewhat interested; and high = very much interested); talk politics (low = almost never or from time to time; high = once or twice a week or every day); and participation (low = two or fewer acts; high = three or more acts, where the acts include voting, belonging to organizations, written or talked to a public official, gone to political meetings, worked in a campaign, and contributed money).

agree on their targets of intolerance, while the diversity of targets noted earlier reflects dissensus among those who are uninterested and un-involved, there exists considerable potential for repression. Clearly, the activists have a greater impact on policies than those who ignore the political process. This is important, because although a dispropor-tionate share of social scientists' concern over the protection of civil liberties has been directed at the intolerance of the non-participants and the alienated segments of society, it is the political activists and elites who have the ability to act on their intolerance.

Tables 4-14B through 4-14D make it clear that it is unlikely that political activists might share a consensus on the targets of intolerance. There are no significant differences among the various groups defined by political interest, and among those respondents with a high level of political interest there exists a high level of dissensus: 37 percent pick communists and socialists, but 36 percent pick radical right groups. Among those respondents who talk politics every day or once or twice a week (the high group), there is a slight tendency to select more right-wing targets than for those who talk about politics less often, but the profiles of these two groups are almost identical. And finally, among respondents with high levels of participation, there is a greater tendency to select right-wing groups, and to select atheists but not communists and socialists, in comparison to those who are less participatory. But again the tendency is weak, and the potential to mobilize the partici-patory and politically interested segments of society around a particular target group appears to be no greater than the potential to mobilize society as a whole.[9]

Overall, education, race, and religion are the three background fac-tors that relate most significantly to target group selection. The distri-butions on a number of other variables (such as sex, class, and political party identification) were examined here, but the profiles within these groups revealed very small departures from the general pattern (Table 4-2). In addition, it is not necessary to present this analysis for the groups selected by repondents on their second round of choices, largely

---

9. Like individuals with these demographic and political attributes, those with varying personalities differed in target selection. We assume, however, that although citizens *could* respond to a demagogic appeal, reflecting their sociological or political charac-teristics (e.g., religion, social class, partisanship, and others), there is little such potential to organize in terms of psychological categories (e.g., self-esteem, self-actualization, or other such characteristics). See Chapters 7 and 8, however.

because these patterns are similar to those reported above for the "least-liked" groups.

It may be useful, however, to report the combinations of groups selected on the first and second rounds by education, race, and religion. We do so in Table 4-15. When the data are combined in this manner, the relationship between education and the target groups selected remains quite strong (see Section A of the table). Thus, those at the lower end of the educational scale were much more likely than those at the higher end (42 percent to 25 percent) to select two left-wing groups as targets, while the latter were more likely to select two right-wing groups. However, respondents across all educational levels were more likely by a wide margin to select two left-wing targets than two right-wing targets, although this margin was smallest among the most highly educated. Besides the selection of two left-wing groups, the other dominant pattern among respondents was to select one group from each end of the spectrum, a pattern that did not vary much in frequency among the three educational groups.

With respect to race, these figures suggest some modification of our earlier conclusions, showing that Blacks overwhelmingly agreed on the selection of right-wing targets. The table does show that Blacks are far less likely than Whites (5 percent to 38 percent) to select two left-wing groups as targets. However, Blacks do not focus their attention indiscriminately on the extreme right. The modal pattern for Black respondents (70 percent) is to select one group from the left and one from the right. Since 77 percent of the Black respondents picked a right-wing group on the first round of choices, it is certain that a very large proportion selected a left-wing group on the second round. The reason Blacks differ so much from Whites on the first choice, then, is because nearly all of our Black respondents selected the Ku Klux Klan as their "least-liked" group (certainly not an illogical choice).

It is also apparent from Table 4-15 that the religious differences noted earlier persist. In addition, some other differences begin to appear between Catholics and Protestants. Again, Jews and the religiously unaffiliated are much more likely than Catholics and Protestants to select right-wing groups. Only 5 percent of the Protestants and Catholics selected two right-wing groups, while 21 percent of the Jewish respondents and 25 percent of those with no religious affiliation did so. On the other hand, Protestants were more likely than any other group to select two left-wing groups as targets. In this sense, they were the most consistent in their two choices. Catholics, very similar to Protestants on the first round of choices, diverged on the second round,

**Table 4-15**        **Combinations of Target Groups Selected, by Education, Race, and Religion (1978 NORC)**

| A. Education | Low | Medium | High |
|---|---|---|---|
| Both Left Wing | 42% | 38% | 25% |
| One Left, One Center | 10 | 14 | 6 |
| One Left, One Right | 39 | 40 | 48 |
| One Right, One Center | 7 | 5 | 6 |
| Both Right Wing | 2 | 3 | 14 |
| N = | 118 | 613 | 444 |

| B. Race | White | Black |
|---|---|---|
| Both Left Wing | 38% | 5% |
| One Left, One Center | 12 | 4 |
| One Left, One Right | 39 | 70 |
| One Right, One Center | 5 | 13 |
| Both Right Wing | 7 | 8 |
| N = | 1028 | 143 |

| C. Religion | Protestant | Catholic | Jewish | None |
|---|---|---|---|---|
| Both Left Wing | 39% | 27% | 18% | 15% |
| One Left, One Center | 9 | 17 | 12 | 9 |
| One Left, One Right | 42 | 45 | 33 | 45 |
| One Right, One Center | 5 | 6 | 15 | 6 |
| Both Right Wing | 5 | 5 | 21 | 25 |
| N = | 739 | 309 | 33 | 81 |

tending to select a centrist group (generally "pro-abortionists") or a right-wing group.[10]

Different demographic groups tend to select different political groups as targets. There is, of course, no reason for everyone to agree on the political groups they dislike, but those who used the Stouffer items to measure tolerance have assumed a certain degree of agreement, since these items specify certain groups presumed to be universally disliked. Our data show in detail that such an assumption is invalid. In the process, we have no doubt illuminated, to some extent, the underlying sources of target group selection processes. To a large degree, the process of selecting a least-liked group is an ideological one, with liberals *tending* to select right-wing targets while conservatives tend to select left-wing targets. Therefore, the factors which underlie polit-

10. We have not included the "other religion" group in Table 4-15.

ical ideology also have their effect on target-group selection. A central part of the process is therefore based on the social groups and norms that individuals come into contact with on a daily basis, and is, more broadly, part of developing a political identity. Thus religious groupings, race, and educational experiences play a major role in the development of political ideologies and identifications, which in turn have their impact on target-group selection. The patterns of groups respondents select coincide to some extent with several variables long thought to account for different levels of tolerance. That is, those groups of citizens thought to be more tolerant, such as the highly educated, turn out to be least concerned about the groups specified in the traditional measures of tolerance. Thus, some of these well established relationships require reconsideration, and it is this reconsideration which forms the core of the next four chapters.

## Levels of Tolerance for the Different Groups

Are there significant variations in the levels of tolerance for these selected groups? Are people more tolerant of political groups on the right than they are of groups on the left? Initially, our concern was to justify our content-controlled measure of tolerance and to describe the distribution of target groups respondents selected. Respondents selecting a particular group can be called "attentive publics"—that is, minorities within the mass public more than casually concerned about a particular group. Since they will be the ones most likely to press for political action against the groups in question, it is important to examine their levels of tolerance. If, for example, those who selected communists as their "least-liked" group are generally tolerant of them, it is unlikely that they will take action against communists, at least in the short run. On the other hand, if these respondents are generally intolerant of communists, some potential for action would exist, given the appropriate circumstances.

The levels of tolerance and intolerance for the different groups were measured in terms of an overall tolerance scale, based on responses to the six political items listed earlier. This scale will be described in considerable detail in the next chapter. Here we note only that the responses to these six questions were summed to create a scale ranging from 6 to 30 (the scores on each item ranged from 1 to 5), with the lower number representing the intolerant end of the scale. Respondents with scores between 22 and 30 were classified as "more tolerant," those with scores from 15 to 21 were classified as "in-between," and those with scores below 15 were classified as "less tolerant." These classifications are similar to Stouffer's, but since the scales are based on different principles, our results cannot be directly compared with his. The average score for all respondents on our scale was 16.1, and since the midpoint was 18, most respondents fell on the intolerant side of the midpoint.

Table 4-16 summarizes the distributions on this scale for respondents selecting each target group. The groups are listed in ascending order according to the degree to which respondents were prepared to tolerate them. The figures for the entire sample are also presented. As the latter figures indicate, only a small proportion of the sample (15 percent) were "more tolerant" according to this classification. The largest proportion (45 percent) fell in the middle of the scale, while a slightly smaller proportion (40 percent) was classified as "less tolerant." This classification thus yields a somewhat smaller proportion of tolerant respondents than might have been expected on the basis of the responses to the individual items presented in Table 3-4. However, this classification requires respondents to provide a consistent set of tolerant responses to qualify as "more tolerant," and such consistency is not necessarily reflected in the distributions of the individual items.

The distributions reveal considerable variation in levels of tolerance from group to group. The proportion of "more tolerant" respondents ranges from 5 percent among those selecting communists to 59 percent among those selecting the John Birch Society. Respondents were clearly tolerant of only two groups, the John Birch Society and "anti-abortionists," and they were generally tolerant, or at least not intolerant, of just two other groups, fascists and "pro-abortionists." Because of the size of the middle category, the proportions of "less tolerant" respondents do not perfectly mirror the proportions of "more tolerant" respondents within the groups. The largest proportion of "less tolerant" responses (53 percent) was found among those who selected communists as a target, which is not very surprising. In addition, significant proportions of those selecting Black Panthers (48 percent), the SLA (37 percent) and the KKK (37 percent) were intolerant. From a political standpoint, the most important of these groups are those who selected either communists or the Ku Klux Klan, since they represent by far the largest numbers of respondents, with 29 and 24 percent of the sample, respectively. One would have to conclude that the people most concerned about these two groups are not very tolerant of them. Additionally, it might be noted that the groups toward which greatest intolerance is shown are those that advocate and have on occasion practiced violence. We shall return to this latter point at greater length in Chapter 7.

**Table 4-16    Levels of Tolerance for Selected Target Groups (1978 NORC)**

| | Communists | Black Panthers | SLA | KKK | Atheists | Socialists |
|---|---|---|---|---|---|---|
| Less Tolerant | 53% | 48% | 37% | 37% | 29% | 19% |
| In Between | 42 | 44 | 44 | 49 | 53 | 71 |
| More Tolerant | 5 | 8 | 19 | 14 | 18 | 10 |
| N = | 442 | 85 | 117 | 358 | 118 | 21 |
| Mean Scores: | 14.1 | 15.1 | 16.1 | 16.2 | 17.3 | 17.6 |

| | Pro-abortionists | Fascists | Birch Society | Anti-abortionists | Entire Sample |
|---|---|---|---|---|---|
| Less Tolerant | 28% | 20% | 14% | 14% | 40% |
| In-Between | 41 | 41 | 27 | 28 | 45 |
| More Tolerant | 31 | 40 | 59 | 58 | 15 |
| N = | 64 | 76 | 22 | 29 | 1357 |
| Mean Scores: | 18.5 | 19.3 | 21.1 | 21.4 | 16.1 |

As a general proposition, respondents were far less tolerant of the political groups on the left than they were of the groups on the right. The three groups toward which respondents were least tolerant were communists and the two New Left groups, the Black Panthers and the SLA. Among the first six groups listed, five are associated with the left and only one, the Ku Klux Klan, is identified with the right. On the other hand, the three groups toward which respondents were most tolerant were fascists, the Birch Society, and "anti-abortionists," the first two of which are clearly associated with the right. Since the selection of target groups is related to ideology, we may infer that people on the left are more tolerant of groups on the right than people on the right are of groups on the left.[11]

The threat of "tyranny of the majority" presupposes that the majority may come to agree on a target of oppression. To evaluate the likelihood of mass movements against any group, we examined target group selection at national, regional, and local levels. We have also looked at the target selection among social and political strata. With one exception the wide disparity in target group selection that characterized the national sample also characterized each of these more restricted groupings. Except for the overwhelming selection, by Blacks, of the Ku Klux Klan, there is no evidence to support the prediction that homogeneous groups are more likely than the national sample as a whole to agree on a scapegoat or target of intolerance.

We have described this pattern as one of "pluralistic intolerance." The diversity of target selection within and across various social, political, and geographic groupings undercuts any cohesive movement against any particular group. Our findings suggest little likelihood of a consensus on a target group. That Blacks select the Klan to a high degree does not seriously undermine this interpretation. Black history suggests that this target selection is more defensive than aggressive.

11. In the previous chapter, and in Chapter 7, we delineate the relationship between respondents' personal political ideology and their selection of target groups. It is indeed true that the two are related.

# The Social Sources of
# Political Tolerance

**5**    In the two previous chapters, assessing the current level of political tolerance in the United States, we concluded that, at the aggregate level, tolerance has not increased, but rather remains quite low. Nevertheless, on individual items and for individual respondents, considerable variation in levels of tolerance persists. For example, in the national sample, almost 60 percent of our respondents were tolerant on the question of whether their least-liked group should have its phones tapped, but, on teaching in public schools, less than 20 percent gave the tolerant response. Thus on each question, there are significant individual differences in tolerance; different items elicit differing degrees of tolerance. The basic question is why tolerance varies so much from respondent to respondent, and why, within this variation, opinion is skewed toward intolerance rather than tolerance.

In this chapter, we describe the political tolerance items in greater detail, and construct and analyze a scale of political tolerance. This provides a more complete picture of the amount and type of variation in political tolerance. We then review, in some detail, various social explanations for this variation. We examine the impact of background or sociological variables, such as education, sex, region, and so on, on tolerance. In the next chapter, we turn to personality-psychological variables, such as self-esteem, dogmatism, and self-actualization, among others, which several researchers suggest are powerful determinants of political tolerance. In Chapter 7, we show that the processes influencing political tolerance are not entirely social and psychological: several of them are political, independent of an individual's social char-

110

acteristics or personality traits. Finally, in Chapter 8, we examine the simultaneous impact of all three sets of variables.[1]


## The Dependent Variable: Degree of Political Tolerance

We asked our national sample nine questions about their least-liked group, six political questions and three social questions. We thus expected in a factor analysis a two factor solution, with the six political items loading on the first factor and the three social items loading heavily on the second. The results of various factor analyses (Table 5-1) confirm these expectations. For example, using an oblique rotation, the first six items load at .40 or higher on the first factor, while none of the social items load above .05 on it; conversely, all three social items load at .54 or higher on the second factor, while none of the political items load above .20 on it. the "teach in schools" question is problematic because it loads .40 on the first factor and .20 on the second factor, perhaps because it has somewhat more social content than the other five political questions.

**Table 5-1**            **Item Analysis of Nine Tolerance Items (1978 NORC)**

| Tolerance Item[a] | Corrected Item-Total Correlation | Oblique Rotation[b] | | Orthogonal Rotation (Varimax with Kaiser Normalization) | |
|---|---|---|---|---|---|
| | | Factor 1 | Factor 2 | Factor 1 | Factor 2 |
| President | .43 | .44 | .07 | .43 | .22 |
| Teach | .50 | .40 | .20 | .44 | .33 |
| Outlawed | .58 | .54 | .14 | .56 | .33 |
| Speech | .60 | .85 | −.13 | .75 | .18 |
| Phone Tapped | .45 | .45 | .09 | .45 | .24 |
| Rallies | .61 | .82 | −.09 | .73 | .20 |
| Dinner | .47 | .05 | .60 | .24 | .58 |
| Next Door | .44 | .00 | .62 | .20 | .58 |
| Dated | .40 | .01 | .54 | .18 | .51 |
| Eigenvalues | | 3.0 | 0.5 | 3.0 | 0.5 |

If we divide the items up into two scales, the first composed of the first six political items and the second composed of the last three social items, the coefficient alphas are .78 and .62 respectively.
[a] See Table 3-3 for the exact question wording
[b] Factor one correlates .64 with factor two in the oblique solution.

1. It is important to remember that very few controls will be introduced in the next three chapters, and largely only bivariate relationships between tolerance and these sets of variables will be examined.

In the oblique solution, however, the two factors correlate .64 with one another, indicating that political and social tolerance (of explicitly political groups) are highly related and that the results using the two sets of tolerance items will not differ greatly. The results of an orthogonal solution (also in Table 5-1) reveal the same pattern of items by loadings, although the loadings of each item on its secondary factor are higher. Nevertheless, it is clear that using the political and social tolerance items separately is justified. Certainly the eigenvalues for the secondary factors are very low (.5), but this is because there are so few social items in the set of tolerance questions.

In the following analysis, we rely primarily upon a six-item political tolerance scale, based on the six political tolerance items in Table 5-1. Since each item has five point agree-disagree response categories, scores on the six item scale range from 6 to 30. The mean score for the six item scale is 16.1, well below the midpoint of 18; and the coefficient alpha, an estimate of reliability, is .78.

In a subsequent chapter we present the results of multivariate analyses that use these tolerance scales as dependent variables. In the next three chapters, however, we review the various findings and explanations proposed by researchers of political tolerance. We also present some simple percentage tables to show precisely how our conceptualization of tolerance relates to prior research findings, and present a simplified version of the dependent variable, collapsing the 24 point tolerance scale into three categories: those respondents who are relatively "less tolerant" (scores of 6–14), those who are "in-between" (15–21), and those who are relatively "more tolerant" (22–30).[2]

Using these three categories, 40 percent of the sample is categorized as "less tolerant," 45 percent as "in-between," and only 15 percent as "more tolerant." (See Table 5-2.) This is consistent with the earlier

2. These categories are not totally arbitrary. If a respondent was uncertain on each of the six political tolerance items, his/her score would be 18, the midpoint of the scale. Of course, respondents could obtain a score of 18 by being tolerant on three items but intolerant on the other three items, and to interpret their score of 18 as neutral would be a mistake. (The fact that the coefficient alpha is relatively high indicates that not many respondents have such response patterns.) Nevertheless, those respondents whose scores are near the midpoint can certainly be classified as "in-between." In creating these three categories of respondents, we selected the midpoint plus or minus three points on the scale to create the "in-between" group. The "more" and "less" tolerant groups are simply those respondents with scores more than three points above or below the midpoint. Our categories are based on items totally different from those used by Stouffer and by Nunn, Crockett, and Williams, and thus no direct comparisons of the percentage "more tolerant" or "less tolerant" can be made between their samples and ours.

Table 5-2          **Levels of Tolerance (1978 NORC)**

|  | N | Percent |
|---|---|---|
| "Less Tolerant" (6–14) | 537 | 40 |
| "In Between" (15–21) | 610 | 45 |
| "More Tolerant" (22–30) | 210 | 15 |
|  | 1357 | 100 |

For 152 cases, there are missing data on at least one of the six political tolerance items.

Table 5-3          **Intensity of Tolerance and Intolerance (1978 NORC)**

| Item | Among Tolerant Respondents, Percent Strongly Tolerant | Among Intolerant Respondents, Percent Strongly Intolerant |
|---|---|---|
| President | 27% | 70% |
| Teach | 14 | 49 |
| Outlawed | 13 | 46 |
| Speech | 7 | 33 |
| Phone Tapped | 24 | 24 |
| Rallies | 5 | 26 |
| Dinner | 8 | 50 |
| Next Door | 10 | 40 |
| Dated | 31 | 51 |
| Mean | 15 | 43 |

analysis, showing that Americans are generally intolerant. In fact, only 5 respondents have the maximum score of 30 and an additional 11 have scores between 27 and 29. On the other hand, 36 respondents have the lowest possible score (6) and an additional 76 score betwen 7 and 9. Thus the distribution is skewed toward the intolerant end of the scale.

We caution the reader to keep in mind, however, that these three categories of tolerance have been created only for the purposes of convenience, to facilitate and simplify the presentation. The multivariate analysis, presented later, is more precise and relies on the full six-item scale, with the scores ranging between 6 and 30. The multivariate analysis makes use of all of the information available, although it may be more difficult to comprehend.[3]

3. Use of the three categories noted in the text causes a loss of information, and in some cases leads to results that differ slightly from those of the multivariate analysis. In such instances, we attempt to reconcile the apparent discrepancies, most of which are minor and can be explained by the fact that those respondents who are intolerant feel more strongly than those who are tolerant (see Table 5-3). Thus when we collapse

Before focusing on the explanatory variables, we should note that the skewed distribution, toward the intolerant end of the scale, partly results from the fact that the intolerant feel more intensely than the tolerant respondents. As noted in Table 5-3, on the average only about 15 percent of tolerant respondents feel strongly about the item in question; fully 85 percent of the tolerant indicate weak rather than strong agreement with statements expressing tolerance toward their least-liked group (or mild *dis*agreement with statements expressing intolerance toward their least-liked group). On the other hand, almost half (43 percent) of the intolerant respondents feel strongly. In no case do more than a third of the tolerant respondents express strong tolerance, whereas in seven of nine instances over a third of the intolerant respondents express strong intolerance. Although we have no data on political elites, this does cast some doubt on the claim that a tolerant minority that feels intensely about civil liberties can sustain a tolerant regime because of the indifference of the intolerant majority. At least attitudinally the reverse appears true in the United States: the supporters of tolerance, at least among the mass public, seem at best lukewarm defenders of the creed, perhaps even uncertain whether they themselves should be tolerant. (See the earlier discussion in Chapter 4.)

In the sections to follow, we review the various findings and explanations proposed by the major researchers on political tolerance. We ultimately present a rather complex multivariate model of our own, more completely specified than previous models. In the meantime, we offer critiques of the works under review, and quote liberally from the existing literature to give the reader an unvarnished view of the interpretations to be found there. For sake of convenience, we discuss the variables included in this model under the general headings of sociological, psychological, and political explanations of political tolerance. Although the categories are somewhat arbitrary, most authors and their explanations fit well into one or another of them.

## Education, Social Status, and Tolerance

Since Stouffer's in-depth empirical treatment of political tolerance, there has been a series of essentially sociological or demographic explanations of political tolerance, which rely on variables such as education, income, and occupation. Stouffer himself first suggested this

respondents into groups based on the tolerance scale, some of this variance between the tolerant and the intolerant disappears, and the distinction between strong and weak tolerance is often lost.

set of explanations, and while he relied almost exclusively on education as his explanatory variable (rather than on any broader conception of social status) he did lay the groundwork for the work that followed.

Stouffer noted a strong positive relationship between education and tolerance of nonconformity. He created a fifteen-item tolerance scale, a modified Guttman scale. Based on this scale, he divided his sample of respondents into three groups, those who were "less tolerant," "in-between," and "more tolerant." Stouffer's three categories are not directly comparable with ours, in terms of the percentage of respondents in each category, but his sample, like ours, was ordered into three groups that differed systematically in their degree of political tolerance. (See Stouffer, 1955, Appendix C for details.) Nunn, Crockett, and Williams (1978) replicated Stouffer's original modified Guttman scale and also replicated his three categories of tolerance (pp. 180–185).

Stouffer found that fully 66 percent of college graduates were "more tolerant," while only 16 percent of those with only a grade school education were "more tolerant." The relationship appeared to be linear, with intermediate educational categories having intermediate levels of political tolerance. Stouffer offered a process explanation for this finding:

> . . . schooling *puts a person in touch with people whose ideas and values are different from one's own.* And this tends to carry on, after formal schooling is finished, through reading and personal contacts. Now, we can plausibly argue that this is a necessary, though not the only, condition for tolerance of a free market place for ideas. To be tolerant, one has to learn further not only that people with different ideas are not necessarily bad people but also that it is vital to America to preserve this free market place, even if some of the ideas traded there are repugnant or even dangerous for the country. The first step in learning this may be merely to encounter the strange and the different. The educated man does this and tends not to flinch too much at what he sees or hears. (P. 127; emphasis in original)

So Stouffer makes an essentially cognitive argument. The citizen must *learn* that a free market of ideas is vital to American democracy and that non-conformists are not necessarily bad. The process of learning is essentially one of being exposed to these non-conformists and their ideas, which higher education does quite well. Stouffer therefore does not relate tolerance to the conditions of work and alienation or to the broader social structure; rather he sticks closely to the purely cognitive functions of education. One learns the abstract principle that free exchange of ideas is necessary and that to be different is not necessarily to be bad and dangerous. This, of course, affects greatly the individual's decision about whether to be tolerant or intolerant.

Prothro and Grigg (1960) did not extend this explanation, although they did tend to reaffirm it. They related education to support of the "basic principles of democracy" and found a substantial relationship, even controlling for income. But the reverse was not true: with education controlled, there was no major relationship between income and support for these basic principles. Hence the impact of other social status variables on tolerance seemed less important.

Nunn, Crockett, and Williams (1978) demonstrate that the relationship between tolerance, as measured by Stouffer's questions, and educational level apparently is even stronger now than it was in the 1950s. While Stouffer found 66 percent of the college educated and 16 percent of the grade school educated to be "more tolerant," Nunn and his associates found comparable percentages for the 1970s to be 84 and 19 percent. So, given the traditional measures, the relation between education and tolerance has increased to some degree.

Nunn and his colleagues basically accept Stouffer's process explanation, although they elaborate it somewhat. They argue that education is important not as a mere indicator of position in the social structure, but because it increases "the likelihood of gaining specific knowledge about civil liberties and the democratic process," it "increase(s) awareness of the varieties of human experience that legitimize wide variation in . . . values," and it makes it probable "that one's cognitive development will be characterized by the flexible, rational strategies of thinking which encourage democratic restraint" (p. 61). Like Stouffer's original statement, this is a purely cognitive explanation.

Nunn and his colleagues attempt to compare the cognitive and social structural explanations of tolerance by examining the direct and controlled relationships between education and occupation, and political tolerance. Like Prothro and Grigg, they find that education continues to relate strongly to tolerance when occupation is controlled, but that the reverse is not true. They find percentage differences in tolerance on the average of 10 percent for occupation controlled for education, but of 45 percent for education controlled for occupation. They believe that if education affects political tolerance merely because it indicates position in the social structure, then the relationship between education and tolerance should disappear once occupation is controlled. Since the relationship not only fails to disappear, but remains stronger than occupation, even under the controlled condition, they conclude that the major impact of education is a direct one and that social or occupational status is not an important variable in explaining political tolerance. Education has its impact, then, not through affording one control and power over the environment and hence a basic self-confidence and assurance, but through cognitive experiences and the development of cosmopolitan values.

Although many other studies have confirmed the relationship between education and political tolerance, few authors have added anything of consequence to the cognitive explanation Stouffer proposed. An exception is a study by Korman (1971) arguing that work experiences, including hierarchical structure, rigidity, and specialization in the workplace, reduce political tolerance. Unfortunately, he lacks data to support his thesis, and in his review of the literature he is unable to discover any directly relevant studies. He does find some indirect evidence, however, in that various studies have shown that "individuals in organizations which encourage self-control evaluate stimulus diversity and ambiguity more positively than those in organizations stressing hierarchical control" (Korman 1971); and "membership in occupations with specialized characteristics is negatively related to tolerance and liking for different occupations and different groups" (Sutton and Porter, 1968; and Korman 1963).

Korman's analysis moves from a narrow conception of education and its cognitive impact to broader notions of occupational structures, workplace experiences, and related variables, all of which have some sort of impact on tolerance and related attitudes. Unfortunately, neither Korman nor any other author has demonstrated that these effects are independent of education. None of these studies explicitly controls education while relating workplace or other status indicators to tolerance. Education may still be the key variable, and our analysis attempts to separate the effects of education from those of status and occupational structure.

Before discussing other factors related to political tolerance, we review some additional work that sets the stage for our empirical analysis. Schuman and Presser (1977) have convincingly demonstrated that the relationship of education to tolerance depends somewhat on the wording of the tolerance questions. In a question wording experiment, they asked one sample of respondents the original Stouffer questions about removing from the library a book written by a communist, and about allowing an atheist to make a speech. Both of these questions are worded in such a way that it is "easy" for the respondents to give the intolerant response. For example, Stouffer's communist-book question is:

> This next question is about a man who admits he is a Communist. Suppose he wrote a book which is in your public library. Somebody in your community suggests the book should be removed from the library. Would you favor removing the book, or not?

A second sample was asked similar questions, worded in a more balanced fashion, making it "easier" for the respondents to give tolerant responses. For example, on the communist-book question, after being told that someone favors removing the book, respondents are told that "somebody else in your community says this is a free country and it [the book] should be allowed to remain" (p. 167). Schuman and Presser's variation on Stouffer's question provides a favorably worded cue for the "tolerant" as well as the "intolerant" position on the issue.

Schuman and Presser created two tolerance indexes, one based on the "harder" Stouffer questions, and the other on the revised questions. Education correlated .51 with the Stouffer questions but only .34 for the "easier" questions, even though the target groups were the same—communists and atheists. Whether our content-controlled strategy should reduce or increase the influence of education is difficult to predict. On the one hand, as noted earlier, Stouffer's questions focused on left-wing targets. We have demonstrated that lower educated respondents are more likely to select left-wing groups as targets, compared with higher educated respondents. Thus while education clearly plays a role in target group selection, it may play much less of a role in determining the degree of tolerance than the Stouffer-based measures have suggested. Stouffer's measures may have caused the lower educated respondents to appear less tolerant than the higher educated respondents merely because they feel more negative about left-wing groups. Perhaps the findings would have been reversed or neutralized if right-wing groups had been used.

On the other hand, Schuman and Presser have found that education becomes less important using more balanced and "easier" measures of tolerance, other things being equal. Our measurement strategy produces lower levels of tolerance than the traditional Stouffer questions (see Chapter 3), although our questions themselves are not necessarily "harder" to be tolerant on than the Stouffer questions. If Schuman and Presser's findings mean that more highly educated people are tolerant whether it is "hard" *or* "easy" to be tolerant, but that less educated people are intolerant when the questions are "hard" and tolerant when they are "easy" then our strategy should produce a stronger correlation between education and tolerance.

Clearly these expectations are contradictory. In fact, our six-item tolerance scale correlates .31 with education, .17 with income, and .16 with occupation; Stouffer's four-item scale correlates .41 with education, .24 with income, and .25 with occupation. Thus the second expectation is more realistic; perhaps if our questions were as "soft" as Stouffer's the correlations with social status would disappear altogether. In any event, when the available target groups cover the ideological spectrum, highly educated respondents will select right-wing targets while uneducated respondents tend to pick left-wing target groups. Beyond target selection, however, although there remains some tendency for the highly educated to be more tolerant, this tendency is not as strong as prior research has suggested. Income and occupational differences almost disappear using the content-controlled strategy.

Lest we overstate the case, Figures 5-1 through 5-3 present the percentage differences in the "more tolerant" and "less tolerant" groups, by education, income, occupational status, and subjective social class.[4] We also include the mean tolerance scores for various groupings of the independent variables. The percentage "more tolerant" increases with both education and income (Figure 5-1) although for education there is a large jump for respondents with some college; the grade school and high school groups do not differ a great deal in percentage "more tolerant." For income, the relationship is more clearly linear, with about equal differences between the lower and middle group and between the middle and upper group. Note that the relatively small correlation between income and political tolerance (about .17) can result in differences in "more tolerant" of almost 17 percent between the low and high income groups.[5] (Among those with low income, approximately 7 percent are "more tolerant" while for those with high income the figure is about 24 percent.)

No group in Figure 5-1 has a higher percentage of "more tolerant" than "less tolerant" respondents. There are several variables, discussed later, so strongly related to tolerance that the dotted line and the solid line in the figure cross, and for the group lowest on the independent variable in question, there are more "less tolerant" than

4. Once again, we must caution that in the figures presented in this chapter and the next, the percent high and the percent low on tolerance refers to the "more tolerant" and "less tolerant" groups as defined by our scale. These percentages are not comparable to the percentages "more tolerant" presented by Stouffer and by Nunn and associates, although Nunn did replicate Stouffer's procedure so their categories are comparable.

5. We detail other similar instances later where the measure of association between two variables is weak, but the percentage differences appear to be quite significant.

"more tolerant" respondents, while for the highest group the reverse will be true. The background variables are not strongly enough related to tolerance for this "crossing" to occur.

Figure 5-1 also presents the mean differences in political tolerance between categories of the independent variables. For example, the mean six item tolerance score for those with a grade school education is 14.0; for those with a high school education, 15.3; and for those with at least some college, 17.8. For income categories, the mean differences are smaller, ranging from 15.0 for the lowest group to 17.2 for the highest group.

To present a more complete analysis, we examine the mean scores on each of the nine individual tolerance items for two educational groups: those with high school education or less, and those with at least some college. We do so to show that although some of the differences on the independent variables appear to be quite large, they

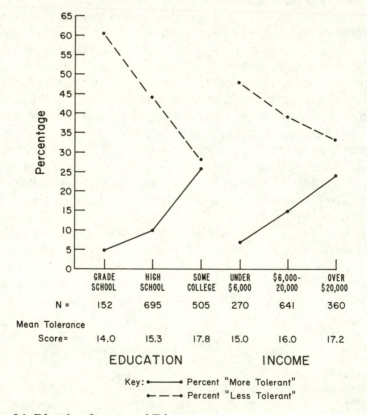

Fig. 5-1. Education, Income, and Tolerance

result from fairly small differences on the individual items that make up the scale.

In Figure 5-2 we plot the average tolerance score for each of the nine questions for the two educational groups, presenting the mean score for each group on each question, with a range from 1 to 5 (strongly intolerant through strongly tolerant).

The low education group's means range from 1.8 (intolerant) on the President and Dated questions to 3.4 (slightly tolerant) on the Phone question. The high education group's means range from 1.8 (intolerant) on the Dated question to 3.7 (slightly tolerant) on the Phone question. There are very few differences within that range, although on most questions the high education group is slightly more tolerant. Moreover, for the low education group, the mean is closest to the "intolerance" category on five questions, and closest to the "uncertain" category on the remaining four; for the high education group, the mean is closest to the "intolerance" category on four questions, closest to the "uncertain" category on four, and closest to the "tolerance" category on one. These differences are marginal, and even the high education group is generally tolerant only on the question dealing with using phone taps. (See Chapter 3 for the exact wording of these questions.) In short, a strong case cannot be made for a tolerant, educated elite, and in the pages to come we attempt to gauge the importance of education, compared with numerous other variables, on levels of political tolerance.

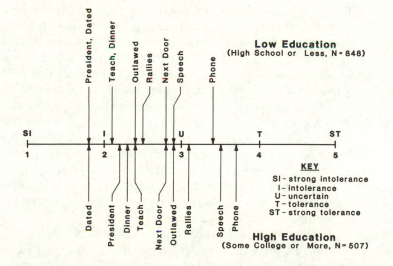

Fig. 5-2. Education and Tolerance

One recent study by Lawrence (1976) examined the role of education in somewhat greater depth, relying on NORC data, which asked respondents whether various groups should be allowed to demonstrate and to petition. (See Chapter 2.) The groups included persons concerned about crime in their community; a group of neighbors; a group calling for the government to stop a polluting factory; a group of black militants; a group of radical students; a group calling for legalization of marijuana; and a group calling for the government to make certain that blacks have open housing in white neighborhoods. Lawrence found that education was significantly correlated with "tolerance" for the latter four groups but not the first three. His interpretation was that the first three groups (anti-crime, neighbors, and anti-pollution) represent "softer issues" while the latter four groups (militants, radical students, marijuana, and open housing) represent "harder issues" and that, as Schuman and Presser found, the highly educated were tolerant on all issues and groups while the lesser educated were tolerant only when it was easy to be so. On harder issues the uneducated were intolerant, producing a stronger correlation between education and tolerance. As we have just seen, however, our own data contradict this interpretation.

In fact, it is likely that Lawrence found education uncorrelated with tolerance of crime, neighbors organizing, and opposition to pollution because these are ideologically neutral issues and groups; by contrast, he found a correlation between tolerance and education with the militant, radical, marijuana, and open housing groups because they are ideologically left-wing. As we have demonstrated, those with less education dislike these left-wing groups more than the highly educated do. Lawrence recognized this, and attempted to control for it by examining what he called the "issue relatedness" of tolerance, controlling for their attitude toward the issue and group in question. Thus he took those who were positively disposed toward open housing, and correlated education with tolerance for the group petitioning or demonstrating about open housing; he repeated this correlation for respondents neutral on the open housing issue; and then again for those negative about open housing. He repeated this procedure for each issue, finding that the correlations were reduced somewhat, although they did not disappear altogether. This is consistent with our results, which show that the correlation is reduced but does not vanish.

Next, Lawrence correlated respondents' postions on the issues in question with their willingness to tolerate various actions by groups on these issues, controlling for education. He found that the correlations are virtually identical within each education level: people at *all* education levels tend to respond to questions of tolerance in terms of their own attitudes toward the groups and issues in question. Thus if people like "radical students," they are more likely to tolerate them, regardless of the respondents' level of education.[6] Our own measurement procedure can be viewed as a more elaborate, careful, and valid way to control for respondents' attitudes toward various target groups.

Although most of the literature has dealt with education as the major social status variable, we noted above that Korman (1971) suggests that occupational status and workplace experience may have a significant impact on political tolerance. In Figure 5-3, we present the relationship between occupational status and political tolerance. Education and income were measured by straightforward questions about number

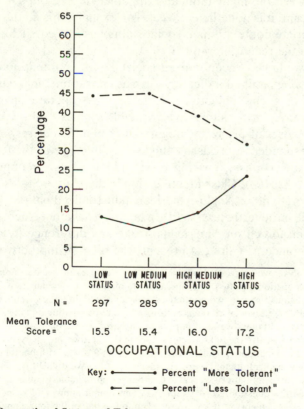

Key: ●———● Percent "More Tolerant"
     ●— — —● Percent "Less Tolerant"

**Fig. 5-3. Occupational Status and Tolerance**

6. Although highly educated respondents are more likely than uneducated respondents to feel positively about radical students and are thus more likely to tolerate them, if they do not like radical students, they are no more likely to tolerate them.

of years of formal education and about family income; occupational status is measured with the Hodge-Siegel Prestige Score, which is assigned to the reported occupation of the respondent or, in case of the unemployed, of the respondent's spouse.[7] (For details see Siegel [1971].)

The correlation between occupational status and political tolerance is .16. The mean tolerance scores range from 15.4 to 17.2 across the status categories, and the percentage "more tolerant" ranges from 10 percent for the low medium status group to about 23 percent for the high status group. The relationship is not entirely linear, as the low medium status group is not significantly different from the low status group. In general, the relationship is not strong, and although the difference between the high status and the other three groups is statistically significant, it is nonetheless weak. We examine this matter further in a multivariate context, since social status has played such a prominent role in the recent literature.

Thus far we have conceptualized social status as a continuous variable and have examined indicators such as education and occupation. The effects of such "objective" variables may operate on political tolerance by creating a "subjective" variable such as "self-perceived" social class, a set of discrete categories in the minds of respondents. We asked respondents to classify themselves into one of the following categories: lower class, working class, middle class, or upper class (Hamilton, 1972: 100). Class identification in the United States is weak in comparison to other Anglo-American industrialized nations (Alford, 1963), but it is nevertheless worth examining whether such identifications, when forced on Americans, make any difference in levels of political tolerance.[8] Figure 5-4 presents the relationship between sub-

7. In our analysis we rely on education, on two measures of socioeconomic status (income and occupational status), and one measure of subjective social status. Thus for socioeconomic status, we use two continuous indicators and do not conceptualize them as measures of discrete social classes; both income and occupational status have continuous values and although we do group them for purposes of convenience in the text in Chapters 4 and 5 we use the full range of values in the multivariate analysis in Chapter 8. The assigned occupational prestige scores range from 9 to 82, with bootblacks given scores of 9 while medical doctors were given scores of 82. We divided the sample into four categories, noted in Figure 5-3, created to produce approximately equal sized groups.

8. We worded the question so as to force the maximum number of respondents to select a social class category: "If you were asked to use one of the four names for your social class, would you say you belong in: the lower class, the working class, the middle class, or the upper class?" From previous experience, we expected that, if given a choice, most respondents would not select any class identification.

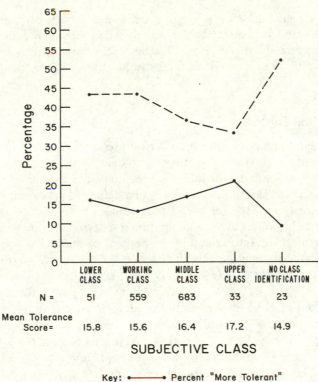

Fig. 5-4. Subjective Class and Tolerance

jective class and political tolerance. The relationship is clearly weak. (Eliminating those with no class identification, the correlation between subjective class and tolerance is a mere .07.) Although the 33 respondents who identified themselves as upper class do appear more tolerant than the remaining respondents, their number is so small that it does not influence the correlation. We conclude that subjective social class is unimportant as a source of political tolerance.

In summary, our conceptualization of political tolerance reveals much weaker correlations between tolerance and various measures of social status than earlier studies found. The relationships between tolerance on the one hand, and income, occupational status, and subjective social class on the other are very weak, although those who are extremely high on each of these latter variables are significantly more tolerant than the remaining respondents. The relationship between education and tolerance is weaker using our measure than with the Stouffer-based measures, but is nevertheless stronger than with the other measures of social status. To the extent that status is important, it appears to be as a cognitive factor rather than a more encompassing structural variable.

## Gender and Tolerance

Although the basis of the social structure and education hypotheses is reasonably well specified, other sociological variables related to tolerance (as measured with older conceptualizations), have been discussed without any theoretical sophistication. For example, in his original analysis, Stouffer found that women were less tolerant than men, and this difference held up under controls for education and political interest. Approximately 35 percent of males but only 27 percent of females could be classified as "more tolerant," and these percentage differences were virtually unaffected by various controls. Unfortunately, Stouffer offered no convincing explanation of this finding. He did offer several potential explanations, including greater religiosity on the part of women, the claim that parents allowed girls less freedom than boys, and the notion that males (more likely to work) would come into contact with diverse people and ideas through their jobs. This last explanation is most consistent with Stouffer's explanation of his education findings, but he ultimately rejected all three explanations as inconsistent with his data. Even among less religious respondents, women were less tolerant than men; women were not greatly different from men on the various personality (or psychological) variables that Stouffer studied, and when they did differ, the women seemed to have characteristics which should predispose them toward more rather than less tolerance; and finally, working and unemployed women did not differ in their tolerance scores.

Nunn, Crockett, and Williams (1978), of course, updated the Stouffer findings. Although they found that both sexes became more tolerant, they also found that sex differences increased: in 1973, 64 percent of males were classified as "more tolerant" whereas only 48 percent of women could be thus classified. The sex differences went from 8 percent in 1954 to 16 percent over the twenty year span. Furthermore, these differences held up even under controls for education, occupation, and age. Nunn et al. are not so reluctant as Stouffer to offer an explanation of their findings:

the most probable basis for the continuing divergence in tolerant attitudes of the main bulk of American men and women . . . [is] inequality between the sexes in American society . . . Representing all the ways in which American men have enjoyed dominion, privilege, responsibility, and diversity both of expectations and of experiences in comparison with women, the concept rationalizes the mystery of men being more politically tolerant than women (p. 119).

This explanation seems inadequate, however. It is beyond question that women were less equal to men in the 1950s than in the 1970s, yet the differences on tolerance grew substantially over the same period of time. The difference should have narrowed if "inequality between the sexes" is the major causative agent in the process. This "inequality of experiences" explanation fits the authors' education explanation: diversity of experience and learning to accept and understand differing points of view could be the common factor operating for both the education and sex differences. Yet the data do not appear to be consistent with so simple an explanation.

In the previous chapter, we found that women were more likely than men to select targets with some religious significance. Fully 21 percent of women selected atheists or one of the abortion groups as their least-liked group, while only 10 percent of men did so. This is consistent with Stouffer's religiosity explanation. Table 5-4 explores this factor.

**Table 5-4        Sex and Target Group Selection (1978 NORC)**

|                          | Women | Men  |
|--------------------------|-------|------|
| Both Left Wing           | 30%   | 37%  |
| One Left, One Center     | 15    | 7    |
| One Left, One Right      | 43    | 43   |
| One Right, One Center    | 7     | 4    |
| Both Right               | 5     | 9    |
| N =                      | 723   | 634  |

While 46 percent of men select two target groups that are ideologically consistent (37 percent select two left-wing groups and 9 percent select two right-wing groups), 35 percent of women do so. On the other hand, 22 percent of women select one ideological group and one abortion group while only 11 percent of men do so. These differences imply that men are more likely to select target groups on ideological grounds, while women are more likely to do so on other grounds. For example, Stouffer found that:

among church goers and non-churchgoers alike a female is more likely than a male to perceive Communist beliefs in terms of hostility to religion. The *reverse* is true about government ownership of property. Males are more likely than females to pick this out as a tenet of Communist belief (p. 169).

Apparently, then, the intolerant males were strongly opposed to communism (and related doctrines) for ideological reasons, but women opposed them on different grounds: their anti-religious character. This explanation may be correct. Although sex differences in tolerance of communists increased slightly over the twenty year period 1954–1973, both men and women became more tolerant in the meantime, probably because communism became less ideologically threatening to men at the same time that it was becoming less religiously threatening to women. (Certainly some men opposed communism on religious grounds, and some women did so on ideological grounds, but we are discussing broad tendencies.)

This finding, then, that women are more likely to select atheists or one of the abortion groups as their least-favorite, simply means that when other available targets engage religious feelings, women will select them instead of communists and socialists. After all, the religious connotation of communism and socialism is less direct than that of atheism or abortion. Women's hostility to these groups may not be totally religious; it may be based on a broader threat—to the family and family virtues and values.

To test this explanation, we examined the relationship between sex and respondents' stated objections to their least-liked group. We asked them what it was about that group that they disliked. After the respondent answered this probe, the interviewer asked if there was anything else they disliked about the group. Both of these questions were repeated for the respondents' second least-liked group. The responses to these questions were then coded into a number of categories, of types of objections. We explore the matter in greater depth in Chapter 7; here, we merely note that one of these categories involves religious objections. Table 5-5 presents the percentage of objections that are religious in nature, by sex. On each of the four probes, females made more religious objections to their least and second least-liked groups. Proportionately, females gave roughly twice as many religious objections as men.

Religiosity may account for the differential selection of target groups by men and women, but it does not necessarily lead to the expectation

Table 5-5    **Religious Objections to Target Groups, by Sex (1978 NORC)**

|  | Male | Female |
|---|---|---|
| Least-Liked Group, First Probe | 7% (622) | 13% (692) |
| Least-Liked Group, Second Probe | 4% (295) | 5% (349) |
| Second Least-Liked Group, First Probe | 6% (562) | 13% (604) |
| Second Least-Liked Group, Second Probe | 3% (237) | 6% (261) |

The N's are in parentheses. For example, the first entry in the table in parentheses means that 622 males gave a first objection to their least-liked group; 7 percent of these objections were religious (and 93 percent were not). Then only 295 males gave a second objection to their least-liked group, of which 4 percent were religious objections while 96 percent were not.

that the latter will be less tolerant of their selected targets than the former. Figure 5-5 shows very little difference between the sexes in tolerance of their least-liked group. The mean score for women is 15.9, for men 16.2; the percentage "more tolerant" among women is 14 percent, for men 16 percent, not a significant difference. The correlation between the tolerance scale and sex is −.06. We therefore conclude that the sex differences in tolerance noted in earlier studies were primarily artifactual, disappearing when the content-controlled measurement procedure is applied.

## Race and Tolerance

Prior research has ignored the question of whether racial minorities (particularly Blacks) are more or less tolerant than Whites in American society. On the one hand, Blacks and other nonwhites might be more tolerant than Whites because they have been the subjects of discrimination and persecution in the United States. Related research has found that Blacks are generally more liberal than whites on domestic issues, and of course more liberal on matters of discrimination and civil rights generally (Erikson and Luttbeg, 1973: 186–188). As objects of much intolerance, Blacks might be expected to defend tolerance generally.

On the other hand, several factors lead to the expectation that Blacks would be more intolerant than Whites. The college educated are somewhat more tolerant than those with less education, and Blacks have a lower aggregate level of education than Whites. Furthermore, since

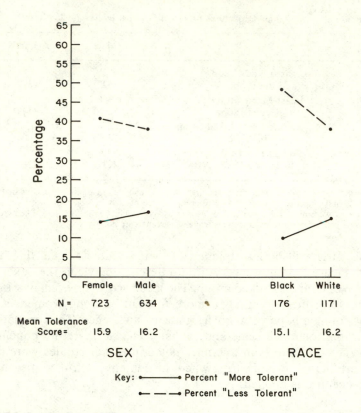

**Fig. 5-5. Sex, Race, and Tolerance**

some radical right-wing groups (particularly fascists and the Klan) have focused their hatred and violence against racial minorities, we might expect the content-controlled measure to reflect less tolerance among Blacks. Since very few Whites have been directly threatened in this way, Blacks should perhaps be less tolerant.

The data in Figure 5-5 show that neither expectation is clearly borne out. Although the mean tolerance score for Whites is somewhat higher than for Blacks, the correlation between race and political tolerance is only − .05. In spite of the fact that only 10 percent of Blacks but 15 percent of Whites are "more tolerant," the relationship is quite weak. The mean for Blacks is 15.1 and for Whites it is 16.2, but even these mean differences tend to disappear once education is controlled. (Data not shown.) In fact, among those with a grade school education, Blacks are significantly more tolerant than Whites. As a result, we shall not include race in the multivariate analysis.

**Aging, Generations, and Tolerance**

In his original analysis, Stouffer found large cohort differences in the degree of tolerance toward communists, atheists, and socialists. The percentage of respondents rated as "more tolerant" ranged from 47 percent of those aged 21 to 29, down to a mere 18 percent of those 60 and over. Since education and age were so highly correlated in his sample, he related age to tolerance, controlling for education, and although the relationship was weakened, it did not disappear. For example, among the college educated, the proportion of those "more tolerant" ranged from 77 percent among those aged 21 to 29, down to 31 percent for those over 60. The comparable figures for respondents with only a grade school education were 24 and 13 percent. Thus, although the education differences were greater, age differences persisted. In fact, aging appeared to make more of an impact on those with higher levels of education than on those with little education.

Although Stouffer did not pursue the implications of these findings at much length, subsequent authors have. Cutler and Kaufman (1975) attempted to compare an aging explanation with a cohort or generational explanation. The aging explanation is that as citizens become older, they become more generally conservative. Since tolerance is clearly a liberal concept, people become less tolerant as they age. This explanation is consistent with Stouffer's findings; the process occurs across all educational levels, since aging is common to all strata. The generational explanation holds that, as new cohorts enter the electorate, their life experiences are different; in consequence they develop different political attitudes. There seems to be a critical stage theory underlying the generational explanation: the historical epoch and the nature of the political times that shape the young adults' first political experiences influence them for a lifetime. People reaching political maturity in the late 1960s are more liberal than people who did so in the 1950s, and will be more liberal throughout their lifetimes. In the present instance, the assumption is that each succeeding generation within the last thirty years or so has become more tolerant than the preceeding one, producing a strong relationship between age and tolerance. This relationship was evident already in the 1950s, as Stouffer's analysis showed.

Cutler and Kaufman (1975) analyzed Stouffer's overall tolerance scale, as well as his three subscales, focusing on each target: communists, atheists, and socialists. They controlled for education, sex, and race, and examined the relationship of age and cohort to political tolerance. Using the 1954 Stouffer data and the 1972 NORC data, they found, as did Stouffer, a significant relationship between age and tolerance in both years. They also discovered, however, that tolerance increased *in all age cohorts,* indicating that in all likelihood aging led to greater liberalism, assuming that tolerance is a liberal attitude. However, the influence was not uniform across all age cohorts; the younger cohorts' level of tolerance increased more than did the older cohorts'. They concluded that:

> Stouffer's prediction, as is the case with most statements of the aging-conservatism hypothesis, would have led us to expect decreasing levels of tolerance, especially among the older cohorts. Since, in fact, tolerant or liberal attitudes have become more prevalent among all cohorts over the 18-year period, it is clear that growing older is not invariably accompanied by more conservative political attitudes in an absolute sense. However, because the older cohorts appear to be more likely than the younger cohorts to adhere to their earlier attitudes, this differential propensity leads to a widening gap between the cohorts. It is in this relative sense that growing old would appear to be accompanied by increasing conservatism (p. 80).

In this sense, aging leads to conservatism, at least relative to the times. Between 1950 and 1970 tolerance became more "fashionable," and so even the older cohorts became more tolerant. However, they did not change as much as the younger cohorts, thus remaining "more conservative" than the changed climate of opinion.

In a related study, Davis (1975) performed a cohort analysis on the same data Cutler and Kaufman used, relying on a more sophisticated methodology that allowed him to break down the increases in intolerance and to assign percentage increases to various causative agents. Since we discussed this study in Chapters 2 and 3, we need only reiterate a few points. Davis found an increase of about 23 percent in tolerant responses; he was able to attribute 4 percent to increased educational levels, about 5 percent to cohort replacement not operating through changes in educational levels, and the remaining 13 percent was "unexplained." In other words, cohort replacement during this 18 year span resulted in higher educational levels in the electorate, which in turn increased tolerance, all else equal, by about 4 percent. Furthermore, the younger cohorts were an additional 5 percent more tolerant than the cohorts they replaced, even controlling for education.

These results all suggest a cross-sectional relationship between age and tolerance, with the older respondents being less tolerant than the younger. This is true even if, as they age, respondents become more rather than less tolerant, because the nature of the times (now more conducive to tolerance) affects the younger cohorts more than the older.

Nunn and his colleagues (1978) also updated Stouffer's analysis of the impact of age on tolerance. They noted that age differences in tolerance increased between 1954 and 1973, and that age was an important variable, even controlling for education. They were more specific, however, than the other authors about precisely what sets the younger cohorts in the 1970s apart from those coming of age in the 1950s:

> Confronting the post-1945 world "anew" meant experiencing the exhilarating "pace of change" and massive "change of scale" associated with those years as merely ordinary; it meant that being a well-educated person was commonplace and that the *experience* of being a highly educated member of an educationally advanced society—surely a unique feature of the post-1945 world—was routine; it meant that living in cities amid many other persons and groups, all expressing a multiplicity of values, was the rule; and it meant that working alongside and in cooperation with tens, hundreds, and even thousands of other persons in large-scale organizations was one's everyday unexceptional lot (p. 89).

Thus the crucial changes in the world include higher educational levels, greater urbanization and concomitant diversity of experience, and change itself, all working to increase political tolerance. It must be pointed out, however, that all of these analyses demonstrating age and cohort relationships with tolerance involve controls for education, so to use educational level as part of an explanation of age and cohort changes in tolerance begs the question.

Nunn, Crockett, and Williams go on to identify the civil rights struggle for Blacks, women, and the poor, as well as the Viet Nam war, as further causes of the increased committment to political tolerance on the part of the post-1950s cohorts. In their own words:

> For many young persons, the war raised moral and political sensibilities to a level of intensity, sustained throughout the latter half of the decade, and forged deep attachments to humanitarian concerns in general and to the issues comprehended by political tolerance in particular (pp. 90–91).
>
> In sum, the fit between societal complexity, diversity, and change, on the one hand, and the emergence of extensive support for traditional civil liberties among the young, on the other hand, seems to us remarkably snug (p. 92).

And, finally, they claim that:

we have found that young Americans have embraced and received a quite basic American political tradition—the attitudes and practices involved in democratic restraint and political tolerance—in unprecedented numbers. Additional data . . . reveal once again the extraordinary tendency for younger Americans to lead all others in expressing politically tolerant views. The cultural legacy of democratic restraint is most prevalent among the young (pp. 93–94).

But the analysis in Chapter 4 suggests that the relationship between age and political tolerance may be another chimera, created by the content bias of the Stouffer questions. For example, among the younger generation (40 and under), only 37 percent select the socialists, communists, or atheists as their least-liked group, whereas among the older generation (over 40), almost half, 48 percent, do so. On the other hand, the younger respondents select a right-wing group 39 percent of the time, whereas only 27 percent of the older generation do so.

It is possible that generational differences, reflecting the times in which the respondents come of age politically, will manifest themselves primarily in the selection of target groups, but not necessarily in the degree of tolerance toward these targets. Thus all of Nunn and his associate's conclusions about increased tolerance among the younger generation are true mainly as they apply to left-wing groups. And, in fact, all of the experiences that they mention—civil rights for Blacks, women, and others, and the Viet Nam war—should make the younger generation more sympathetic toward left-wing groups. One might expect, then, an increase across the generations in the selection of right-wing targets, and *perhaps* few generational differences in tolerance toward least-liked groups.

The results in Figure 5-6 show that the content-controlled procedure did not totally reduce the age related variation in political tolerance. The percentage "more tolerant" ranges from about 21 percent for those under 31 years of age, to 7 percent for those over 60; the mean tolerance scores for these two groups are 17.1 and 14.4, respectively. So, although younger respondents are more hostile to the right-wing groups and older respondents to the left-wing groups, the young continue to be somewhat more tolerant than the old. These differences are further reduced by controls for education, but do not totally disappear.

Our argument about the content bias of the earlier measures of tolerance (Chapter 3) is, however, partially true regarding the impact of age on tolerance. The correlation between age and Stouffer's tolerance scale in our national sample is $-.33$; using our content-controlled measure, age and tolerance correlate at $-.21$. The relationship is reduced considerably once left and right-wing groups are put on an equal basis.

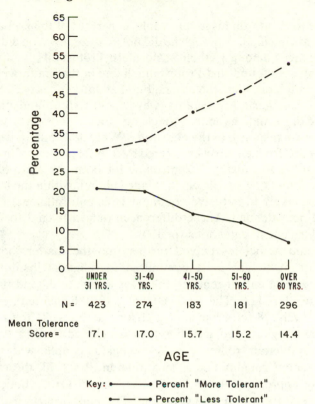

| N = | 423 | 274 | 183 | 181 | 296 |
|---|---|---|---|---|---|
| Mean Tolerance Score = | 17.1 | 17.0 | 15.7 | 15.2 | 14.4 |

AGE

Key: •——————• Percent "More Tolerant"
     •— — — —• Percent "Less Tolerant"

**Fig. 5-6. Age and Tolerance**

Certainly the differences are not great enough to argue that the Viet Nam War and the civil rights struggle produced a generation of youth committed to protecting unpopular groups' civil liberties, replacing an earlier generation more willing to violate these protections. Note that even among the younger age groups (Figure 5-6), the percent "less tolerant" is considerably larger than the percent "more tolerant," again illustrating that the age-tolerance relationship, although real, is weak. It is, nevertheless, strong enough to warrant further multivariate analysis.

## Religion and Tolerance

Stouffer found that religion and religiosity made a difference in tolerance of ideological non-conformity. For example, among people who had attended church in the last month, 29 percent could be classified as "more tolerant" on his index, while 36 percent of the non-attenders could be so classified. Although he did not analyze Jews, he did examine the differences among Catholics, northern Protestants, and southern Protestants. He found that Protestants living in the South were significantly less tolerant than the others, but that differences between Catholics and northern Protestants were inconsistent and small. He explained these findings about "religiosity" in terms of perceived threat to religion. In response to the question, "What do Communists believe in?" the most frequent answer, offered by fully 24 percent of his sample, was "hostility to religion." Controlling for both sex and political interest, he found that people who attended church within the last month were more likely to perceive communists as anti-religious than those who had not attended. These differences ranged from 3 to 7 percent for various control categories (p. 170).

Nunn and associates delved further into the matter, noting that "Americans who are most committed to religious institutions are among the most enthnocentric—the least willing to extend the benefit of the doubt" (p. 122). They showed that in 1954 the percentages "more tolerant" were 28 for Protestants, 31 for Catholics, 71 for Jews, and 49 for non-religious people. Thus they concluded that, in 1954, Jews were more tolerant, followed by non-religious people, with Catholics and Protestants roughly tied as least tolerant. By 1973, these percentages were approximately 46 for Protestants, 59 for Catholics, 88 for Jews, and 87 for non-religious people. The rank order remains about the same, except now the non-religious people are as tolerant as the Jews, and Catholics have become more tolerant than Protestants.

Nunn et al. also found that the differences in tolerance between those who were active religiously persisted into the 1970s, and in fact the differences had expanded since 1954. As noted above, in 1954 the percentage tolerant among religiously active people was 29, while for the inactive it was 36; by 1973, these percentages were 48 and 62 respectively. The authors conclude that:

> The evidence is striking. Traditional Christians, who participate actively in their churches and who find themselves with limited resources to comprehend and affect the larger world, closely link God and political authority and are also likely to see political nonconformity as the work of the Devil. When the effects of education, gender, size of residence, participation in voluntary associations, and age are accounted for . . . the correlation of religious orthodoxy . . . and tolerance of non-conformists is .19 (without adjustments it is .35). (p. 140).

So the most significant factor affecting intolerance appears to be religious traditionalism, a diagnosis also made by other writers. (See, for example, Hofstadter, 1961.)

Again, some of these religious differences may result from the questions' content-bias. First, to find that Jews and non-religious people are most tolerant of communists, atheists, and socialists may not prove the point at all. Certainly, one expects non-religious people to be most tolerant of atheists, since many non-religious people are themselves atheists. In addition, Jews have historically been sympathetic to left-wing groups, particularly in comparison with Protestants. A much stronger test, of course, is to examine the degree to which Jews are tolerant of fascists and Nazis, as witnessed by events in Skokie, Illinois, in 1978. Table 4-12 showed that Jews and non-religious people were much less likely to select the traditional left-wing targets, and much more likely to select right-wing targets, than Catholics or Protestants. Fifty-one percent of Jews and 56 percent of non-religious people selected a right-wing group as their least-liked while only 32 and 31 percent of Protestants and Catholics did so. Moreover, since most Blacks are also Protestants and over 70 percent of Blacks selected a right-wing target, the figure for White Protestants is lower.

Although the results are somewhat mixed, they continue to demonstrate the usefulness of the content-controlled measure. We have ordered the religious groups (Figure 5-7) from Protestant, to Catholic, to Jewish, to other religious groups, and finally non-religious respondents. In terms of the percentage "more tolerant" we find almost no difference among the Protestants, Catholics, and Jews, and even their mean tolerance scores are similar. Thus the content bias of the original Stouffer question is clear, since, using our measure, Jews are not more tolerant than Protestants or Catholics. (In fact, their mean score is lower than the Catholics' mean score.) We continue to find, however, that people who adhere to no particular religious faith are more tolerant than the more religious respondents, and in fact the differences are quite large. Although only about 12 percent of Protestants, Catholics, and Jews are in the "more tolerant" category, fully 44 percent of the non-religious respondents are "more tolerant"; the means range from 15.4 for Protestants to 19.6 for the non-religious group. And, for the first time, we discover a group of respondents for whom the "more tolerant" group outnumbers the "less tolerant" group; it does so for both the "other religions" and the "no religion" groups. Unfortunately we have no measure of the religiosity of our denominational respondents, but our two main conclusions are clear: prior research indicating that Jews are more tolerant than Protestants and Catholics is mislead-

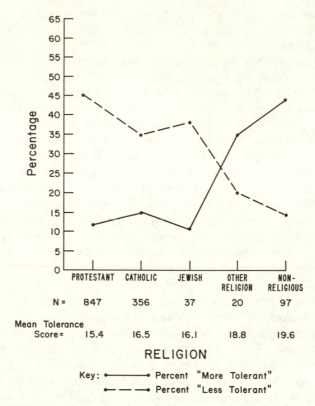

Fig. 5-7. Religion and Tolerance

ing, because of the content-bias of the questions asked; and, as Nunn et al. suggest, less religious respondents are considerably more tolerant than those with some denominational affiliation.

When the various Protestant denominations are analyzed separately, few significant differences appear among them. The traditional wisdom that says Presbyterians and Episcopalians should be more tolerant than Baptists, Methodists, and Lutherans, since their religious doctrine is more liberal, proves generally untrue, although again there is some weak tendency for Presbyterians to be less likely to select the traditional left-wing targets and more likely to select right-wing targets. This is not true for Episcopalians, however, as they differ little from the other denominations. The only major difference in tolerance scores among the Protestant denominations is that the Baptists are less tolerant than the others. The mean score on the six item scale is 14.2 for the

Baptists and very close to 16 for each of the other denominations. So, on an ordinal scale, the Baptists are the least tolerant, with 14.2; Jews, other Protestants, and Catholics each with about 16; and non-religious respondents with 19.6.[9]

## Urbanization and Tolerance

Stouffer found that city size was important in understanding political tolerance. In metropolitan areas, 39 percent of respondents could be classified as "more tolerant"; in other cities, 30 percent; in small towns, 25 percent; and finally, on farms, only 18 percent could be so classified. This finding held up under controls for region, and to a lesser extent, for education. Stouffer saw this relationship as a result of contact with diverse ideas, an explanation similar to that offered for the education relationship. As he put it:

Owing to the relatively high rural birth rate and to changes in technology which shrink the percentages of rural population with every successive Census, the population flow is mainly from the country to the city and the city suburb. Consequently, many city dwellers have lived in two worlds of values—those of their childhood in the country and those of their adulthood in the city. The reverse is rare. The shock of exposure to two value systems could have an effect on tolerance not unlike the effect of formal schooling as described above. It is precisely in those parts of the country where most people are natives of their type of community, if not actually of the same county in which they now reside—such as farm areas, especially in the South—that tolerance of "dangerous" ideas seems to be most difficult (p. 127).

Nunn and associates found that the percentage more tolerant had increased in each category, but that the differences among city size categories persisted. In metropolitan areas, 66 percent were tolerant in 1973; in other cities, 50 percent; in small towns, 42 percent; and in farm areas, 30 percent. Following the familiar pattern, the differences among categories increased somewhat between 1954 and 1973. They

9. To maximize the relationship with tolerance, we coded Baptist 1, non-religous people 3, and all other groups as 2. When this is done, the correlation with the six item tolerance scale is .26. Thus, although religion appears to be an important variable in understanding political tolerance, it is primarily a secular detachment from religion that is important, not whether one is Jewish, Catholic, or Protestant, although target selection does depend upon such denominational factors. And, of course, this is a zero order relationship, without any controls.

controlled for the effects of education, region, exposure to mass media, gender, and occupation and still found "persisting relationships" between city size and tolerance. Their explanation was similar to Stouffer's, relying primarily on the notion of "incongruent experiences."

Our own results, in Table 5-6 and Figure 5-8, are striking, as only in large cities over 250,000 do more respondents select right-wing than left-wing targets; in the very small towns and the open countryside, respondents are overwhelmingly concerned with left-wing groups, the traditional ones studied by Stouffer and by Nunn and his colleagues. On the basis of content bias alone, one certainly expects the residents of smaller locales to be less tolerant on the Stouffer items. People in large cities divide evenly in choosing left- and right-wing groups, and in fact even people who live in suburbs around these large cities divide evenly in choosing left- and right-wing targets. As one travels from the center city to the suburb and toward smaller and smaller towns, one finds more concern with the traditional left-wing targets and less concern with the right-wing targets.

Figure 5-8 collapses several of the categories from Table 5-6 for ease of presentation. It is clear that although the residents of towns of less than 2,500 are less tolerant than the rest of the respondents, there are no significant differences among the remaining groups. The mean six-item tolerance score ranges from 16.2 in towns of 2,500–50,000 to 16.9 in unincorporated SMSA's, and four of the five groups have means of 16.2 or 16.3. Given the strength of earlier findings, it is remarkable that, for our respondents, it makes no difference whether they live in

**Table 5-6**      **Ideological Groups Selected as Least-Liked, by Size of City**

| City Size | Percent Selecting Communists, Socialists, or Atheists | Percent Selecting Birch, Klan, or Fascists | N |
|---|---|---|---|
| Over 250,000 | 23% | 47% | 279 |
| 50–249,000 | 42 | 24 | 146 |
| Suburb of Large City | 36 | 33 | 290 |
| Suburb of Medium City | 41 | 23 | 74 |
| SMSA Unincorporated | 37 | 27 | 166 |
| 10–49,000 | 47 | 29 | 80 |
| 2,500–9,999 | 48 | 24 | 94 |
| 1,000–2,499 | 50 | 23 | 75 |
| Open Country | 50 | 17 | 153 |

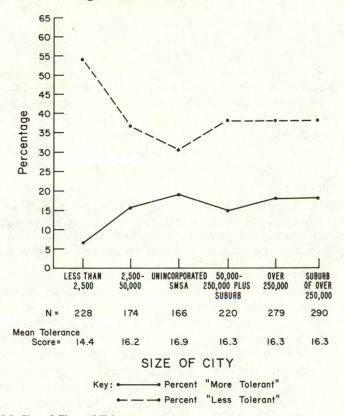

| N = | 228 | 174 | 166 | 220 | 279 | 290 |

Mean Tolerance
Score= 14.4   16.2   16.9   16.3   16.3   16.3

SIZE OF CITY

Key:  ●————● Percent "More Tolerant"
      ●— —● Percent "Less Tolerant"

**Fig. 5-8. Size of City and Tolerance**

cities of 2,500 or cities over 250,000; they are equally intolerant. They do, of course, differ in the particular target groups they select.

When size of city is coded zero for those in towns of less than 2,500 and one for everyone else, the correlation with our tolerance scale is -.16, hardly much of a relationship. City size is so unimportant as a determinant of political tolerance (as opposed to a determinant of target group selection), that it is not included in the multivariate analysis.

## Region and Tolerance

Stouffer also found some very significant regional differences in tolerance of ideological nonconformity. He found that the percentage classified as "more tolerant" was 49 in the West, 39 in the East, 33 in the Middle West, and 18 in the South. Thus the South was the clear exception, the most intolerant region, a finding that held up under controls for urban-rural location and for education. Stouffer offered little by way of explanation of this finding.

Nunn also explored regional differences in tolerance, finding the percentages tolerant to be 71 in the West, 65 in the East, 54 in the Midwest, and 40 in the South. The regional differences appear to be quite stable then, with tolerance, as measured by Stouffer's questions, going up about the same amount in each region. Although there are significant differences among the other three regions of the country, Nunn et al. focused on the distinction between the South and the non-South, suggesting that:

> Localism, defined as a market preference for and identity with the locale of one's birth, is joined in the South with an insularity of mind that is slow to change, actively belligerent toward the new, and openly intolerant toward a diversity of viewpoints (p. 105).

This is not a flattering protrait of the South.

Again, Southerners may not be significantly less tolerant than other respondents, but merely more hostile toward communists, socialists, and atheists. Table 5-7 confirms this latter suspicion. In the East, more respondents select groups of the radical right than of the traditional left wing. In the other three regions, the reverse is true, especially in the Midwest and South. Once the differences in target group selection are taken into account, some regional differences in tolerance persist, although they are not large. As Figure 5-9 shows, the East and West are still slightly more tolerant than the Midwest and the South, although the differences among means are all less than two points on a 24 point scale.

In terms of percentage "more tolerant" on the scale, the low is about 12 percent in the South, the high is 20 percent in the East—not a very great range. The safest conclusion is that the regions differ only insig-

**Table 5-7**          **Tolerance By Region**

| Region | Percent Selecting Socialists, Communists, or Atheists | Percent Selecting Birch, Klan, or Fascists | N |
|---|---|---|---|
| East | 29% | 36% | 315 |
| Midwest | 40 | 26 | 390 |
| South | 44 | 30 | 312 |
| West | 37 | 31 | 340 |

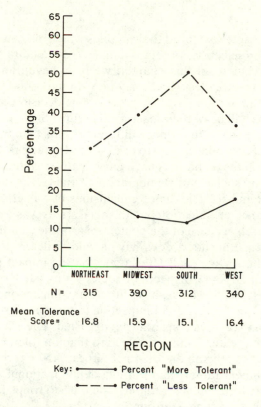

Fig. 5-9. Region and Tolerance

nificantly. The South *is* significantly different from the other regions, however, in the percentage "less tolerant" on the six point scale. So, although the mean differences among the regions are not very great, it is true that, relative to other regions of the country, in the South more respondents fall toward the bottom of the tolerance scale.

Once education is controlled (data not shown), the regional differences disappear for the most part. Among those with a high school education or less there are no differences in the mean tolerance scores among the Midwest, South, and West; respondents in the East are still somewhat more tolerant. Among those with at least some college there are no differences among the East, Midwest, and West; those in the South are still somewhat less tolerant. It is most certainly true that a large part of the regional differences Stouffer and Nunn and his associates noted result from the content bias of their questions.

## Conclusions

The previous chapter explored the variables which play an important role in target group selection. Foremost among these factors were race, education, and religion. In this chapter, we have begun an intensive examination of the variables which may play an important role in the second stage of the decision-making process, the decision of how tolerant respondents will be of their least-liked groups. Since the content-controlled measure seems to produce different results than the Stouffer measures, it is not only appropriate to re-examine the factors underlying tolerance and intolerance, but it is necessary. In this chapter, therefore, the importance of social and demographic variables in determining tolerance was examined. The major conclusions of this effort are:

1. The importance of education and of social status was exaggerated in previous research because of the content-bias of the traditional measures of tolerance. Education does have a role in determining levels of tolerance, although we shall later argue that its impact is indirect and relatively minor. Other aspects of social status, such as income, occupation, and subjective class, have little if any impact on tolerance.

2. Religion and age have a slight impact on tolerance—certainly considerably less than previous research has suggested. The effect of these variables is much greater on target selection than on tolerance *per se*. The major impact of religion on tolerance appears to be through a sort of secular detachment rather than through denominational training or theology. Age has little impact, although the oldest groups are slightly less tolerant than the youngest groups.

3. Urbanization, region of the country, and gender have no impact on tolerance, although, as with the other demographic variables, they do strongly affect target group selection. A great deal of their apparent impact on tolerance seems to be "explained away" as a content-bias in previous investigations.

Generally, this investigation suggests that the social and demographic variables, taken as a whole, have very little impact on tolerance. It does appear that the content-controlled measure not only provides a better, more valid measurement procedure than the Stouffer items, but that it also leads to somewhat different substantive conclusions. As a result, in the next two chapters, we shall turn our attention to the role played by psychological and political variables in the development of political tolerance.

# The Psychological Sources
# of Political Tolerance

**6** The previous chapter considered the social forces which may underlie political tolerance. The most general conclusion from that analysis is that these social forces affect target group selection more than they do tolerance. What, then, are the forces which more directly affect the degree of political tolerance among the electorate? There has been a considerable body of research examining personality-based variables, such as self-actualization (Knutson, 1972), authoritarianism (Sanford, 1973), dogmatism (Rokeach, 1960), and self-esteem (Sniderman, 1975), to name just a few. It is, however, difficult to categorize the psychological explanations which underlie these empirical examinations of the role of personality in determining political tolerance and intolerance. There are several reasons for this. First, a number of findings have been presented with little or no accompanying explanation or justification. Thus, Stouffer briefly presented evidence that individuals' tendencies to categorize rigidly, their child-rearing attitudes, and their degree of optimism were related to their tolerance.[1] Unfortunately, he did not pursue the implications of these findings, although he did analyze the relationships of education and age

1. Stouffer's measure of tendency to categorize rigidly was a question asking respondents to agree or disagree with a statement to the effect that people can be divided into the weak and the strong. We might label this a measurement of dichotomous thinking; in any event, it is an item closely related to the items used to measure constructs such as dogmatism, closed-mindedness, authoritarianism, and so on. His measures of child-rearing attitudes included an item designed to measure *authoritarian* child-rearing attitude, and one designed to measure *conformist* child-rearing attitude. His optimism item was merely a statement asking respondents to judge whether life is likely to be better or worse for them personally in the next few years.

with the psychological variables. Apparently, he believed that education and age affected tolerance partly by shaping rigidity of cognition,
attitudes toward child-rearing, and optimism-pessimism about the future.

Similarly, in a study of 733 New York City adults, Zalkind, Gaugler
and Schwartz (1975) found moderately strong correlations (ranging
from .25 to .44) between measures of flexibility, independence, and
self-reliance on the one hand, and Stouffer's measures of civil liberties
on the other, but failed to offer an explanation for their findings. They
presented their results without much analysis or comment, and advanced and tested no particular theoretical structure.

Psychologists have developed numerous theories and frameworks,
many of which offer very different and often competing perspectives
on tolerance. The situation is empirically complicated as well because
very similar variables have been used as indicators for disparate concepts, making it difficult to interpret the literature. In addition the broad
pattern of interrelationships among psychological variables makes it
difficult to determine the independent effect of each variable. The sections to follow focus on several major psychological explanantions of
political tolerance. We set out, as clearly as possible, their theoretical
and conceptual underpinnings.

## Maslow's Need Hierarchy and Tolerance

Perhaps the most completely developed psychological explanation
of tolerance is Jeanne Knutson's (1972), based on Maslow's need
hierarchy. Since this explanation derives from the general literature
relating psychological needs to political behavior, we review that literature *briefly* and then discuss the applications of Maslow's work to
tolerance.

In the literature on political psychology, there has been considerable
emphasis on the relationship between personal needs and political attitudes. (See Lane, 1969, for a full discussion.)[2] Among more recent

2. Lane finds ten personal needs most useful for his work with college students, and
he "uncovers" important relationships with political ideology for the need for affiliation
and the need for autonomy, among others. Additional recent efforts to relate personal
needs to political behavior include the Georges' (1956) analysis of Woodrow Wilson,
relating his need for affiliation and for self-esteem to his inflexible political style; Barber's
(1972) analysis of twentieth-century Presidents, relating the need for affection and for
self-esteem to Presidential performance and decision making; Lasswell's (1948) analysis
of local officials, relating low self-esteem to a compensatory drive for power; Renshon's
(1974) analysis of the need for personal control, relating it to political efficacy, political
participation, and various political attitudes.

efforts, Knutson (1972) impressively merges Maslow's need hierarchy with empirical research dealing with dogmatism, authoritarianism, manifest anxiety, intolerance of ambiguity, anomie, alienation, and political efficacy. Her conceptualization is convincing in part because it ties together these obviously related concepts and findings. Put broadly, and perhaps oversimply, her argument is that certain personality types exhibit intolerance (conceptual, political, social, or personal intolerance). She argues that using Maslow's need hierarchy we can provide a coherent interpretation of this prior research.

Maslow's need hierarchy posits individual evolution from satisfying lower to satisfying higher psychological needs. His needs, from most basic to most complicated, are physiological, security and safety, affiliation and love, self-esteem, and actualization. We will not discuss Maslow's theory in detail, since our purpose is to test a rather narrow model relating the need hierarchy to political tolerance. Briefly, however, persons whose physiological needs have not been satisfied are preoccupied with meeting them. The higher level needs, although present, will not be activated; concern with physiological needs will deter empathy with the concerns of those who have progressed beyond this stage (Knutson 1972: 26). Since tolerance of unpopular causes and points of view is psychic activity directed toward others (and toward the abstract notions of equal protection of the laws and of due process), and is unrelated to narrow concern with survival, we expect that persons who have not progressed beyond this elementary stage of psychic development will be more intolerant than those who have moved on to other concerns.

If physiological needs are met satisfactorily, the need for safety and security becomes paramount. At this point, the individual is concerned with order and is often quite rigid in attitude and behavior. Predictability becomes a central concern, and the individual wishes to control and reduce all potential threats from the environment. Again, we expect that persons so preoccupied are generally "law and order" types, and their concern with preventing chaos and preserving predictability and order will lead them to be intolerant of those who express disagreement with them, especially over such issues as the legitimacy of the current regime and system of laws. Abstract concepts of freedom and equality seem unrelated to their primary goals, and indeed many of these people are likely to be "undemocrats" (Lane, 1962).

If the growing child has both of these lower needs met reasonably fully, the need for affection and love is activated. Individuals who do not have this need met develop the belief that they are unlovable and lose the capacity to accept and care for others. There is an absence of empathy and a strong tendency toward self-centered activity. Under these conditions, one may find such individuals unable to understand and accept the motives of those who espouse contrary views. Those who disagree are seen as evil, and motivated by illegitimate concerns. Thus, according to Knutson, persons who feel unloved become somewhat authoritarian and undemocratic to alleviate their anxiety.

If the need for affection is generally satisfied, the need for self-esteem is activated. Certainly, feeling loved and appreciated is a necessary precondition, in developing a positive self-concept. However, a positive self-image also includes a feeling of self-worth and of accomplishment. This need for self-esteem has been examined as a possible source of ambition for political power (Lasswell, 1948). Without going into details, suffice it to note that persons suffering a lack of self-esteem appear to lack the ability to enjoy success, tend to project their own shortcomings and motivations onto their self-defined "enemies," and tend to suspect the motivations of those who challenge their values and power (George and George, 1956). These are aspects of intolerance.

Maslow's highest need, self-actualization, involves vague concepts such as "realizing one's potential" and "accepting oneself for what one is." According to Anderson (1973) the distinguishing characteristics of actualizers include: acceptance of self and of others, problem-centering rather than ego-centering, autonomy and resistance to enculturation, appreciation and richness of emotional reactions, increased creativity, democratic character structure, deep interpersonal relations, and so on. Clearly, such persons ought to be the most politically tolerant of all of Maslow's groups we have discussed. As Knutson (1972) puts it:

> it has been repeatedly found that tolerance correlates with optimism, leadership roles and education. I would suggest that self-actualization is the most common (and causal) factor behind all three of these relationships (p. 95).

In summary, then, according to Maslow's need hierarchy, persons in the four groups below the actualizers will be generally intolerant. It is not clear precisely what kind of variation in tolerance to expect between levels of deprivation, although one might expect a monotonic relationship between the need hierarchy and tolerance, because each succeeding level of the hierarchy involves less "concern with self" but more "concern with self in relationship to the environment" (Knutson, 1972). One might assume, therefore, that humans begin the journey to actualization as politically intolerant and become less so at each step along the way. Only through considerable psychic development do people become tolerant of those whose views they oppose strongly. That progression could, of course, be uneven since the need levels involve more qualitative than quantitative differences. There may well be some threshold effects, relating to the development of empathy and psychic security, that cause uneven changes in tolerance.

Unfortunately, Knutson's empirical measure of individuals' positions on Maslow's continuum is seriously deficient. She provides no item analysis; she uses the same items to measure more than one level of need; and she defines self-actualization as a low score on her scales, which are designed to measure the other need levels. Using that definition of actualization, she finds almost 45 percent of her sample to be self-actualizers, while Maslow suggests that actualizers constitute a much smaller segment of the population. Furthermore, Knutson has no clear and useful measure of political tolerance. In short, her contribution is conceptual rather than empirical.

Two empirical analyses are relevant to this discussion. Inglehart (1977), studying changing values in Western Europe, uses Maslow's theory both to guide the research and to develop a values measurement instrument. He provides considerable evidence that the shift from "materialist" to "post-materialist" values parallels the progression along the need hierarchy, and that changes in the distribution of these values in society correspond well to predictions derived from Maslow's theory. Inglehart offers, however, no direct evidence linking these values with political tolerance. Marsh (1977) employs a similar value ranking technique in his study of protest potential in Great Britain. He goes one step further and distinguishes between Inglehart's political values and a set of "personal" values closer to the need hierarchy formulation. The evidence again suggests the utility of the need hierarchy theory, although the fit is significantly better for the personal values measure. Somewhat surprising, however, is the low correlation between the personal and political value measures ($r = .22$). Evidently, there is far from a perfect relationship between psychological progression along the need hierarchy and the political values a person holds, and this may be of some consequence in the present context.

These two studies buttress confidence in the usefulness of Maslow's need hierarchy, by demonstrating the role of value hierarchies in the measurement of need levels. The relationship between the need hierarchy and political tolerance, though, awaits empirical confirmation.

In the national survey, we attempted to measure respondents' positions on the need hierarchy by asking them to select their most important value from a list provided them. We selected one value that measured each level on the need hierarchy (following Inglehart, 1977).

The values are listed in Table 6-1, along with the need level they purport to measure and with the percentage of the national sample selecting each as most important.

The relationship between position on the need hierarchy, as measured by these values, and political tolerance is generally monotonic, although there is a strong (step function) increase in tolerance between the safety and security need level and affiliation and love need level (see Figure 6-1). The percentage "more tolerant" ranges from about 8 percent for those at the lowest need level to 29 percent for those at the highest, while the respective means on the six item tolerance scale are 14.9 and 18.0. Among those at the need-for-esteem level, there are equal proportions of "less" and "more tolerant," while for the self-actualizers there is a larger proportion of "more" than "less tolerant" respondents. Among the sociological background variables, only in the case of religion was there a category with a larger group of "more" than "less tolerant" respondents. Using a scoring system of 1 to 5 for the five need levels, there is a correlation of .24 between position on the hierarchy and political tolerance.

## Socialization, Authoritarianism, and Tolerance

Knutson conceptualizes Maslow's need hierarchy to provide a uni-dimensional interpretation of previous research on authoritarianism, intolerance of ambiguity, and tolerance, among others. Many researchers reject her unicausal explanation and focus more distinctly on the socialization process *not* as it relates to the satisfaction of a particular need hierarchy, but as it affects, to use the psychoanalytic terms, impulse control and the regulation of the instincts. Maslow clearly departs from traditional psychoanalytic approaches, but considerable work on

**Table 6-1**          **Values and Maslow's Need Hierarchy**

| Need Level | Value | Percent of Sample |
| --- | --- | --- |
| Physiological Needs | Comfortable Life | 24 |
| Safety and Security Needs | Security | 31 |
| Affiliation and Love Needs | Affection | 19 |
| Esteem Needs | Esteem | 20 |
| Self-Actualization | Originality | 6 |

N = 1509
Respondents were asked to select which of these five values is most important to them.

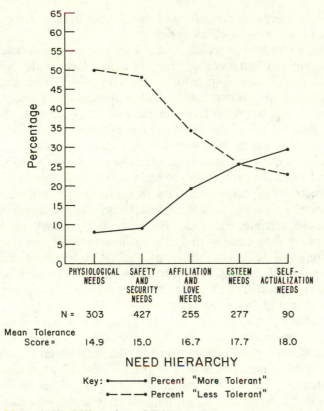

| N = | 303 | 427 | 255 | 277 | 90 |

| Mean Tolerance Score = | 14.9 | 15.0 | 16.7 | 17.7 | 18.0 |

NEED HIERARCHY

Key: •———• Percent "More Tolerant"
•— —• Percent "Less Tolerant"

**Fig. 6-1. Maslow's Need Hierarchy and Tolerance.**

the authoritarian personality has been done from a more orthodox psychoanalytic perspective.

Without detailing the voluminous authoritarian personality literature (Sanford, 1973), we summarize briefly its basic ideas and their relation to political tolerance. In essence, the authoritarian personality construct is a trait approach—it assumes personality to be a collection of traits within the individual. The trait of authoritarianism consists of a number of characteristics, including authoritarian submission, a basic need both to obey those in authority and to command subordinates; aggression toward outgroups, expressing underlying hostility toward those in authority, repressed and redirected toward weaker scapegoats, i.e. Jews and Blacks; conventionality, overemphasis on traditional middle class values; anti-intraception, hostility toward theoretical, intellectual, or impractical ideas; stereotyped thinking, intolerance of ambiguity, and a strong tendency to think in terms of black and white categories; exaggerated concern with the sexual immorality of other people; and other similar characteristics.

According to traditional psychoanalytic theory, these characteristics have their origin in childhood. Fathers of authoritarians are stern and aloof; discipline is harsh and enforces conventional values; and there is a strong emphasis on impulse control. Although the etiology of authoritarianism can be put in terms of the conflicts of the id, ego, and superego, the process of development can be simply stated as one in which the developing child first learns that its impulses are generally bad and to be suppressed; then begins to deny that it has these impulses (i.e. normal sexuality; rebellion toward unbending authority); and finally redirects its repressed hostility from the overbearing father to various minority groups, justified because these scapegoats supposedly embody these terrible impulses. For example, authoritarians hate Blacks because they believe that Blacks, unless tightly restricted by White society and law, will follow their primitive impulses. This is a mere projection of the authoritarian's own impulses, which must be denied and repressed. The ultimate villain, of course, is a too restrictive and conventional childrearing practice.

The relationship of authoritarianism to political tolerance is probably close. Since the authoritarian syndrome includes aggression toward outgroups, stereotyped thinking, and intolerance of ambiguity, one might argue that tolerance is part of the personality itself and not a political attitude affected by personality. This is debatable, but our position is that tolerance is an attitude rather than a personality trait and that the two may be separated analytically without serious distortion. As noted in Chapter 3, the same respondents vary in the extent to which they tolerate different acts of the same target group. If tolerance were a part of authoritarianism, we would not expect to find such variation in responses of the same individuals because the target group would generate a common response to its acts.

More serious, from our point of view, are some criticisms of the authoritarianism research, two in particular, both of which deal with the measurement of authoritarianism. The first of these relates to Adorno's F scale (for fascism), developed to measure authoritarianism. This scale has been attacked for its criteria of item selection, and for the unidirectionality of its items, which results in an obvious response set bias.

The second criticism is more than methodological, although it again relates to the use of the F scale. It has been argued that the original authoritarianism research, and the resulting F scale, have an ideological bias not unlike that in the more traditional measures of political tolerance. Specifically, the F scale items are appropriate to measure authoritarianism on the political right but not on the left. Conceptually, however, there is no reason why left-wing belief systems cannot be rigid or authoritarian. The traditional conceptions and measures of authoritarianism primarily tap negative attitudes toward Jews and Blacks. But any measurement instrument purporting to measure general authoritarianism should either be content free, or balanced to measure left-wing authoritarianism as well. Viewed in context, it is clear why Adorno et al. conceptualized authoritarianism as they did, but we should not add an ideological bias to our measures of personality, since we have taken special care to remove it from our measurement of tolerance.

One major alternative to the F scale is Rokeach's (1960) work on dogmatism, discussed in detail in the next section. Another strategy is to employ a more indirect measure that taps a central aspect of the authoritarian syndrome. To accomplish this, we have included three items from Rosenberg's (1956) faith in people scale and two items from Martin and Westie's (1959) threat orientation scale. Since an important characteristic of the authoritarian personality is distrust of other people, their motives, and their impulses, we deem this an appropriate, if simple, measure of the affective component of authoritarianism. These items and their scale characteristics are presented in Table 6-2.

## Dogmatism and Tolerance

Rokeach (1960) has developed a major theoretical formulation to deal with the conceptualization and measurement of dogmatism or, alternatively, rigidity of thought. Rokeach is among those highly critical of the content biases in authoritarianism research, but goes well beyond this to challenge the Freudian interpretation of rigidity Adorno et al. used. According to Rokeach, rigidity, or dogmatism, is to be understood in terms of an individual's cognitive processes. He focuses on the "belief system," the total organization of the person's beliefs about the (political) world, and then goes on to make the important distinction between a belief system and a disbelief system: the former represents all the beliefs a person accepts as true while the latter is composed of a series of subsystems containing all the beliefs rejected as false. This conception of cognitive organization along a belief-disbelief dimension provides the bridge between cognitive activity and tolerance. Thus, for example, someone whose belief system contained support for democracy as a form of government would have disbelief systems that re-

**Table 6-2**              **Faith in People (Trust) (1978 NORC)**

| Statement[a] | Percent Distrust | Corrected Item-Total[b] |
|---|---|---|
| Some people say that most people can be trusted. Others say you can't be too careful in your dealing with people. How do you feel about it? | 51% | .41 |
| Would you say that most people are more likely to help others or more likely to look out for themselves? | 64 | .34 |
| If you don't watch yourself, people will take advantage of you. | 74 | .55 |
| If a person doesn't look out for himself, nobody else will. | 69 | .50 |
| Life is basically a struggle for survival. | 71 | .51 |

The last three items are five-point agree-disagree scales.

[a] The first three items are from Rosenberg's (1954–55) "faith in people" scale while the latter two items are from Martin and Westie's (1959) threat orientation scale.

[b] Coefficient alpha for a simple additive scale based upon these five items after they are standardized (to correct for the varying standard deviations) is .69. The range for the unstandardized data is 5–19, with a mean of 9.8 (well below the midpoint of 12) and a standard deviation of 2.8. The higher the score the higher the faith in people, or trust, so the sample as a whole is rather untrusting.

jected, to some extent, other forms, such as socialism, fascism, and communism.

Everyone, therefore, should exhibit some rejection of those ideas inconsistent with their system. The exact magnitude of rejection should vary considerably, however, reflecting individual differences in closed-mindedness, or dogmatism. While Rokeach relates dogmatism to a number of the other characteristics of belief systems, the important point for the present analysis is that the degree of rejection in disbelief systems is hypothesized to be a direct function of an individual's level of dogmatism; open-minded people will be much less hostile to beliefs different from their own. This conception of dogmatism, or rigidity, as a characteristic of belief systems yields a view of the "prejudiced personality" that clearly avoids the ideological bias of authoritarianism research by being, potentially at least, free of any specific political content.

Rokeach argues that belief systems serve two often conflicting purposes: to support the cognitive need to know and understand the world, and to defend against threatening aspects of reality. To the extent that the second purpose is dominant, the belief system will become dogmatic and the tendency to reject disbelieved views will be strong. Such rejection therefore serves as a cognitive defense mechanism against perceived threat. Such threat may be short-term and external, or long-term and internal, resulting from anxiety caused by feelings of isolation, helplessness, or low self-esteem.

In terms of the present analysis, disbelief systems can translate into political intolerance, which will vary with two factors: the extent of dissimilarity between disbelief and belief systems, and the level of dogmatism. Since the content-controlled measure of tolerance attempts to assure the selection of a maximally dissimilar "disbelief system," the first factor should be relatively well controlled. Individual differences in dogmatism should therefore be an important determinant of expressed political tolerance. Seven items from the dogmatism scale (listed in Table 6-3, along with their scale characteristics) were included in our national survey.

In relating trust and dogmatism to political tolerance, we discover large differences in tolerance across categories of the independent variables. For purposes of convenience, we have divided the respondents on the trust and dogmatism scales into three groups, labeled high, medium, and low.[3]

Among those high in trust, about 32 percent are "more tolerant," whereas for those low in trust, only 10 percent are so. The relationship between trust and tolerance is moderate; the correlation is $-.20$. Clearly, respondents who lack trust in other people are slightly less tolerant than trustful respondents.

The mean tolerance scores range from 13.7 for the high dogmatism group to 19.3 for the low dogmatism group, a large and significant difference (see Figure 6-2). The percentage "more tolerant" ranges from 5 percent for the former to 35 percent for the latter; in the low dogmatism group, the percentage "more tolerant" outnumbers the proportion "less tolerant" by 35 to 15 percent. The zero order correlation between dogmatism and tolerance is $-.36$, the strongest correlation thus far encountered among the independent variables examined.

3. To collapse the dogmatism scale into three groups, we combined scores 7–16 as low, 17–25 as medium, and 26–35 as high. Although any such groupings are to some extent arbitrary, we did select the midpoint of the scale (21) as our starting point, and went 4 points in either direction to create the medium group. The low and high groups each have ten possible values in their range, and generate approximately equal size groups.

For trust in people, we categorized scores 5–8 as low, 9–12 as medium, and 13–19 as high. We made the high trust category wider than the low trust category, because the distribution is skewed toward the low end, and even with this unequal category width, the low trust group has almost twice as many respondents as the high trust group.

Table 6-3          Dogmatism Items (1978 NORC)

| Statement | Percent Dogmatic | Corrected Item-Total Correlation[a] |
|---|---|---|
| Of all the different philosophies which exist in the world there is probably only one which is correct. | 21% | .53 |
| To compromise with our political opponents is dangerous because it usually leads to the betrayal of our own side. | 34 | .50 |
| A group which tolerates too many differences of opinion among its own members cannot exist for long. | 64 | .41 |
| There are two kinds of people in this world: those who are for the truth and those who are against the truth. | 52 | .56 |
| Most of the ideas which get printed nowadays aren't worth the paper they are printed on. | 37 | .54 |
| In the long run the best way to live is to pick friends and associates whose tastes and beliefs are the same as one's own. | 50 | .37 |
| Most people just don't know what's good for them. | 47 | .47 |

Each item has five response categories, the same ones used for the tolerance items. The percentage dogmatic is the percent who agree strongly or agree with the statement.
[a] Coefficient alpha for a simple additive scale based upon these seven items is .77. The scale range is 7–35, with a mean of 21.1 (almost exactly at the midpoint of the scale), and a standard deviation of 4.7.

This provides some support for the dogmatism-authoritarianism explanation of tolerance.

## Social Learning Theory and Tolerance

Perhaps the simplest and clearest statement relating social learning theory to the development of political tolerance is Zellman's (1975):

The basic proposition of social learning models is that children's attitudes are developed as a fairly straightforward response to environmental inputs and experiences . . . low levels of support for concrete civil liberties in children are quite understandable in light

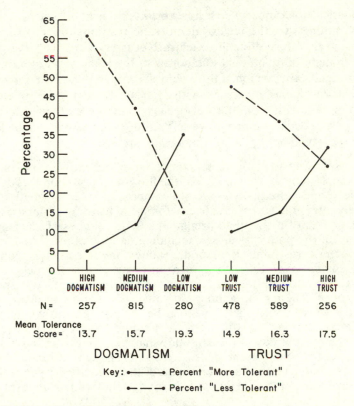

Fig. 6-2. Dogmatism, Trust in People, and Tolerance.

of their collective socialization experience. Civil rights in real-life situations simply are not modeled for children. For example, we tell children that it is wrong (and un-American) to assume guilt until such guilt is proven; yet few children are assumed innocent of wrongdoings or mischief until proven guilty. Similarly, we tell children that we should not assume guilt by association; yet most children have been at some time warned about and punished for associating with persons disapproved of by their parents. So while children learn slogans like "free speech for all," they are also learning that often such slogans have no meaning. This argument is compatible with findings that tolerance increases in adulthood, as the individual's social environment presumably becomes more "tolerant" (p. 36).

Paul Sniderman (1975) provides a more comprehensive treatment of the relationship between social learning theory and the development of political tolerance. He finds a strong correlation between self-esteem and political tolerance, which he explains in terms of social learning theory, noting that the idea of democratic restraint (tolerance) is abstract and therefore difficult to learn. Not everyone is capable of abstract thought, and although the norms of the society may be tolerant ones, a significant portion of the electorate will neither learn nor adhere to them. Particularly persons with low self-esteem will "reject the norms of democratic politics not because they are motivated to do so but largely because their negative self-attitudes have impeded the learning of these values" (p. 178). Sniderman argues:

> Persons high in self-esteem, compared to those low in self-esteem, are more likely to be exposed to the flow of information through the society, and more likely as well to comprehend the information they receive. It is the superior capacity for social learning of persons with high self-esteem . . . that strengthens their chances of learning the norms of the political culture, including, among others, the ideas of democratic restraint. Democratic values are intrinsically complex and change over time; they turn on abstract ideas which require discrimination and training in order to be correctly applied in specific situations. Then, too, democratic values involve a pluralistic set of beliefs which sometimes appear to be inconsistent rather than mutually reinforcing . . . In short, democratic values for a variety of reasons are not easy to learn, and whatever affects an individual's capacity for social learning also affects his chances of learning these values. Self-esteem is a determinant of the capacity for social learning, and thus, of the likelihood of learning democratic values (p. 207).

He suggests that low self-esteem leads to intolerance because it interferes with social learning; he includes a measure of anomie as an index of a person's capacity for social learning. He also argues that self-esteem interferes with the motivation to learn norms and ideals such as tolerance, and he measures this interference by a rejection-hostility scale (see pp. 210–211). Thus self-esteem interferes with both citizens' capacity *and* motivation to learn the societal norms, including tolerance.

Sniderman analyzes the relationships among procedural rights, tolerance, self-esteem, anomie, and hostility. He is often vague about the exact measures and scales used to measure each of these concepts. For example, his procedural rights scale

> . . . ask(s), among other things, whether the government has the right to arrest a person on mere suspicion, if people ought to be compelled to testify against themselves, whether congressional committees investigating "dangerous subversives" must stick to the

rules, or if convictions obtained by illegal evidence should be struck down (p. 196).

He does not, however, list the exact items used in the scale. The same is true for his tolerance scale, which he notes:

> is a gauge of the importance a person attaches to freedom of opinion and of advocacy. The low scorer on this scale is likely to agree with an assertion such as, "The idea that everyone has a right to his own opinion is being carried too far these days," while the high scorer is likely to agree with a sentiment such as "People who hate our way of life should still have a chance to talk and be heard" (p. 197).

Sniderman uses three different measures of self-esteem—scales of personal unworthiness, status inferiority, and interpersonal competence—that correlate highly with one another and produce similar results. We selected the personal unworthiness scale, in the interests of parsimony, as the best measure of self-esteem, with the most in common with the traditional conceptions of the authoritarian personality. Furthermore, it seems more directly related to political tolerance.[4]

Sniderman's theoretical construction is clever and convincing. Unfortunately, it was impossible for him adequately to test it, using his survey data. We are in a similar situation, and we focus on self-esteem as a personality trait of interest in the study of political tolerance, but omit the social learning explanation as part of our model. Although it is a plausible explanation, the type and amount of data necessary to an appropriate test are not available.

The items that make up Sniderman's personal unworthiness (self-esteem) scale are presented in Table 6-4, while the relationship between self-esteem and political tolerance is documented in Figure 6-3. We have also categorized self-esteem scores as low, medium, and high.[5] Among those low in self-esteem, about 7 percent are "more tolerant," while among those high in self-esteem, 34 percent are "more tolerant"; the means are 14.3 and 18.6, respectively, and once again, among those high in self-esteem, there are more respondents in the "more" than in

4. Both Sniderman's self-esteem scale and Rokeach's dogmatism scale are subject to some positive response set bias because in every case, agreement reflects the high dogmatism/low self-esteem end of the scale. See Tables 6-3 and 6-4. Any respondents with a tendency to agree with a statement that seems somewhat reasonable to them will have high dogmatism and low self-esteem scores.

5. We categorized scores 8–21 as low, 22–29 as medium, and 30–40 as high in self-esteem. The distribution is skewed upward, so to obtain a sufficient N in the low esteem group we made the lowest category width greater than the others.

Table 6-4          Self-Esteem Items (1978 NORC)

| Statement | Percent Low Esteem | Corrected Item-Total Correlation[a] |
|---|---|---|
| I do many things which I regret afterwards. | 42% | .41 |
| I never try to do more than I can, for fear of failure. | 33 | .37 |
| A large number of people are guilty of bad sexual conduct. | 48 | .41 |
| There is no such thing as being "too strict" where conscience and morals are concerned. | 50 | .27 |
| I think that in some ways I am really an unworthy person. | 18 | .32 |
| When I look back on it, I guess I really haven't gotten as much out of life as I had once hoped. | 34 | .40 |
| People today have forgotten how to feel properly ashamed of themselves. | 56 | .44 |
| I often have the feeling I have done something wrong or evil. | 20 | .42 |

Each item has five response categories (although McClosky used just two), the same ones used for the tolerance items. The percentage low in self-esteem is the percent who agree strongly, or agree, with each statement.
[a] Coefficient alpha for a simple additive scale based upon these eight items is .69. The scale ranges from 8 to 40, with a mean of 25.5 (just above the midpoint of 24) with a standard deviation of 4.9.

the "less tolerant" group. The correlation betwen esteem and tolerance is .28.[6]

## Conclusions

In this chapter and the previous one, we have reviewed previous efforts to relate social background variables and personality variables to political tolerance. Most recent efforts have concentrated on back-

6. We note that all of the zero order correlations presented thus far are uncorrected, and that, particularly in the case of the personality variables, the scales themselves are indirect and often only moderately reliable measurement devices. Most of the reliability coefficients for these measures are around .70, and, if we were to correct the correlations for attenuation from unreliability of measurement, the zero order correlations would be considerably increased. For example, computing a simple correction for attenuation (Nunnally, 1976) increases the correlation between self-esteem and political tolerance from .28 to .38, while that between dogmatism and tolerance goes from −.36 to −.46. The multivariate analysis presented in Chapter 8 incorporates measurement error into the analysis.

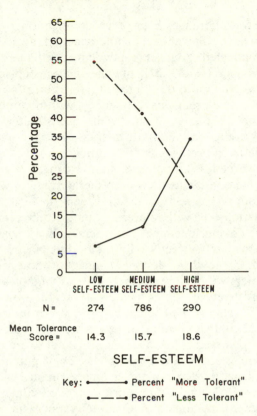

Fig. 6-3. Self-esteem and Tolerance.

ground variables, such as education, religion, region, and so forth. But whatever their emphasis, all recent works on the determinants of tolerance have ignored at least one whole class of variables, either the psychological or the social factors underlying tolerance.

We have examined the bivariate impact of various social and personality variables thought to influence levels of political tolerance and intolerance. Having reconceptualized tolerance, and developed an alternative measurement approach consistent with that reconceptualization, we found that among the social background variables: (1) education continues to have some impact on the level of tolerance, although somewhat less than prior research has suggested; (2) social status variables, including income, occupation, and subjective social class, have very weak relationships with political tolerance ($r = .17$, .16, and .07 respectively); (3) there are no differences in levels of tolerance by degree of urbanization, by region of the country, or by gender, controlling for differences in target group selection; (4) religion and age continue to have some impact on tolerance, but again less than prior research has indicated. Younger respondents continue to be more tolerant than older ones ($r = -.21$), but the relationship is smaller than that found using the more traditional Stouffer items ($r = -.33$). There continue to be some religious differences, with nonreligious respondents being the most tolerant, but while the Stouffer measure indicates that Jews are among the most tolerant, ours shows them to be indistinguishable from Protestants and Catholics.

The personality variables, on balance, show stronger relationships than the demographic ones. Maslow's need hierarchy ($r = .24$), trust ($r = .20$), dogmatism ($r = -.36$), and self-esteem ($r = .28$) all have strong bivariate relationships with tolerance. Since Stouffer, and Nunn and his associates, did not examine these personality variables, we cannot compare our results directly with theirs, but our multivariate analysis, in Chapter 8, shows the dominant impact of these variables.[7]

In the next chapter, we explore several political variables that underlie tolerance. Most recent efforts have totally ignored the political sources of tolerance, almost as if tolerance were an attitude without any specific political content or context. Our criticism focuses on two aspects of the previous studies of tolerance. First, all were based on underspecified models, and ignored whole classes of potentially important variables. Thus most parameter estimates in such works are biased and misleading. Second, prior work employed content-biased measures and conceptualizations of political tolerance. Our empirical analysis demonstrates that some prior findings are totally wrong (gender, city size) and others are misleading (education, region). In general, the social background variables are most heavily influenced by content-bias. In Chapter 7, we examine in depth a third class of variables, those explicitly political. In Chapter 8, we attempt to analyze the simultaneous impact of all three sets of independent variables—sociological, psychological, and political—on tolerance. At that point, we shall be in a position to judge the extent to which current conclusions in the literature are misguided.

7. As we show in Chapter 8, these four psychological variables are highly related to one another, especially self-esteem and dogmatism. The corrected correlations among these variables reach into the .60s and .70s, and thus we cannot examine their separate impact on political tolerance, but must treat them as multiple indicators of the same underlying personality dimension.

# Political Explanations
# of Tolerance

7

The previous chapters discussed some of the social and psychological sources of tolerance; it is appropriate at this point to take up some of the major political explanations of the concept. "Political" explanations account for political behavior by more or less conscious choices made to pursue political purposes or in light of the consequences of political processes. Since tolerance is so much a part of liberal political doctrine, and since it is often said to arise from participation in liberal political processes, we should attempt to understand it in these terms.

In order to do so, we shall first turn to the explanations that respondents themselves provide for their own opinions. As we shall see, many respondents justify their selections of target groups in terms of the standard assortment of liberal concepts, such as rights, equality, democracy, and procedural fairness. After considering these open-ended responses, the analysis focuses on the following political factors: political ideology (in the liberal-conservative sense), political participation, perceptions of threat from dissident groups, and tolerance as an abstract set of political principles. All of these factors are prominently discussed in the literature on tolerance, and the presentation that follows will provide an opportunity to discuss the controversies that are raised in this literature.

## Some Limits to the Analysis: The Political Context

Before proceeding to the empirical analysis, we might briefly indicate what our results can and cannot demonstrate. Readers should remember that we are dealing with the opinions that respondents provided at one point in time; hence, the national political con-

163

text was similar for all respondents. Since we were unable to vary the political context with a cross-sectional design, we cannot know how respondents might have answered our questions under conditions of more or less intense political conflict. By and large, 1978 (the year our survey was completed) was relatively tranquil politically in the United States, at least insofar as civil liberties issues were concerned.[1] Both the diversity of the targets selected in our survey, and the general level of tolerance we discovered probably reflect this context to some degree.

Therefore, our analysis cannot address the question of how such opinions change or remain stable in response to changing political contexts. It is safe to assume that the relative difficulty involved in being tolerant changes with political circumstances. The political context can influence both the levels and the character of tolerance in three general ways: (1) in the degree to which dissident groups are perceived to threaten important values; (2) in the choice of groups against which intolerance is directed; and (3) in the relative importance of the issues at stake in political conflicts. To a considerable extent, the level of tolerance at a given time will depend on the willingness of groups to negotiate their differences peacefully, a willingness which is in turn based on the more fundamental agreement that the core interests of contending groups are not to be threatened. While socio-psychological factors may account for such changes in the scope and depth of conflicts, the political process can generate a momentum of its own, as groups begin to take action in anticipation of what other groups are going to do. The way in which this kind of dynamic mobilizes and reinforces intolerance is difficult to study with our research design, which is cross-sectional and which focuses entirely on individual level variables.

It might also be noted that tolerant norms may appear to prosper at a particular time only because serious threats to the regime have been eliminated or neutralized. Societies may appear to tolerate groups only after they have so thoroughly intimidated and controlled them that they no longer constitute serious threats to the regime. After such groups have been tamed, so to speak, they can be safely tolerated.

Consistent with our earlier conceptualization of political tolerance, we presume that genuine tolerance exists only in the face of a real objection to a group or idea. If there is no threat from any political

1. Some might object to this generalization (which is only an impression) by citing the controversy over homosexual rights or the attempted march by Nazis in Skokie, Illinois, as evidence that civil liberties issues were very important in 1977 and 1978. Nevertheless, our impression is that these years were relatively tranquil compared to other periods in American history.

group, then the society and its citizens may appear to be tolerant because it is "easy" to be tolerant. Qualitative political judgments of this kind, though important to attempt, are difficult to make and must be based on a different kind of evidence than that presented here.

A comprehensive political account of the sources of tolerance and intolerance would have to consider these questions. The most appropriate ways to do so would be through historical case studies, or through some type of philosophical or theoretical analysis. The present study focuses heavily on factors that account for tolerance and intolerance in individuals. In this sense, the design of the study precludes examining system level factors that might help to explain the general level of support for tolerant political norms. Our results, then, may overstate the role of these individual level factors and understate the role of those factors operating at the system level.

## Objections to Target Groups

Robert Lane, in his study (1962) of fifteen working men, demonstrated that ordinary citizens, when given the opportunity, can provide detailed explanations for their political beliefs, a truth often obscured in mass surveys that force respondents to answer batteries of questions without much opportunity for reflection. Given the nature of our study, we could not probe in detail into the reasons underlying the answers that respondents gave to our questions. Since intolerance is often thought to be an ignorant or unreflective response to some vague and exaggerated threat, such a detailed analysis would advance our understanding of this problem a great deal. But in the present study, we could not be quite so ambitious.

After respondents had identified their "least-liked" group, however, they *were* asked, "What is it about this particular group that you dislike?" As expected, they gave a wide range of answers, which we grouped (see Table 7-1) into different categories under the headings of political, economic, religious, and miscellaneous objections. As is indicated in the table, the political objections were subdivided into four categories: (1) those which were ideological in nature, (2) those reflecting a civil libertarian concern that the group in question is bigoted or hostile to minority rights, (3) objections containing references to the tactics and methods employed by the group, and (4) objections portraying the group as "Anti-American." Examples of statements for each coding category are also presented in Table 7-1. The largest number of responses fell under the heading of "Civil Liberties Concerns." In the sample, 27 percent gave this objection as a first response and

**Table 7-1    Reasons Given for Disliking Target Group**

| | First Response | Second Response | Example from National Survey |
|---|---|---|---|
| I. Political Objections | | | |
| A. Ideological (Rejects goals of group and its form of government; group is too radical, too conservative, oppressive) | 22% | 16% | "I dislike the fascists because of their historical background of having a master race and that some people have the power to say who is supreme. They have a belief in a totalitarian society." |
| B. Civil Liberties Concerns (Group rejects civil liberties, against minorities; it is anti-pluralist | 27 | 26 | "The communists want to control people's lives. They lack freedom of speech and freedom of the press." |
| C. Tactics and Methods (Group is violent, destructive, takes law into its own hands) | 19 | 22 | "I dislike the tactics and methods the SLA employs. I don't like the violence with which they accomplish their goals. And they get a lot of attention. That's all—basically their methods, the bloodiness." |
| D. Anti-American (Group rejects U.S. system, it is bad for the country) | 3 | 8 | "The communists are against everything this country is about." |
| II. Economic Objections (Group is exploitative, it doesn't respect property rights, it is against free enterprise. | 2 | 4 | "The communists want to take away free enterprise. They control the distribution of capital." |
| III. Religious Objections (Group is anti-religious, it doesn't believe in God) | 10 | 4 | "The atheists don't believe there is a God and they don't believe in any form of religion. They are against all religions and don't want anybody else to believe if they can help it." |
| IV. Miscellaneous Objections (Group members have bad traits—they are lazy, mean, cruel; respondent just doesn't like them) | 17 | 20 | |
| N = | 1314 | 652 | |

Excluded from this tabulation are 42 responses concerning pro-abortionists. Also excluded in both columns were those who gave no response. About half of those who gave answers listed only one objection.
The coding scheme in this table was suggested to us by Paul Sheatsley, who supervised the coding of the open-ended questions.

26 percent as a second response. Such responses typically contained references to the group in question as bigoted, anti-pluralistic, and antagonistic to the rights of others. This, in a sense, highlights the "paradox" of tolerance discussed earlier, since large numbers of respondents oppose groups because they believe these groups pose a threat to the norms of tolerance. A large number of respondents also cited the tactics and methods used by the groups in question. The Ku Klux Klan and the New Left groups, in particular, were perceived as violent, destructive, and lawless. A significant proportion also gave ideological reasons for disliking a group. That is, they objected to the goals of the group, which they often described as too radical, too conservative, or as simply oppressive.

The reasons for disliking the various groups were far from uniform. Table 7-2 presents the distributions of responses for the target groups selected. As expected, ideological reasons were most often given for opposition to communists and fascists, which makes sense given the highly ideological goals of these groups. In addition, people frequently objected to these two groups on civil libertarian grounds. On the other hand, those who selected one of the New Left groups or the Ku Klux Klan frequently cited the methods these groups used as a reason for disliking them. This was especially true of the New Left: 63 percent of those selecting either the Black Panthers or the SLA provided this rationale. In addition to tactical objections, a large proportion (41 percent) of those selecting the Ku Klux Klan also cited civil liberties

**Table 7-2**        **Reasons for Disliking Target Groups, by Groups Selected**

|  | Group Selected | | | | |
|---|---|---|---|---|---|
|  | Communists | Atheists | New Left Groups | Fascists | KKK |
| I. Political Objections | | | | | |
| A. Ideological | 38% | 3% | 13% | 46% | 6% |
| B. Civil Liberties | 33 | 3 | 4 | 25 | 41 |
| C. Tactics and Methods | 3 | 2 | 63 | 8 | 26 |
| D. Anti-American | 5 | 1 | 3 | 7 | 1 |
| II. Economic Objections | 5 | — | 1 | — | — |
| III. Religious Objections | 7 | 86 | — | — | — |
| IV. Miscellaneous Objections | 9 | 5 | 16 | 14 | 27 |
| N = | 441 | 119 | 202 | 76 | 358 |

First objections are presented here.
  Those choosing Socialists, the John Birch Society, and the two abortion groups as targets were excluded from these calculations because of small N's.

concerns as a reason for opposition. Again, these responses are perfectly consistent with what we know about these groups—namely, that they use inflammatory methods in the service of obscure objectives. Perhaps the most unsurprising figure in the table is that nearly all (86 percent) who selected atheists gave religious reasons for doing so. To summarize, the reasons given for objecting to these groups are not random or illogical, but make perfect sense in light of the faces these groups present to the public.

By far the most ambiguous comments were made by those who selected communists as their least-liked group. These respondents expressed a view of communism as oppressive and dangerous, but their comments were singularly free of references to specific threats posed by communists. In addition, few references were made to the Communist Party of the United States or to domestic communists; instead, the term "communists" was interpreted in international terms (that is, in terms of foreign governments) or in abstract ideological terms. The following comments were quite typical:

> I don't like their philosophy of taking over and dividing the people and then ruling them by a centralized form of government. And I don't like the way they infiltrate democracies and get the people to fight among themselves.

> They can take over a country without shooting a gun. They are not for the people and not out in the open. Lots are in this country now.

> I don't like their way of government. It is too powerful for the people. They don't give their people any say so at all.

> The communists talk out of one side of their mouth and mean the other. You can't trust them. They have no feelings for the common people. It is a dictatorial outfit.

> I don't like their methods. If America doesn't wake up they will get control. All of the above groups [i.e. those listed on the questionnaire] are part of communism [sic] who work under a liberal label.

Civil libertarians have long been worried about the tendency of "anticommunists" to express their opposition in general terms, arguing that since these objections lack specificity, they can be extended to embrace anyone or any group that shares something in common with, or is sympathetic to, communism (a tendency well expressed in the last of the comments quoted above). For this reason, many believe that intolerance of communists poses a more potent threat to civil liberties than does intolerance of other groups, especially those on the right. Moreover, it is sometimes argued, communists at least pretend to sup-

port democracy and civil liberties, while extremist groups on the right
do not. While some support for this view may be found in the responses
to our questionnaire, it should also be noted that these responses are
not entirely unfocused. Many respondents oppose communism because
of the ends it pursues. But many also repudiate it because it uses
undemocratic means to achieve these ends.

There was a similar tendency among those selecting fascists (or Nazis) as a target to denounce them as undemocratic and oppressive. By
and large, however, these respondents focused on more specific griev-
ances, such as anti-semitism, racial hatred, and the provocative tactics
used by this group. In addition, there were several references to the
attempt by the Nazi Party to hold a march in Skokie, Illinois, a suburb
of Chicago in which thousands of survivors of Nazi concentration
camps live. The following is a sample of comments:

> I dislike the Nazis appearing in public places. I dislike reminding war
> survivors of the bad times they experienced. I dislike their whole
> philosophy of life—it is a similar mentality as the Ku Klux Klan.

> I do not like their anti-semitism. Any group that goes out to persecute
> another group is stupid. I just don't like them.

> I guess I don't like them because of Hitler and the way he wanted
> to kill off the race because he thought they weren't good enough to
> live in the world.

> The Nazi party is a continuation of the German Nazis that were in
> power during World War II and stand for things I don't believe in—
> that one group of people is better than another. They tried to do
> away with Jews and feel that the pure German race is the only race
> fit to survive.

> The Nazis believe in arbitrary oppression. They will arbitrarily op-
> pose anyone who opposes their views. I dislike their whole anti-
> democratic methodology.

The perception of arbitrary oppression runs through these comments
about fascists and Nazis. Fascists attack people on the basis of their
religion or race, which is seen as a purely arbitrary basis of attack.
Their intolerance is seen to have a clear focus. A vigorous response
to these provocations is thus seen as a necessary means of self-defense.
By contrast, those who selected communists as a target view communism as a more inclusive threat to everyone's freedom.

The comments about the Ku Klux Klan are very similar to those
about fascists and Nazis, as one might expect. Respondents uniformly
condemned the Klan for its doctrine of white supremacy and for its

persecution of Blacks. Some recalled unfortunate experiences at the hands of the Klan, while many others based their judgments on what they had read about its activities. Many of those who selected the Klan were themselves Black; hence, their comments sometimes reflect a very personal sense of persecution. Their hostility is therefore not difficult to understand. Some representative comments:

> I dislike the way they destroy and spread hate against the Blacks and the awful ways they carry out these premeditated burnings, murders, and the worst kind of abuse. What happened in the 1950s and 1960s could have made one die with heartache. All those horror stories of dragging men through the streets until their skin tore off. That kind of horror.

> The Klan has absolute hate for Blacks and other minorities for no other reason than the color of their skin. I dislike the way they take the law into their own hands.

> This is an unfair organization. It stands for White supremacy. They have dirty low-down ideas and they carry them out!

> I think they're ignorant—the killing of Black people just because they're Black. They are stupid and ignorant—using terror and mass hysteria to do all kinds of terrible crimes.

> I dislike their idea of White supremacy. They believe that Whites are better than Blacks or anyone else. I dislike their economic views that a Black should always be a slave and a White man always a master. No other person can climb out of their economic class.

> They seem to be out to destroy all minorities. They don't represent any good to the country. They are always burning peoples' houses and making minority people suffer. This should not be allowed.

> I come from an area where the KKK was very strong and I do not believe in what they stand for. They are totally against any race that is not White, specially the Blacks. They believe Whites are better than anyone else. I dislike the way they go about showing their dislike of other races, through torture, murder, and destruction.

> They are pro-WASP. I mean that they feel America should be for White Christians. They are "night-riders." They take Negroes and bind them.

> I don't like the way they treat people. Aren't they the ones that had something to do with Martin Luther King's death? I think they were and you shouldn't do that to anybody.

Many respondents quoted in the preceding pages turned out to be intolerant of either communists, fascists, or the Ku Klux Klan. That is, they believed that members of these groups should not be fully free to organize, run for office, or speak in public. Yet, as has been noted, the perceptions of the threat posed by these groups are not at all uniform. Communists are thought to pose a broad threat to freedom, while fascists, Nazis, and the KKK unjustly attack specific groups. Some will perhaps say, on the basis of such responses, that there is a fundamental difference between intolerance of communists and intolerance of fascists, Nazis, or members of the KKK that renders one form of intolerance more justifiable, or less reprehensible, than the other. Thus, those on the left might say that intolerance of communists represents an attack on an ideology (a system of ideas), and is not as justifiable as intolerance on the part of those defending themselves against racists and anti-semites. On the other hand, those who react against communism might say that this doctrine poses an ideological threat to the concept of tolerance itself, which makes it more dangerous than the attacks of right-wing extremists, since the latter are directed against particular groups and not against the concept of constitutional rights *per se*. Each faction's fundamental claim is that one form of intolerance is legitimate while another is not.

The complaints that people have about the New Left groups (the Black Panthers and the SLA) do not raise comparable questions. By and large, respondents did not attack the goals of these groups, which they did not profess to understand, but rather opposed their violent tactics. The following are representative comments:

> They [the SLA] are totally anti-social. They are out to destroy society by any means possible. They would kill anybody to meet their goals.

> The SLA is capable of robbing, murdering, raping, and being able to get away with it. The group itself needs to be demolished.

> It's their [the SLA's] violence. That's the group with the Patty Hearst thing. That's it, the violence. They take all the worst of those other groups and roll it into one.

> They [the SLA] have total disregard for people other than themselves. They threaten violence for its own sake.

> I don't like their [the Black Panthers'] militance. The way this group constantly uses violence to build a party. I don't like the influence they seem to have on the young Blacks, the kids.

> I dislike their [the Black Panthers'] militant attitude. From what I read in the paper, it is a very small minority that tries to take over and make themselves a majority.

> Well, they [the Black Panthers] take the law into their own hands and do things in their own creed. They are very radical. They don't have God in view at all. They want to turn to a lower type of man, more animal like than human.

> The Black Panthers scare the living daylights out of people. They do terrible things. They ride motorcycles. One had to leave the country. They are just bad.

For these respondents, objections to these groups have little to do with the issue of tolerance for dissent. The groups are seen as lawless and violent, and their methods are not distinguished from their goals. Respondents do not view them as dissenting groups, which have a right to express their opinions, but as lawless groups, which deserve to be destroyed. They are not seen as attacking any particular targets, as do the Klan and the Nazis; nor are they thought to have any clear ideological goals, as do the communists. The threat they pose lies in their unlawful or provocative behavior rather than in their political objectives. This is surely one reason why they seem so threatening, and why respondents were so reluctant to tolerate them.

We should add that some objections to the Black Panthers were based solely on racial considerations which have little to do with the methods the group uses. Some respondents expressed their hostility to the group with words that reflected prejudice more than anything else. A few of the clearest examples:

> They're Black. If they went back to Africa, they'd be worse off. They think we owe them a living and we don't.

> They're Black. Blacks have been given too much already. I hate Blacks and that's it.

The objections levelled against atheists were also very predictable. Most respondents who selected atheists as a target criticized their anti-religious doctrines and their persistence in propagating their views. Though respondents sometimes conceded their right to hold such views, they nevertheless preferred that atheists would remain silent. Some representative comments:

> I don't like their idea that there is no God. I also don't like their speaking their piece. Even though its their rights, I don't like it.

> Wherever you hear of atheists you hear of trouble. I'm afraid they may sway my son.

What was surprising about these responses, however, was the often expressed sentiment that atheists violate the rights of believers through their attacks on public expressions of support for religion.

> They are placing their beliefs over everything else. This minority is trying to *take our rights away* because they do not want us to believe our beliefs. They don't want us to have prayers in our schools, "In God We Trust" on our coins. They are trying to keep us from doing what it is in our rights to do. [Respondent's emphasis]

> Atheists do not believe in anything. I dislike them because that one atheist woman was able to take prayer out of the schools.

> Atheists don't believe in God and I do not like them saying that children cannot pray in school. We cannot have released time for religious training in schools because of them. It hurts the children in schools.

According to these respondents, it is not they who are violating the rights of atheists, but the other way around. Moreover, atheists constitute a minority that has succeeded in depriving the majority of its religious freedoms. Atheists not only hold reprehensible doctrines, but also have great political influence. (There is no mention of the fact that the decisions in the areas of school prayer and released time were not solely the work of atheists but were made by the Supreme Court and have since been ratified, albeit tacitly, by Congress.)

A small proportion picked either "pro-abortionists" or "anti-abortionists" as the most objectionable group. Unlike the groups discussed above, these two groups cannot be placed easily along the left-right dimension, since attitudes about abortion derive from sources other than those that define the left-right dimension. The comments made about these groups mirrored very closely the opinions on the issue that are expressed in the popular media or in political debate. The antagonists tend to speak to one another in the language of "rights," which is reflected in the statements below. On the one side, abortion was frequently characterized as murder or an infringement on the rights of the unborn:

> I don't believe in it. Abortion means killing unborn babies. They (the pro-abortionists) are pushing their views. They are making abortion easy and it is being paid for with tax money.

> They are reaching for a controlled society and it comes as close to being fascist as anything in the modern world. It is exactly what Hitler tried to do in order to produce a superior race.

> I don't believe that you have the right to take the life of a child. They believe in taking away life, which is the same as murder.

On the other side, "anti-abortionists" were said to deprive women of their freedom of choice:

> I don't like the idea that a particular group has the authority to say what other women can do with their bodies. A woman should have the right to have a child or an abortion.

> They [the anti-abortionists] are always trying to decide if a woman should or should not have a child. I think this group just meddles into other women's business. We should have a right to do what we want.

The latter argument is similar to the argument for tolerance: people should be allowed to express themselves or to conduct their own business so long as they do not injure others. Abortion, like the expression of opinions, is in the domain of individual choice. Those who oppose abortion, who selected "pro-abortionists" as a target, see it differently. Abortion does infringe on the rights of another party and is therefore wrong. It is not simply a matter of individual choice; therefore, the analogy with tolerance does not hold. Often, supporters of abortion (that is, of less restrictive abortion laws) emphasize the connection between this issue and the larger question of tolerance, a connection their opponents deny. Given this connection, it is perhaps not surprising, as was shown in an earlier chapter, that those who selected "anti-abortionists" as a target were more tolerant than those who selected "pro-abortionists."

It is, of course, difficult to derive firm generalizations from brief quotations like those reported in the preceeding pages. But though these responses are unsystematic and lacking in detail, we can extract a few tentative conclusions. At the most obvious level, respondents tended to express their opposition to target groups in the standard language of a liberal society. According to them, these groups either threaten the rights of minorities, threaten the principles of a liberal political system, or simply break the law. Few respondents expressed their disapproval in terms that clearly suggested some non-liberal perspective. Thus, we did not find any references to communists as "representatives of the working class" or to fascists as the "vanguard of reaction," to borrow a few terms from the Marxist vocabulary. No one bothered to examine the historical or economic function of the Ku Klux Klan or the New Left, or of any other group for that matter. The language of rights and democratic procedure was clearly the dominant mode of expression.

In addition, the greater part of the sample interpreted the actions of these groups as outside the domain of legitimate dissent. That is, respondents did not view these groups as organizations with opinions to present and with a legitimate right to be heard, but rather as threats to their *own* rights. This was especially true of perceptions of groups on the extreme right, which do not hide their dislike of Jews, Blacks, or Catholics. In this sense, then, these respondents did not view these groups within a framework that would make the concept of tolerance meaningful. Other values were believed to be at stake besides those of free expression and free assembly. Obviously, before an appeal can be made to tolerance, people must be persuaded that it is an overriding value and that the expression of political opinions need not threaten their vital interests. Unfortunately, the latter claim is not always true, or at least many of our respondents did not believe so.

Many scholars have written about the "mobilization of bias" in American politics (Schattschneider, 1960), or about the intolerant character of American liberalism (Hartz, 1955). They have tried to show that American institutions, while apparently neutral in the eyes of those governed by them, actually define as illegitimate political goals that are inconsistent with liberal assumptions. Yet the concept of tolerance, viewed abstractly, stands for procedural neutrality. In practice, however, those who pursue political goals that conflict with the liberal value of individual rights are themselves seen as intolerant, since they threaten these rights. From this standpoint, tolerance can be extended safely to those who fit within the liberal consensus, that is, to those who do not threaten the liberal conception of rights. Hence, while many think of tolerance as a procedural value to be applied equally to all political doctrines, in practice it is interpreted and applied only insofar as it does not threaten the principles underlying the liberal regime.

## Tolerance and Ideology

Tolerance is preeminently a liberal concept, in the broader sense of the term "liberal," which we take to refer to the doctrine of natural rights and natural equality that served as the theoretical foundation for representative democracy. As a historical matter, the growth of liberalism has been associated with the spread of tolerant political norms, so much so that the terms "democracy" and "tolerance" have come to be closely identified.

This connection is obvious in contemporary formulations of liberal theory. Modern theories of pluralism, for example, rest heavily on the concept of tolerance and, in part, on the empirical findings concerning tolerance reported earlier. Lowi (1969) has identified the liberal foundations of pluralism in (1) its assumption of a self-regulating society, (2) its differentiation between the political and economic spheres, and (3) its description of the political process in terms of conflicts and compromises among organized groups. Though this theory offers no substantive definition of a public interest, the polity is assumed to be held together by a consensus around procedural norms that allows interested groups access to institutions and to channels of persuasion (Truman, 1951). Hence, the existence of tolerant political norms, either in the mass public or among elites, is an important empirical condition on which this theory rests. In this sense, pluralism, like earlier versions of liberal theory, assigns considerable importance to procedural norms.

At the individual level, the relationship between tolerance and ideology is somewhat more complicated, in that both liberals and conservatives tend to share the general assumptions of liberalism as it is more broadly understood. As a consequence, the United States is often described as a uniquely liberal regime (Hartz, 1955). Thus, conflicts between liberals and conservatives in the United States tend to take place within this broader liberal framework. Since nearly everyone in the United States is a liberal in some sense, the relationship between tolerance and ideology in individuals has to be conceived much more narrowly.

From this narrower standpoint, the differences that do exist between liberals and conservatives are sometimes thought to account for the differences in the degree to which individuals accept tolerant norms. At times, the terms "tolerance" and "liberalism" are used interchangeably so that the acceptance of tolerant norms is said to be a liberal position and the rejection of such norms, or their more guarded acceptance, is said to be a conservative or an "illiberal" position (see Lipset and Raab, 1970: 432–433). This connection is often made, with considerable justification, where questions of race intersect with those of tolerance, since racial issues are often posed in terms of civil rights or civil liberties. Those who make the connection, however, are usually careful to distinguish between economic and non-economic issues, where the former refers to questions of the distribution of wealth and the latter to those of cultural conformity and non-conformity. In this sense, tolerance is understood to be part of the social or the non-economic dimension of domestic liberalism. In such formulations, liberalism is not generally understood as a causal factor; rather, tolerance is *defined* as an aspect of non-economic liberalism. This is in part because the substantive issues raised in this connection, such as the legalization of drugs, the acceptance of cultural non-conformity, and tolerance for communists, socialists, or atheists, are so clearly associated with the left.

The impression that there is a relationship between liberalism, narrowly understood in terms of social or economic issues, and the acceptance of tolerant norms is also reinforced by the historical consideration of extremist movements in the United States. Lipset and Raab (1970: 5), in their historical survey of such movements, define extremism as the rejection of democratic procedural norms. While they acknowledge that many left-wing groups in America have fit this definition, they assert (p. 3) that "extreme *rightist* movements have been more indigenous to America and have left more of a mark on its history" (emphasis theirs). They thus focus almost exclusively on right-wing insurgencies, among them the anti-Masonic and anti-Catholic movements before the Civil War, the Ku Klux Klan, the Coughlinite movement of the 1930s, the John Birch Society, and the (George) Wallace movement of the 1960s.

All of these movements, according to Lipset and Raab, represented attempts to restore a social order thought to be disintegrating. The reactionary character of these groups is thus explained in terms of their declining social and political status, suggesting that the moralistic conceptions of politics and conflict found in these movements result from frustrations over declining social status. These are then projected into the political arena as attacks on those groups displacing them. Thus, these movements are supported by those who are displaced by, or who are unable to come to grips with, the process of social development. Instead of adapting to this process, they try to arrest it politically. Their grievance, therefore, is not fundamentally with the groups they attack but rather with the historical process itself.

Whatever the merits of this account (for criticisms, see Rogin, 1967), there is much truth to the claim that the most powerful extremist movements in the United States have risen disproportionately from the right. Yet the explanation itself helps to reveal the connection between ideology and tolerant norms. In terms of this account, intolerance is part of a general attempt to arrest politically the process of change and development. Those who find this process alarming, therefore, are most likely to reject tolerant norms. For those, among whom we might count Lipset and Raab, who view the historical process as more benign, tolerant norms are seen as instruments of progress. Tolerance, both in spirit and practice, allows emerging social groups room to grow and to express their interests socially and politically, thus providing momentum for further change in both spheres. It is not an accident, therefore, that tolerance has become associated with liberalism and social change, while intolerance has become associated with the right, and with attempts to control the momentum of change.

These associations between ideology and tolerance were indirectly reinforced by earlier empirical work on tolerance. The use of left-wing groups as points of reference against which to measure tolerance was certain to create the impression that intolerant attitudes are concentrated on the right. Though Stouffer and others did not make systematic attempts to measure the relationship between ideology and tolerance, one can safely assume that those on the right were the ones most intolerant of communists, socialists, and atheists. This impression is reinforced by the fact that some of the strongest correlates of tolerance, such as residence outside the South and in urban as opposed to rural areas, are also related in a consistent manner to the liberal-conservative dimension.

We can test this suspicion because our questionnaire contained two sets of items dealing with atheists and communists identical to the ones Stouffer used in his study. The proportions of tolerant responses to these items by ideological groups (using the measure of ideological self-placement described in Chapter 3) are presented in Table 7-3. As noted earlier, these questions, when posed in 1978, elicited large proportions of tolerant responses, as is evident from the table. However, liberals were consistently more tolerant on these items than self-identified moderates and conservatives. The differences are not especially large, but they are consistent. The average proportion of tolerant responses across the four items was 78 percent for liberals and 62 percent and 61 percent, respectively, for moderates and conservatives. The simple correlation between the self-placement index and a tolerance scale based on these items was $-.19$, which reflects a moderate relationship between ideology and tolerance of atheists and communists. Assuming that this relationship would have been found in the earlier surveys, readers were perhaps justified in inferring that those on the left are more tolerant than those on the right.

We may now consider whether these impressions concerning the relationship between tolerance and ideology hold up under closer scrutiny. Since our measure of tolerance is neutral (in ideological terms) in that it allows respondents to choose targets on both the left and the right, we expect that the relationships to be reported will not be quite as strong as they would have been had we relied on the traditional

Table 7-3          **Relationship between Ideology and Tolerance Using Atheists and Communists as Points of Reference (Percent Giving Tolerant Responses)**

| Question | Ideology (Self-Placement Index) | | |
|---|---|---|---|
| | Liberal | Moderate | Conservative |
| If a person wanted to make a speech in your city against churches and religion, should he be allowed to speak or not? | 80% | 63% | 62% |
| If some people in your community suggested that a book he wrote against churches and religion should be taken out of your public library, would you favor removing it or not? | 75 | 60 | 60 |
| Suppose an admitted communist wanted to make a speech in your community, should he be allowed to speak or not? | 78 | 60 | 59 |
| Suppose he wrote a book which is in your public library. Somebody in your community suggests that the book should be removed from the library. Would you favor removing it or not? | 78 | 63 | 62 |
| N = | 329 | 512 | 451 |
| Average: | 78% | 62% | 61% |

measures. Nevertheless, given what has already been said about ideology and tolerance, we advance the tentative hypothesis that those on the left will be more tolerant of extremist groups on the right than those on the right will be tolerant of corresponding groups on the left.

Two measures of ideology, in the left-right sense, have been adopted. The first is an index of ideological self-placement, to which we have already referred. This is a seven-point liberal-conservative scale on which respondents were asked to locate themselves. The scale ranges from extremely liberal on one end to extremely conservative on the other. The second measure is based on four domestic social-welfare questions commonly used in national election surveys. These questions probed respondents' opinions about the role of the federal government in the areas of job security, medical protection, the welfare of racial minorities, and school integration. The underlying dimension in these four items concerns the role of the federal government, the general issue over which liberals and conservatives have divided in the postwar period. The responses to these items have been cumulated to form a scale of domestic ideology. This is a substantive measure of ideology, based on responses to substantive questions, in contrast to the first

Table 7-4 Distributions of Respondents by Ideology

A. The Self-Placement Index

| Position | Percentage of Respondents |
|---|---|
| 1 (extremely liberal) | 3% |
| 2 | 9 |
| 3 | 11 |
| 4 (mid-point) | 36 |
| 5 | 18 |
| 6 | 12 |
| 7 (extremely conservative) | 2 |
| Don't Know | 11 |
| N = 1509 | |

B. The Domestic Issues Scale

| Issue | Liberal | Moderate | Conservative | Corrected Item-Total Correlation |
|---|---|---|---|---|
| Job and Standard of Living | 27% | 26% | 47% | .46 |
| Medical and Hospital Costs | 43 | 19 | 38 | .34 |
| Black Welfare | 38 | 29 | 33 | .49 |
| School Integration | 40 | 14 | 46 | .38 |

The percentages are for those respondents with opinions. Those with no opinion ranged from 3 to 8 percent. Each item is a seven-point scale and the scores on each have been added to create a domestic issues scale. The coefficient Alpha for this scale is .63.

measure, which simply reflects the self-placement of respondents. The major problem with the domestic issues scale, for example, for the present analysis, is that the items dealing with Black welfare and school integration are dangerously close to, and are likely to be confounded with, the tolerance-intolerance dimension for those who chose a target with a racial connection, such as the KKK or the Black Panthers. Obviously, neither of these measures is ideal—ideology is a particularly difficult concept to capture in a single scale—but each taps a different aspect of the left-right continuum.[2]

2. A third measure of ideology was also used in the study, though it will not be brought into play until Chapter 8. As we demonstrated in Chapter 3, and will show again in a moment, respondents at the liberal end of the spectrum were most likely to select targets from the right, and vice versa. It is therefore possible to contrive a measure of ideology based on the target groups selected. Thus, those who chose two right-wing groups were classified as the most liberal, while those who chose two left-wing groups were classified

We said in Chapter 3 that ideology is strongly associated with the kinds of target groups respondents select. The point can be made again somewhat differently using the domestic issues scale as a measure of ideology. Using this scale, the responses to the four questions were summed and respondents were classified on the basis of their overall scores as liberal, moderate, or conservative (see the note to Table 7-5). The relationships between ideology and the target groups selected are presented in Table 7-5. It is readily apparent that liberals tended to select groups on the right while conservatives selected groups on the left. Among conservatives, 75 percent selected one of the groups on the extreme left (communists or socialists, atheists, or one of the new left groups); among liberals, 59 percent selected one of the groups

Table 7-5        **Ideology and Target Group Selected (Domestic Issues Scale)**

| Target Group Selected | Ideology | | |
| --- | --- | --- | --- |
| | Liberal | Moderate | Conservative |
| Communists and Socialists | 21% | 32% | 44% |
| Atheists | 4 | 9 | 10 |
| New Left Groups (Black Panthers, SLA) | 7 | 15 | 21 |
| Radical Right Groups | 59 | 34 | 17 |
| Pro-abortionists | 5 | 5 | 5 |
| Anti-abortionists | 2 | 3 | 2 |
| Others | 1 | 3 | — |
| | 99% | 101% | 101% |
| N = | 293 | 512 | 372 |
| Row %: | 25 | 44 | 32 |

The domestic issues scale was based upon four items, each of which allowed scores ranging from 1 to 7. Thus, the overall scale ranges from 4 to 28. The cutting points for this table were as follows: 4 to 12, liberal; 13 to 20, moderate; and 21 to 28, conservative.

as the most conservative, on a three-point ordinal scale. Those who picked one group from each end of the spectrum were placed in the middle of the scale. This procedure creates a surrogate, rather than a direct, measure of ideology, since ideology cannot be adequately defined in terms of the political groups that people dislike. However, such patterns are bound to be related to ideology. The distribution in the sample among these categories was as follows:

| Target Groups Are: | | Percentage of Respondents |
| --- | --- | --- |
| Both Right-Wing | Liberal | 7% |
| Mixed | Moderate | 59 |
| Both Left-Wing | Conservative | 34 |

on the extreme right (the KKK, the John Birch Society, or fascists). Moderates, meanwhile, fell in between, though they too were more likely to select groups on the left than on the right. When the distibution is arrayed in terms of the self-placement index, the pattern remains intact, though it is not quite so clear: 66 percent of the conservatives selected target groups on the left, while 53 percent of the liberals selected groups on the extreme right (data not shown). These patterns underscore again the inadequacy of those earlier measures that used only groups on the extreme left as points of reference in measuring tolerance.

It might be noted that there is a strong asymmetry in this pattern of results. Despite the relationship between idelogy and target groups selected, a substantial proportion of liberals (32 percent) selected one of the groups on the left, but only about half this many conservatives (17 percent) selected corresponding groups on the extreme right. There thus appears be more antipathy among liberals toward extremist groups on the left than there is among conservatives toward such groups on the right. This asymmetry may reflect either a greater inclination among liberals to reject extremist politics, regardless of the ideological source, or a more general perception among both liberals and conservatives that extremist groups on the left are more dangerous than those on the right.

The hypothesis that tolerance increases as we move across the spectrum from right to left can be tested in several ways. The figures in Table 7-6 show the proportions of tolerant responses among liberals, moderates, and conservatives to the six questions dealing with procedural liberties. The measure of ideology used is the self-placement index, which incorporates more fully the dimension of social liberalism and conservatism generally thought to be related to tolerance. As the data suggest, liberals are more likely to provide tolerant responses on our content-controlled measure than either moderates or conservatives. As with the Stouffer measures, these differences are not especially large, though they are consistent. The average proportion of tolerant responses across all six items is 48 percent among liberals, 37 percent among conservatives, and 36 percent among moderates. The pattern is evident on each of the individual questions as well. In examining these figures, readers should remember that the overall proportion of tolerant responses among all three groups is quite low. On only two of the six questions—those dealing with free speech and with the tapping of telephone conversations—were the proportions of tolerant responses greater than 50 percent. Obviously, despite the general relationship between ideology and tolerance, there is a substantial amount of intolerance on both the left and the right.

It should be emphasized that this relationship is much stronger using the self-placement index than it is using the domestic issues scale. Since the latter emphasizes the economic dimension of the left-right scale, it does not generate any significant differences between liberals and conservatives with respect to tolerance. This becomes clear in Figure 7-1, which presents two summary measures of tolerance for each measure of ideology. The proportion of those who are "more tolerant" and "less tolerant" are based on the distributions on our overall tolerance scale, discussed in Chapter 5. The mean scores on this scale are also presented in the figure. As the display indicates, those who were classified as liberal on the self-placement index were more likely than conservatives to be tolerant: 24 percent of the liberals were "more tolerant," compared to about 15 percent of the conservatives. The mean scores on the overall tolerance scale, which ranges from 6 to 30, were 17.6 for liberals and 15.7 for conservatives. The simple correlation between the self-placement index and the overall tolerance scale was −.15, indicating that tolerance scores decline slightly as one moves across the spectrum from left to right.

These differences disappear when the domestic issues scale is used to measure ideology. When respondents are grouped on this measure, 18 percent of the liberals were classified as "more tolerant," compared to about 14 percent of the conservatives; and 39 percent of the liberals were "less tolerant" compared to about 44 percent of the conservatives. Similarly, the mean scores on the overall tolerance scale were very nearly the same for all three ideological groups. Moreover, the

**Table 7-6**       **Tolerance and Ideology (Self-Placement): Percent Giving Tolerant Responses to Specific Questions**

| Question | Ideology | | |
|---|---|---|---|
| | Liberal | Moderate | Conservative |
| 1. President | 29% | 15% | 16% |
| 2. Teach | 26 | 20 | 19 |
| 3. Outlaw | 42 | 28 | 31 |
| 4. Speech | 68 | 51 | 55 |
| 5. Phones Tapped | 73 | 67 | 60 |
| 6. Rallies | 48 | 33 | 38 |
| Average: | 48% | 36% | 37% |
| N = | 321 | 489 | 441 |

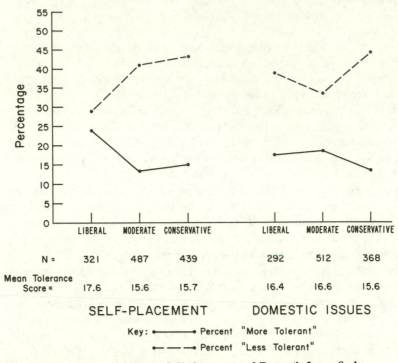

Fig. 7-1. Tolerance and Ideology: Self-placement and Domestic Issues Scale

simple correlation between the tolerance scale and the domestic issues scale was smaller ($-.05$) than that for the self-placement index.

These figures therefore suggest that the relationship between tolerance and ideology depends heavily on the social as opposed to the economic aspect of the liberal-conservative dimension. This is certainly consistent with what has been written about the subject elsewhere. Obviously, a more reliable measure of social ideology might strengthen this relationship still further.

We assume that the tendency of liberals to be more tolerant than conservatives derives from the fact that liberals are more tolerant of extremist groups on the right than conservatives are of extremist groups on the left. Some evidence for this interpretation is provided in Table 7-7, though the patterns presented are far from conclusive. This table presents the proportions of respondents classified as tolerant and intolerant, by ideology and by the target group selected. Very few respondents, liberal or conservative, were "more tolerant" of communists or socialists. However, only 3 percent of the conservatives were "more tolerant" of these two left-wing groups, while about 33 percent of the liberals were "more tolerant" of the three groups on the extreme right. This pattern points to a degree of asymmetry in levels of tolerance between the left and the right. It is interesting to note, however, that

Table 7-7          **Tolerance and Ideology by Target Group Selected: Percent "More Tolerant" and "Less Tolerant"**

| Group Selected | | Ideology (Self-Placement) | | |
| --- | --- | --- | --- | --- |
| | | Liberal | Moderate | Conservative |
| Communists or Socialists | Percent "More Tolerant" | 6 | 6 | 3 |
| | Percent "Less Tolerant" | 40 | 53 | 56 |
| | N = | (71) | (181) | (162) |
| Atheists | Percent "More Tolerant" | 5 | 14 | 28 |
| | Percent "Less Tolerant" | 35 | 30 | 26 |
| | N = | (20) | (44) | (47) |
| New Left Groups | Percent "More Tolerant" | 20 | 14 | 15 |
| | Percent "Less Tolerant" | 37 | 38 | 42 |
| | N = | (35) | (74) | (78) |
| Radical Right Groups | Percent "More Tolerant | 33 | 13 | 15 |
| | Percent "Less Tolerant" | 23 | 37 | 37 |
| | N = | (168) | (147) | (115) |

liberal respondents were far more tolerant of these groups on the right than they were of the two groups on the left. In addition, a larger proportion of liberals (33 percent) was tolerant of the groups on the right than was the case among conservatives (15 percent). Hence, liberals are more tolerant than conservatives both of groups on the left and those on the right. Among those who selected New Left groups as targets, there was hardly any difference between liberals and conservatives in levels of tolerance, though again liberals were slightly more tolerant. Among those who selected atheists, on the other hand, conservatives were more likely to be tolerant than liberals, a difficult finding to explain given the above patterns. In summary, then, the relationship between tolerance and ideology seems to reflect two factors: conservatives focus heavily on communists as targets and are highly intolerant of them; and, though liberals focus heavily upon radical right groups as targets, they are much more tolerant of these groups than conservatives are of communists or socialists.

These results, though suggestive, should be regarded as preliminary. Since we have not yet controlled the relationship for additional variables, it may be strengthened or weakened when such controls are introduced, particularly because the influence of ideology is likely to be confounded with that of other variables, such as age, education, or religion. Nevertheless, these patterns do reveal that the levels of tolerance among liberals, moderates, and conservatives are only *marginally* different. Whether these patterns reflect other factors is a question that will be taken up in a later chapter.

## Political Threat and Tolerance

Previous studies have shown that the level of intolerance in individuals is directly related to perceptions of threat posed by dissident groups (see Stouffer, 1955: Chapter 8). Thus, intolerance arises from perceptions that dissident groups threaten important values or constitute a danger to the constitutional order. That this proposition should have been verified is hardly surprising, since persons intolerant of a group should feel that it poses some threat or danger. Yet it is also true that many people who perceive dissident groups as threatening are nevertheless prepared to tolerate them and to defend their procedural claims. It is appropriate, therefore, not only to test this general proposition once again with our data but also to examine a related question about the kinds of people prepared to tolerate dissident groups in the face of their own perceptions that such groups pose serious threats.

It is worth noting before we proceed that various legal doctrines hold that individuals may be deprived of civil liberties if their actions pose a "clear and present" danger to the constitutional order. Such doctrines formulate, in constitutional terms, the kinds of political calculations that individuals may make when deciding whether dissident groups should or should not be tolerated. These doctrines, however, usually distinguish between "threats to the constitutional order," which need not be tolerated, and "threats to important values," which may merit constitutional protection. This is a highly theoretical problem, and we do not expect our respondents to make such judicial discriminations. Our discussion will therefore proceed without any systematic attempt to keep separate these different notions of threat.

As an independent variable, "threat" may be understood in either psychological or political terms. From a psychological standpoint, some people may be predisposed to perceive threats whether they exist or not, while others may be predisposed not to see them even when they do exist. Thus, to the extent that perceptions of threat are controlling, people may be psychologically inclined to be either tolerant or intolerant. From a more political view of the matter, perceptions of threat might be understood to arise from evaluations of the political strength of and the dangers posed by dissident groups. In this sense, perceptions of threat may arise directly from the immediate political environment, and may be expected to ebb and flow with the degree of political unrest in the society. Obviously, both of these are partial views, and each no doubt captures part of the truth. For our purposes, there is no *a priori* reason to insist on either the political or the psychological view, even though we have included this discussion among the political explanations of tolerance.

The clearest demonstration of a relationship between threat and tolerance may be found in Stouffer's study (1955: Chapter 8), in which he reported a strong relationship between the perceived danger of communism and tolerance. He found that among respondents who were more interested in political issues, only 25 percent of those who thought domestic communism posed a very great danger could be classified as "more tolerant," whereas among those who thought it posed no danger, 42 percent were "more tolerant." The corresponding figures among those less interested in politics were 16 and 46 percent. This relationship held up when controls were introduced for other variables, such as education, age, region, sex, and religiosity.

The most alarming aspect of this, for Stouffer, was that many respondents who perceived no danger from domestic communism were nevertheless very intolerant, implying that no amount of education or information about the real dangers posed by domestic communists could ever eliminate intolerance, since many people seemed to be intolerant regardless of their perceptions of danger:

> There is a relationship between perception of internal communist danger and tolerance, but not high enough to suggest that changes in perception of danger alone would automatically and simultaneously result in changes in tolerance. The two variables do have something in common. But tolerance and intolerance may be a disposition too deeply rooted in a man's or a woman's personality structure to be responsive to a merely negative information program which minimizes the internal Communist risk, even if the facts should justify such an interpretation of the risk (p. 193).

However, on the more optimistic side, Stouffer also found that the better educated respondents were the most likely to discount their perceptions of threat in deciding whether to tolerate communists. This implied, in turn, that even though education could not eliminate these perceptions of threat, it could still promote tolerant attitudes in the face of these perceptions.

We tried to measure the threat posed by each respondent's least-liked group by presenting a series of semantic differential items about the group in question. This is a different measure than that used by

Stouffer, but (as will be shown) it produces roughly similar results. We began with eight adjective pairs, listed in Table 7-8. Respondents were asked to rate, on scales ranging from 1 to 7, their target group on each adjective pair. The means and standard deviations are also presented in the table for each pair, and these can be compared with the results from our local sample (presented in Table 3-5). As the figures indicate, respondents tended to rate the groups toward the undesirable end of each scale. Hence, the means tend to cluster between 5 and 6 on each adjective pair.

When the responses were factor analyzed, the six adjective pairs with the highest mean scores loaded heavily on the first factor extracted, while the two remaining pairs (strong-weak and important-unimportant) loaded on a second factor (see Table 7-8). The correlation between the two factors was $-.04$, indicating that they are quite independent of one another, and also that the factor pattern matrix would be the same for virtually all methods of factor analysis. As the individual item correlations suggest, the six adjective pairs composing the first factor are most strongly related to tolerance. These six correlations cluster very closely, ranging from $-.28$ to $-.32$. The two remaining pairs are not as closely associated with the tolerance scale; the correlations between tolerance and the strong-weak and the important-unimportant scales are .10 and .18, respectively. As a consequence, the first factor tends to be systematically related to our tolerance scale, while the second is not. To make the presentation more compact, therefore, the analysis to follow will be based on the six pairs composing the first factor, which will be used as our central measures of threat.

It might be noted that these six pairs involve different kinds of evaluations of the target groups than do the remaining two pairs. That is, the six pairs evaluate the goals of the target groups, while the two remaining pairs evaluate the strength or importance of these groups. This suggests that differences in levels of tolerance reflect more the threat that target groups are thought to pose to citizens than the real strength or importance of these groups. This is consistent with Stouffer's observation that intolerance cannot be eliminated by simply convincing citizens that extremist groups are in fact powerless to achieve their objectives.

There was considerable variation in the degrees of threat associated with different target groups. Table 7-9 presents the mean scores for the different target groups on a composite scale of threat (ranging from 6 to 42). It also presents the proportions of respondents selecting each

Table 7-8    Perceived Threat and Tolerance

| Adjective Pairs[a] | Mean | Standard Deviation | Factors[b] | | Zero-Order Correlation With Tolerance |
|---|---|---|---|---|---|
| | | | Factor 1 | Factor 2 | |
| Strong-Weak | 3.8 | 2.0 | .08 | .51 | .10 |
| Honest-Dishonest* | 5.4 | 1.7 | .64 | −.03 | −.30 |
| Trustworthy-Untrustworthy | 5.5 | 1.8 | .65 | −.10 | −.32 |
| Predictable-Unpredictable | 5.2 | 2.1 | .39 | −.11 | −.31 |
| Safe-Dangerous* | 6.0 | 1.4 | .69 | .20 | −.31 |
| Important-Unimportant | 4.3 | 2.2 | −.09 | .48 | .18 |
| Non-violent–Violent | 5.6 | 1.8 | .60 | .14 | −.29 |
| Good-Bad | 6.1 | 1.4 | .62 | −.03 | −.28 |
| Eigenvalues: | | | 2.2 | 0.6 | |

[a] All adjective pairs were presented in terms of seven-point scales. The items with asterisks were reversed in the questionnaire in order to balance their presentation. In the table they are presented so that the higher score is always toward the "undesirable" end of the scale.
[b] The factor analysis was conducted with an oblique rotation with Kaiser normalization. Since the correlation between the factors is low (−.04), the factor pattern matrix will be nearly the same for all methods of factor analysis.

Table 7-9 **Target Groups Selected and Perceptions of Threat**

| | Threat[a] | | | |
|---|---|---|---|---|
| Groups Selected | Mean Score | Percent "High" | Percent "Low" | N |
| New Left Groups | 37.3 | 93 | 7 | 192 |
| Communists | 35.0 | 80 | 20 | 407 |
| KKK | 34.6 | 79 | 21 | 333 |
| Fascists (Nazis) | 31.4 | 61 | 39 | 72 |
| Socialists | 29.7 | 61 | 39 | 18 |
| Pro-abortionists | 28.8 | 41 | 59 | 56 |
| John Birch Society | 28.5 | 43 | 57 | 21 |
| Atheists | 27.8 | 39 | 61 | 106 |
| Anti-abortionists | 25.9 | 32 | 68 | 25 |
| Total Sample | 33.8 | 74 | 26 | 1254 |

[a] The measure of threat is a cumulative scale ranging from 6 to 42. It is based upon the responses to the six adjective pairs composing Factor 1 in Table 7-8 above. Those with scores of 30 and higher on this scale were classified as "high" and those with scores of lower than 30 were classified as "low."

group that were classified as "high" or "low" on this overall scale.[3] The scale combines the responses to the six adjective pairs that made up the first factor, discussed immediately above. As the figures indicate, the New Left groups were believed to pose the greatest threat, followed by communists, and by two groups on the extreme right, the KKK and fascists. Overall, 93 percent of those who selected one of the New Left groups thought that it posed a great threat, while the corresponding figures for those who selected communists, the KKK, and fascists were 80, 79, and 61 percent, respectively. Conversely, atheists, the Birch Society, and the two abortion groups were thought to pose the least threat. These rankings on the threat scale correspond roughly to the rankings presented earlier on the tolerance scale. As was shown in Chapter 4 (see Table 4-15), respondents tended to be least tolerant of the New Left groups, communists, and the Ku Klux Klan, and most tolerant of the two abortion groups and the John Birch Society.

3. This scale was divided as follows: those who had cumulative scores of 30 and higher were classified as "high" and those who had scores of 29 and below as "low." Only two categories were used because the distribution was heavily skewed toward the high end of the scale. Roughly 75 percent of the respondents were classified as "high" (see Figure 7-2), despite the fact that the cutting point was decidedly closer to the higher end of the scale. The distribution made it difficult to create substantively meaningful categories while maintaining some variation among them. The same observation applies to the "general principles" scale, discussed below (see Footnote 7).

We have been unable to find any variable, besides tolerance, that is systematically related to our measure of threat. All of the variables we have discussed are randomly associated with perceptions of threat. Table 7-10 presents the simple correlations between the cumulative measure of threat and six other variables. These correlations are uniformly low. Perceptions of threat do not vary significantly with education, participation, age, ideology, or with the two psychological variables included in the table. The fact that threat does not vary with self-esteem and dogmatism is worthy of attention, for it might have been expected that those who are low in self-esteem or high on dogmatism would be most likely to perceive threats from the political environment. But there is no evidence for this hypothesis. The correlations in the table indicate that perceptions of political threat arise independently of these particular psychological processes. We cannot identify, with the information at hand, the sources of these perceptions, though we infer that they reflect, in some degree, political judgments about the values for which target groups stand and the amount of influence held by these groups.

The relationship between tolerance and threat can be explored in various ways. The correlations reported in Table 7-8 clearly indicate that tolerance is associated with perceptions of threat from dissident groups, and we can demonstrate this again from a different angle. Figure 7-2 presents the proportions of respondents who were classified as "more tolerant" and as "less tolerant" by the level of peceived threat. The threat scale was collapsed into just two categories (high and low) because it is heavily skewed toward the high end, which makes finer discriminations pointless. The percentages show clearly that intolerance increases with the level of threat. Among those who were classified as high on threat, 49 percent were "less tolerant" and

**Table 7-10        Sources of Threat: Simple Correlations Between Threat and Six Selected Variables**

| Variable | Correlation | N |
|---|---|---|
| Education | .07 | 1249 |
| Participation | −.02 | 1242 |
| Age | −.10 | 1254 |
| Ideology (self-placement) | −.06 | 1162 |
| Self-Esteem | .11 | 1248 |
| Dogmatism | −.11 | 1250 |

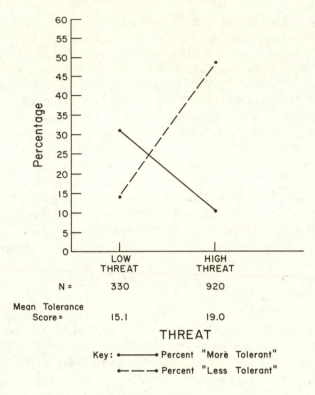

Fig. 7-2. Tolerance and Threat

only 10 percent were "more tolerant." Among those low on threat, only 14 percent were "less tolerant," while about 30 percent were "more tolerant." In other words, about three times as many respondents were tolerant among those "low" on threat than among those "high" on threat.

Stouffer argued that education plays an important role in giving people the capacity to tolerate extremist groups in the face of their perceptions that such groups are dangerous or threatening. Commenting upon his findings, he concluded that:

> Thus we see how education is related to the capability, if one perceives great internal Communist danger, of being relatively tolerant in spite of it. In other words, there is something about people with more schooling which equips them to make discriminations, to appreciate the principles of civil rights, and to handle a value conflict in a more tolerant way than others (p. 202).

Although those with more education were no more (or less) likely than others to perceive threats from extremist groups, they were much more likely to discount such perceptions of threat in deciding whether to tolerate such groups. However, Stouffer appears to have misinterpreted his findings, since, on our reading of his data, threat had about the same effect among the highly educated as among the uneducated.

Our own data indicate that the relationship between tolerance and threat holds up after we control for other variables, including education. This was to be expected, since threat is not related to any of the other variables considered in our study. The figures in Table 7-11 are the simple correlations between tolerance and threat, within various control groups. The correlation between these two variables for the entire sample is .43, and the correlations within the various control groups cluster very closely around this figure.

Stouffer's conclusion that education reduces the influence of threat is thus not confirmed. Threat seems to have the same influence among the highly educated as among the less educated: it reduces tolerance, and it does so to a similar degree. It is true that among those "high"

**Table 7-11        Tolerance and Threat: Correlations Within Control Groups**

| Group | Correlation | N |
|-------|-------------|---|
| Entire Sample | .43 | 1250 |
| Education | | |
|    Grade School | .40 | 124 |
|    High School | .48 | 635 |
|    Some College | .39 | 242 |
|    College Degree | .39 | 244 |
| Sex | | |
|    Male | .43 | 591 |
|    Female | .44 | 659 |
| Ideology (self-placement) | | |
|    Liberal | .46 | 307 |
|    Moderate | .38 | 447 |
|    Conservative | .43 | 404 |
| Political Participation | | |
|    Low | .44 | 650 |
|    Medium | .44 | 499 |
|    High | .40 | 89 |
| Religion | | |
|    Protestant | .43 | 799 |
|    Catholic | .46 | 328 |
|    Jewish | .40 | 34 |

on threat, the highly educated are more tolerant than the less educated. This is also what Stouffer found. However, he erroneously concluded that educated respondents were tolerant in spite of this perceived threat *because* of their education. This inference was unwarranted, because the differences in tolerance between the educated and the uneducated respondents were the same for both the high and the low threat groups. The safest conclusion to be drawn is that the effects of education and threat are independent of one another.

In comparison with the other independent variables, threat emerges as one of the most important determinants of tolerance. This may come as no surprise, since the very notion of intolerance seems to presume a threat of some kind, but it does raise a difficult theoretical problem. Because we have been unable to discover any other factors to account for perception of threat, it must be regarded as a truly independent determinant of tolerance and intolerance.

## Tolerance and Political Involvement

Beginning with Stouffer's study in 1955, most empirical analyses of American political behavior have reported strong relationships between political involvement and support for "democratic" political norms. Stouffer, comparing the responses of various types of community leaders with those of rank-and-file citizens, found on almost every question relating to tolerance that the community leaders were more supportive of civil liberties than the mass public. On an overall scale of tolerance, Stouffer reported (p. 51) that about 66 percent of the community leaders could be classified as "more tolerant," compared to only 31 percent of the national rank-and-file. Thus, he concluded that:

> Without exception, each of the 14 types of community leaders tends to be more willing to respect the civil rights of Socialists, atheists, and those suspected of disloyalty who deny they are Communists, and self-avowed Communists than either the rank-and-file in the same cities as the leaders or the national cross-section (p. 57).

Nunn, Crockett, and Williams (1978) examined a similar sample of community leaders in their 1973 survey, finding that approximately 83 percent of the community leaders could be classified as "more tolerant," while only 56 percent of the national cross-section could be so classified. Thus, the differences in tolerance between elites and rank-and-file citizens remained quite constant, though the overall levels of tolerance among both groups increased over the 19 year period. However, the authors also found that these differences disappear when controls are introduced for education, sex, region, exposure to news media, city size, and occupation. This is consistent with Jackman's (1972) conclusion that the differences in tolerance between Stouffer's samples disappear once controls are introduced for education. It is difficult to sustain the argument, then, that community leaders are more tolerant than their followers simply as a result of their community involvement and participation. They appear to be more tolerant for other reasons: they are more educated, come from higher status backgrounds, are more likely to live in large cities, and so forth.

McClosky (1964), in his study of national party convention delegates and the general electorate, found that the former were much more tolerant than the latter. He introduced no controls for background differences between the two samples, so we cannot tell whether these differences "wash out" as they do in the Stouffer and the Nunn et al. samples. McClosky's study is most interesting, however, for his interpretation of the findings:

> Democratic viability is, to begin with, saved by the fact that those who are most confused abut democratic ideas are also likely to be politically apathetic and without significant influence. Their role in the nation's decision process is so small that their "misguided" opinions or non-opinions have little practical consequence for stability. If they contribute little to the vitality of the system, neither are they likely to do much harm (p. 376).

The obvious, and the most important, implication to be drawn from these findings is that the democratic system is preserved by an activist political elite that, contrary to the electorate at large, accepts the norms of civil liberties and is prepared to apply them in specific circumstances.

Others have disputed this interpretation, though they have not generally disputed the findings on which it rests. When survey results are cited showing that leaders are more tolerant than rank-and-file citizens, these critics usually respond by saying that citizens would become more tolerant if they were given the opportunity to participate in politics. For example, Pateman argues that:

> Once the participatory system is established . . . it becomes self-sustaining because the very qualities that are required of individual citizens if the system is to work successfully are those that the process of participation itself develops and fosters; the more the individual citizen participates, the better he is able to do so. The human results that accrue through the participatory process provide an important justification for a participatory system (1970: 25).

Pateman, and others, believe that the give and take required of those who participate in politics teaches citizens about different points of view, the necessity of bargaining and compromise, and the value of civil liberties. Thus, the remedy for intolerance is to encourage participation rather than to restrict it. In other words, this dispute revolves around the causal interpretations of empirical findings and not around the validity of the results themselves.

The most important question to reconsider is, of course, the empirical claim that leaders are more tolerant than the mass public. If this claim is invalid or if it must be substantially qualified, then the causal dispute is moot. From a certain view of democracy, it is preferable, if one has to choose, that elites be more tolerant than the electorate at large, whether or not this greater tolerance is the *result* of community involvement. From this standpoint, the relative intolerance of rank-and-file citizens must be a lesser cause of concern.

We do not have an elite sample, so we cannot compare results across samples using our measure of tolerance. However, we can examine differences within our mass sample in levels of tolerance controlling for political participation and interest in politics. In his original analysis, Stouffer found that those more interested in politics were more tolerant than those who were less interested, though he used this only as a control and did not address its significance in and of itself. Similarly, Nunn and his associates analyzed a variable they called "interest in current events." Using Stouffer's data, they found that, in 1954, 36 percent of those most interested in current events were "more tolerant," while this was true of only 25 percent of those who were less interested; the figures from their 1973 survey were 62 and 47 percent, respectively. They also found that organizational membership and activity were strongly related to political tolerance.

In our survey, we included two measures of political involvement, the first a political participation scale and the second a political information scale. The scales, along with the distributions of responses to individual questions, are presented in Table 7-12.[4] The participation scale arrays respondents in terms of a wide range of political activities, from voting to working actively in an election campaign. The information scale taps their knowledge of fairly straightforward political details.

The linear relationships between our measures of tolerance, on the one hand, and participation and information, on the other, are weak.

4. These questions were posed in a yes-no format. The scales were created by summing responses to the items. The participation scale ranged from 0 to 6 (there were six items) and the information scale from 0 to 5 (there were five items here).

The simple correlation between the overall tolerance scale and the participation scale is .15, and that between tolerance and the information scale is .17. The relationships between tolerance and political involvement are thus positive but not particularly strong.

The most interesting aspect of these relationships, however, cannot be uncovered by linear measures of association alone. The influence of participation on tolerance, at least in Stouffer's formulation, is expected to operate most clearly at the highest levels of participation— that is, among those who can be regarded as community leaders. Since these comprise only a tiny fraction of any population, one cannot test the proposition adequately by looking at the linear correlation between tolerance and political involvement. Given the limitations of our sample, we must try to identify those few respondents whose participation scores are highest and compare their levels of tolerance with the rest of the sample.

Accordingly, the participation and information scales were divided into three categories, from lowest to highest. On the participation scale, the highest category consisted of those who said that they had participated in at least five of the six acts listed in Table 7-12. The middle category consisted of those who participated in at least two of these acts (but not more than four), while the lowest category consisted of those who participated in none, or in only one, of the acts.[5] Only about 7 percent of the respondents fell into the highest category, which we assume is a rough surrogate for an elite stratum. The information scale was recoded similarly: those who answered at least four of the items correctly were placed in the highest category, those who answered two or three questions correctly in the middle category, with the remainder in the lowest category. This classification was substantially less selective, as roughly a third of the respondents fell into the highest category.

The relationships between tolerance and these two scales are depicted in Figure 7-3. As will be seen from the pattern on the left-hand side of the figure, those in the highest category of participation are substantially more tolerant than the rest of the sample. About 37 percent of this select group (N = 95) were "more tolerant," compared to only about 12 and 17 percent of the low and medium categories, respectively. Thus, even with our measure of tolerance, those with the highest rates of participation tend to be the most tolerant.

This pattern is not quite as clear on the information scale, probably because it is not as selective as the participation scale. Nevertheless,

5. In other words, those with scale scores of 5 or 6 were classified as "high," those with scores of 2, 3, or 4 as "medium," and those with scores of 0 or 1 as "low."

**Table 7-12**          **Participation and Information Scales**

A. Participation Scale

| Items | Percent Yes | Corrected Item-Total Correlation |
|---|---|---|
| Contributed Money | 19 | .46 |
| Worked in Campaign | 13 | .41 |
| Gone to Meetings or Rallies | 20 | .50 |
| Written or Talked to Public Official | 31 | .47 |
| Belong to Organizations That Take Stands | 15 | .35 |
| Voted in Last Four Years | 73 | .28 |
| Coefficient Alpha for Scale = .68 | | |

B. Information Scale

| Items | Percent Correct | Corrected Item-Total Correlation |
|---|---|---|
| Know Vice-President | 79 | .45 |
| Know Number of Senators per State | 52 | .47 |
| Know Length of Term for U.S. House | 30 | .32 |
| Know Which Party Controls House | 69 | .42 |
| Know U.S. Secretary of State | 34 | .43 |
| Coefficient Alpha for Scale = .66 | | |

those in the highest category of this scale also tended to be the most tolerant. Thus, about 23 percent of this group were "more tolerant," compared to 8 and 14 percent of the low and medium categories, respectively. Both with respect to participation and information, then, we find stronger relationships with tolerance than the zero-order correlations suggested.

Does political involvement itself generate tolerance or are these relationships the result of some other factor or factors? Education is one factor often said to account for the relationship between tolerance and involvement reported in other studies (see R. Jackman, 1972).[6] It is appropriate, then, to control the relationship between participation and tolerance for level of education. (See Table 7-13A.) The figures in each cell of the table are the proportions of respondents classified as "more

6. We controlled for education because Jackman's analysis (1972) proved that it is important. There are, of course, other factors that might have been considered.

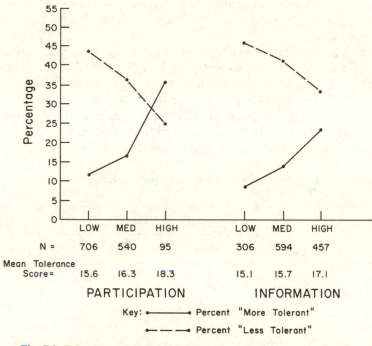

Fig. 7-3. Tolerance and Political Involvement: Participation and Involvement

tolerant.'' The relationships between participation and tolerance, at each educational level, appear in the percentages read across the table. The correlations listed in the right-hand margin measure the relationships between participation and tolerance at each level of education. The relationship between education and tolerance, for level of participation, can be assessed by reading the percentages down the columns. The correlations across the bottom of the table measure the relationship between education and tolerance, by level of participation.

As a rule, the relationships are stronger down the columns than they are across the rows of the table, indicating that education, and not participation, is more closely associated with tolerance. The relationships between participation and tolerance are all very weak, except among respondents at the highest level of education (college graduates). Within this group, the correlation between the two variables is .18, still not particularly high. On the other hand, the levels of tolerance increase more rapidly and more steadily as we move from the lowest level of education to the highest. This is true for respondents at the low and medium levels of participation, but not for those at the highest level.

The correlations between education and tolerance within the first two groups are .33 and .29, respectively, but only .13 for those at the highest level of participation.

In Table 7-13B, the relationship between tolerance and participation is controlled for dogmatism. In general, the results parallel those reported above for the education control. Within the categories of dogmatism, the relationship between participation and tolerance is weak, the correlations being .00, .10, and .12 for the high, medium, and low categories, respectively. On the other hand, the relationship between tolerance and dogmatism is much stronger across the three categories

**Table 7-13A**     **Tolerance and Participation Controlled for Education: Percent "More Tolerant"**

| Education | Participation | | | |
|---|---|---|---|---|
| | Low | Medium | High | $r$ |
| Grade School | 4 | 8 | * | .05 |
| | (97) | (51) | | |
| High School | 8 | 10 | 22 | .08 |
| | (419) | (239) | (27) | |
| Some College | 21 | 15 | 33 | .01 |
| | (75) | (124) | (15) | |
| College Graduate | 25 | 35 | 45 | .18 |
| | (75) | (125) | (51) | |
| $r =$ | .33 | .29 | .13 | |

N's are in parentheses
* Insufficient number of cases

**Table 7-13B**     **Tolerance and Participation Controlled for Dogmatism: Percent "More Tolerant"**

| Dogmatism | Participation | | | |
|---|---|---|---|---|
| | Low | Medium | High | $r$ |
| High | 2 | 7 | 18 | .00 |
| | (158) | (83) | (11) | |
| Medium | 11 | 11 | 33 | .10 |
| | (433) | (330) | (46) | |
| Low | 28 | 37 | 43 | .12 |
| | (113) | (126) | (37) | |
| $r =$ | $-.28$ | $-.38$ | $-.29$ | |

N's are in parenthesis

of participation, these correlations being $-.28$, $-.38$, and $-.29$ in the low, medium, and high categories, respectively. These two analyses, taken together, suggest that participation does not have a direct influence on the level of tolerance.

All this suggests that political activists tend to be more tolerant than others because they differ from non-activists in other relevant characteristics. For example, among the select group of activists in our sample, 56 percent are college graduates, compared to only about 18 percent in the sample as a whole. There are comparable differences with respect to other important variables. Political activists are thus highly distinctive with respect to a number of factors that are in turn related to tolerance. Thus, the relationship between participation and tolerance is probably spurious, and it is doubtful in any case that it is strong enough to justify the claims made for the salutory effects of political participation.

These findings do not give us a clear basis to decide between the two theories discussed earlier in this section. Activists tend to be more tolerant than others, yet a large portion of them are nevertheless intolerant. This latter consideration makes it doubtful that the system as a whole would be made more tolerant by insulating leaders from pressures from below, leaving aside the question of whether this could be accomplished in the first place. Moreover, the greater tolerance of activists seems not to reflect participation itself but rather other characteristics of these people. Hence, increased participation, in conventional forms of political activity, will probably not make citizens significantly more tolerant.

A complicating factor is that activists and non-activists tend to select different kinds of groups as potential targets. Activists are more likely to select groups on the extreme right while non-activists are more likely to select groups on the left. Given the differences in tolerance between activists and non-activists, the participatory system brings into play conflicting and compensating tendencies. Those who are in a position to do something about their beliefs tend disproportionately to select groups on the right, but they are more likely to be tolerant of them. Those who are less influential, on the other hand, tend to be more hostile to groups on the left, and they are more likely to be intolerant. This is not to say, however, that the value of participation should be judged in terms of its possible consequences for tolerance alone. Other consequences must be considered, as well as the possibility that participation, like tolerance, may be a good in itself.

We leave for a later chapter a more precise measurement of the relationship between participation and tolerance. The question can only be settled through a multivariate analysis, which will be undertaken in Chapter 8. We conclude for the moment, however, that other factors account for much of the apparent connection between these two variables.

### Support for the General Norms of Democracy

One of the major conclusions of previous studies (Prothro and Grigg, 1960; McClosky, 1964) is that there is little relationship between support for the general principles of democracy, as they conceived of them, and the application of these principles in specific situations. Members of the mass public were found to be very supportive of the general principles, yet at the same time they were generally willing to suspend them in hypothetical situations involving communists, atheists, or other controversial groups.

We have already criticized the methodology on which these conclusions were based. Briefly, the investigators simply compared the differences found in their samples between the marginal distributions for the abstract questions and for the specific items. The consensus in favor of the abstract statements and the lack of any such consensus on the specific formulations indicated that there was no relationship between the two. A more appropriate way to approach the problem is to measure the relationship between the degree to which individuals support the abstract principles and the degree to which they apply them in practice. In reformulating the problem, then, we may pose two questions: (1) Is the level of support for the general principles of democracy and civil liberties still as high as it was in the 1950s? (2) Is there any significant relationship between the degree to which individuals support these general principles and their willingness to apply them to political groups they oppose?

To answer the first question, we repeated in our survey two of the questions used by Prothro and Grigg and five used by McClosky. These items, along with the distribution of responses in our survey, are summarized in Table 7-14. The items range from the more to the less abstract. The first four items express democratic principles in highly abstract form, while the last three are more specific and, hence, more controversial. The distributions of responses to these seven items are all very close to those reported in the earlier studies, despite Prothro and Grigg's use of local rather than national samples, and the passage of nearly twenty years. It is still true that the overwhelming proportion

**Table 7-14    Support for General Principles of Democracy**

| General Statement | Agree | Uncertain | Disagree | Percent Agree Prothro-Grigg or McClosky | Correlations with Six-item Tolerance Scale (specific acts) |
|---|---|---|---|---|---|
| 1. People in the minority should be free to try to win majority support for their opinions. | 89 | 9 | 2 | 94-98 | .14 |
| 2. Public officials should be chosen by majority vote. | 95 | 3 | 2 | 94-98 | .14 |
| 3. No matter what a person's political beliefs are, he is entitled to the same legal rights and protections as anyone else. | 93 | 4 | 3 | 94 | .22 |
| 4. I believe in free speech for all no matter what their views might be. | 85 | 7 | 9 | 89 | .23 |
| 5. If someone is suspected of treason or other serious crimes, he shouldn't be entitled to be let out on bail. | 62 | 11 | 26 | 69 | −.25 |
| 6. When the country is in great danger we may have to force people to testify against themselves even if it violates their rights. | 35 | 16 | 48 | 36 | −.27 |
| 7. Any person who hides behind the laws when he is questioned about his activities doesn't deserve much consideration. | 52 | 16 | 32 | 76 | −.29 |

N = 1509

The first two questions listed are taken from the Prothro-Grigg (1960) questionnaire, while the last five are taken from McClosky's (1964). Our questions were presented in the form of five-point agree-disagree scales. The figures in the table are the percentages that agree or strongly agree with the statements versus the percentages that disagree or strongly disagree. In the original studies, these questions were presented dichotomously so that respondents either had to agree or disagree.

of the American public supports the principles of minority rights, majority rule, equality under the law, and free speech when these principles are posed in an abstract form, as they are in the first four items in the table. On each of these items, the difference between the percentages giving the tolerant and intolerant responses is greater than 75 percent. These are clearly consensual norms now, as they were nearly a generation ago.

The last three items in the table, borrowed from McClosky's study, are more specific than those discussed above and touch on issues that are perhaps less fundamental to democratic procedure, such as the right to bail and protection against self-incrimination. McClosky regarded these items as "specific applications" of fundamental principles, although we have already noted (in Chapter 2) that the principles underlying the items are ambiguous. In addition, the items are formulated so that these values collide with other important values, such as national security (see items 5 and 6, for example). Because the items express more specific and more controversial situations, they do not generate the consensus that the more abstract statements produce.

The second general question to be investigated has not yet been satisfactorily addressed. In previous studies, investigators assumed that since the percentages of tolerant responses fell off so drastically when the items became more specific, there was in fact little relationship between support for abstract principles and the willingness to apply them in practice. They therefore implied that support for the abstract principles does not constrain or guide responses to specific circumstances. The implicit conclusions that endorsement of abstract principles has no influence on political behavior is not justified on the basis of the evidence presented. Although the marginal distributions of responses to the two types of questions may vary substantially, it does not follow that there is no relationship, at the individual level, between abstract views and responses to specific situations. There may be a relationship between the two, though perhaps not a very strong one. Since neither McClosky nor Prothro and Grigg tried to measure this relationship, we can only speculate about what they might have found.

Among recent writers, only Lawrence (1976) has been sensitive to this problem, as he tried to measure the relationship between respondents' positions on the general norms of tolerance and their willingness to apply them in practice. He concluded that the Prothro-Grigg and McClosky questions were necessarly consensual because of their ambiguity and their abstract character. He therefore argued, we believe correctly, that a certain inconsistency between abstract norms and specific applications was built into the earlier research designs. Thus, he tried to frame questions neither so vague and consensual nor so specific as those used in the earlier studies. Using such items, he found considerable consistency between support for general norms and their application to specific circumstances, concluding that: "Large majorities of the population in fact apply their tolerant general norms consistently on even the hardest . . . issues" (p. 93).

There are thus two important differences between Lawrence's analysis and those of the earlier writers. First, Lawrence used "general norm" questions which were less abstract and thus less consensual; second, he actually measured the relationships between responses to the general statements and responses to the more specific situations. His finding that there is a moderate relationship between the two could be attributed to the nature of his questions. Certainly, highly abstract items, of the kind used in the earlier surveys, are bound to widen the gap between general principles and specific applications. However, it is difficult to discern the impact of the different question formats, since neither McClosky nor Prothro and Grigg reported the relationships between responses to their two sets of questions. As a result, we have no basis for comparison.

It is not a novel proposition that abstract beliefs influence responses to practical situations. Nor is it surprising to find that there is not a one-to-one relationship between the two. As noted earlier, competing values usually operate in practical circumstances, so that people are forced to find some compromise between or among them. Hence, we suspect that the stronger their commitment to the abstract norms of tolerance, the more willing people should be to act on these norms. It is not hard to show, with our data, that there is a relationship between the two. Table 7-14 presents the simple correlations between the various questions measuring support for the general norms and our six-item tolerance scale, which is based on responses to specific situations and political groups. These correlations, while not particularly high, are all in the expected direction. In interpreting these correlations, readers should bear in mind that there is little variation in the responses to the first four items (note the distributions in the table), a circumstance that will usually reduce the size of the correlations.

These relationships are presented differently in Figure 7-4, which shows the proportions of respondents classified as "less tolerant" and as "more tolerant," by degree of support for the abstract norms. In this figure, six of the abstract items were combined into a single scale

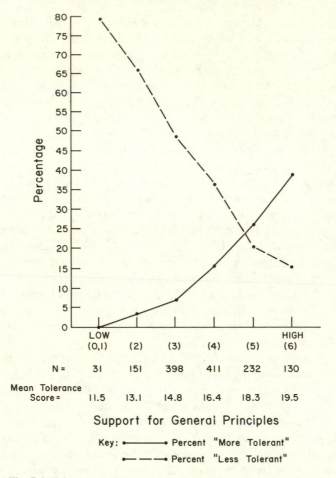

Fig. 7-4. Tolerance and Intolerance by Support for Abstract Principles

to measure support for the abstract norms.[7] The figures clearly reflect a strong relationship between the abstract and specific formulations of tolerance. Among those whose support for the norms was weakest, none was classified as "more tolerant," while among those whose

7. This scale was based on six of the items listed in Table 7-14. Item 2 in that table was omitted because it was unrelated to the other items in the scale. The "General Principles" scale was based on the number of those items answered with tolerant responses. Thus, the scale ranges from 0 to 6, though in Figure 7-4 the two lowest categories were collapsed. The scale was constructed in terms of the number of tolerant responses given, instead of in terms of the cumulative scores from each item, since this method produces a wider distribution of respondents. In the multivariate analysis in Chapter 8, however, we use the cumulative scores.

support was strongest, 39 percent were so classified. The proportions of those classified as "more tolerant" increase steadily as we move up the scale of support for the general norms. Clearly, then, we must conclude that those who endorse the abstract norms are most likely to be tolerant in practical circumstances. Though this conclusion runs counter to that implied by McClosky and Prothro and Grigg, it is possible that they might have concluded differently if they had examined the problem in the way that we have here, especially since we relied on many of their items.

This conclusion, however, leaves a great deal unsaid on this thorny issue of the relationship between principles and behavior. As a normative matter, we do not mean to say that people should be narrowly consistent in their beliefs and behaviors, since there is bound to be some tension between abstract beliefs and the requirements of practical situations. As a practical matter, people will come to different conclusions regarding the proper way to implement political principles. Moreover, we cannot address with the information at hand the actual relationship between principles and behavior, since our measures of the latter consist of responses to survey questions rather than actual behavior. Social-psychologists have discussed the attitude-behavior controversy at length in recent years (for a review, see Schuman, 1972, and Oskamp, 1977), and there is little that we can add to this discussion beyond the general points raised in Chapter 2. We should remind the reader in closing, however, that these particular findings bear more on the question of constraint between abstract and specific attitudes than they do on the attitude-behavior controversy.

## Summary and Conclusions

This chapter has examined several political variables often said to be related to tolerance, among them, ideology, perceptions of threat from target groups, political involvement, and support for the abstract principles of democracy. The results of the analysis support the following conclusions:

1. There is a weak, though consistent, relationship between ideology and tolerance. Liberals tend to be more tolerant than conservatives, but only when a self-placement measure of ideology is used. When economic issues are used to distinguish liberals and conservatives, this relationship disappears. Apparently, then, the relationship between tolerance and ideology is relevant to the social or non-economic dimension of ideology. Liberals (defined in non-economic terms) tend to pick right-wing groups as targets and conservatives pick left-wing groups. Lib-

erals tend to be slightly more tolerant of the right than conservatives are of the left. In addition, liberals tend to be more intolerant of groups on the extreme left, such as communists, than they are of groups on the extreme right.

2. Political involvement is also weakly related to tolerance. The more people participate in politics, the more likely they are to be tolerant. However, the linear relationship between participation and tolerance, though positive, is weak, so we cannot make a great deal of it. However, when we compared a very narrow stratum of activists to the rest of our sample, we found large differences in levels of tolerance. The activists tended to be much more tolerant than the rest of the sample, though further analysis revealed that this relationship reflects other factors associated with participation. Nevertheless, it is true, as others have argued, that activists are more tolerant than non-activists.

3. The degree to which respondents perceived a threat from their target group was strongly and consistently related to tolerance. Persons who see a group as a serious threat are very likely to be intolerant of it, regardless of the nature of the group. However, given our methodology, which allowed respondents to select their least-preferred group, most people in our sample perceived their target group as very threatening, which accounts, in part, for the high levels of intolerance we found. In addition, perceptions of threat were unrelated to all other variables considered in the study, and thus they cannot be explained in terms of the psychological or social variables discussed earlier in Chapters 5 and 6.

4. Finally, the degree to which respondents endorsed several abstract statements expressing democratic principles was related to the degree to which respondents were prepared to tolerate their least-liked groups in practical circumstances. Thus, those who endorsed the abstract principles of free speech, minority rights, and the right to run for office were most likely to permit members of their least-liked groups to do these things. In this sense, abstract principles may constrain or guide responses to practical circumstances in which dissident groups might be involved.

# A Multivariate Model
# of Political Tolerance

8

The major studies of political tolerance, reviewed in the previous chapters, share several characteristics which limit their usefulness in understanding the sources of political tolerance. First, they rely on content-biased measurement procedures, and thus have spawned misleading conclusions. Second, they focus on one set of independent variables, thus analyzing incomplete and misspecified models. Stouffer (1955), for example, focuses primarily on bivariate relationships between social variables and tolerance. For the most part, he ignores the political and psychological sources of tolerance. Nunn, Crockett, and Williams (1978) follow Stouffer, failing to include psychological variables in their analysis. On the other hand, Sniderman's (1975) model consists solely of psychological independent variables. In short, there has been no comprehensive effort to include, in one multivariate model, variables from the social, psychological, and political explanations of tolerance. In the previous chapters, we attempted to overcome the first problem, that of content-bias. In this chapter, we attempt to overcome the second problem, that of incompletely specified models. We examine the role of social, psychological, and political variables in respondents' decisions of first, which target group to select, and second, how far to tolerate that target group. We shall focus most of our attention on the latter.

In general, we assume that social variables are causally prior to psychological variables. Social background variables, such as education, religious affiliation, age, and so on, generally shape the environment in which individuals operate and, at a very general level, shape the contours of perception. Thus, for example, if social class, broadly conceived, has an impact on political tolerance, this impact is not likely to be a direct one, but rather operates by shaping life's experiences and the manner in which individuals perceive and interpret these experiences. Thus high levels of social status may produce economic and personal self-satisfaction, and this satisfaction in turn may affect whether one has a "need" to perceive the world in dichotomous terms and to be intolerant toward groups and ideas which fall in the "wrong" category. Although it is, in theory, possible for social variables to have a direct impact on tolerance (and, in fact, many previous authors have assumed it is so; see Chapter 5), we presume it is influenced more heavily by other sets of variables, psychological and political.

## A Model for the Analysis of Political Tolerance

In Chapter 3, we presented a framework within which to analyze political tolerance. In that discussion, we asked four questions: What is political tolerance? How tolerant is the U.S. public? What are the targets of attitudinal intolerance, and how are they selected? Once a target is selected, how do individuals decide to tolerate, or refuse to tolerate, that group? We attempted to provide answers to these questions, addressing the first in Chapter 1, the second in Chapter 3, the third in Chapter 4, and now, the last question in Chapters 5–8. The last question is the most difficult to answer, and Chapters 5–7 have merely set up the problem in a way that will allow us to attempt an answer in this chapter.

We present the model in two stages, to avoid confusion, since it is complicated, with many hypothesized relationships. Fortunately, we have already provided detailed discussions of the relationships between each set of independent variables, and the dependent variable, political tolerance, in previous chapters. Here we merely refer the reader back to those discussions.

Figure 8-1 presents the hypothesized relationships among the political variables that relate directly to tolerance. The social and psychological variables are clustered as causes of these political variables. We assume the immediate causes of tolerance to be twofold: adherence to the general norms of democracy, and the perceived threat from target groups. As noted earlier, McClosky (1964) and Prothro and Grigg (1960) argued that there is little relationship between support for general norms of democracy and the actual application of these norms. However, Lawrence (1976) did find a direct relationship, and our analysis supports him. The extent of perceived threat of the target group should also lead directly to political tolerance (see the discussion in Chapter 7): the

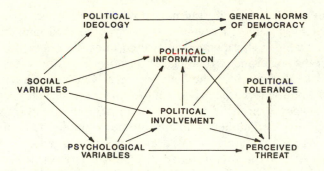

Fig. 8-1. Preliminary Model of Tolerance

greater the perceived threat to personal values, the less tolerant individuals should be of the threatening group.

The major causal processes affecting support for the general norms of democracy and perceived threat by the target group are primarily political, although perceived threat is subjective and may be affected by psychological variables. All things equal, certain personality types may be more likely to perceive a threat; psychological security (personality) and perceived threat could be related. In addition, people who are more heavily involved in politics, and who are therefore knowledgeable about politics and the political system, should both subscribe to the general norms of democracy, and provide a realistic assessment of the threat posed by their least-liked group. Since the official political norms of society are tolerant ones, persons actively involved in the political process should be likely to learn and subscribe to them. Furthermore, even controlling for political involvement, liberals ought to be more likely to subscribe to these norms than conservatives. There is no reason to expect, however, that political ideology should be directly related to perceived threat, since there are manifest groups to threaten both liberals and conservatives.

Political ideology, information, and involvement are conceptualized as products of social and psychological variables. We expect that only one direct relationship exists among these *political* variables—that political involvement leads directly to more political information, above and beyond that expected given a respondent's level of education, social status, and psychological characteristics. Those involved, for whatever reason, in the political process, frequently talk about politics and absorb more knowledge about the political system and the political process.

In Figure 8-2, we specify the nature of the social background and psychological variables, as well as their hypothesized impact on the political variables. The major unanswered question about this model is whether the social and psychological variables have any direct impact on political tolerance, or whether they merely have indirect effects through the political characteristics of the citizenry. Certainly, previous research suggests direct effects, but none of that research involved completely specified models with appropriate multivariate controls. In addition, it relied on content-biased measures of tolerance.

Although it may be important to distinguish between the affective and cognitive aspects of personality, our initial model considers personality (psychological security) as a single, more general, variable. Personality, as we have conceptualized and measured it, can be expected to have a direct impact on political ideology, political information, political involvement, and perceived threat. Those respondents who are more dogmatic, lower on the need hierarchy and lower in self-esteem, should be more conservative than their opposites. Further, respondents with these characteristics should be unlikely to become involved in politics, and even if involved, should acquire less information about the political system than their counterparts. (See Sniderman, 1975, on social learning theory.)

The four social background variables in our model are education, social status, age, and secular detachment from religion.[1] Education is expected to have a major direct impact on three variables: political information, political ideology, and personality. Certainly education ought to increase knowledge of the political system and the political process. Highly educated respondents ought to know more about the social, economic, and political systems *in general* than those with little education. Education might be expected to have two opposite effects on ideology, leading to greater economic conservatism, but also to greater social liberalism (Erikson and Luttbeg, 1973; Ladd, 1978). Thus the exact composition of our political ideology variable will determine the direction of the relationship between education and ideology. As our political ideology measures are coded to indicate those who are most conservative, we have called the ideology construct conservatism. As education's impact is to produce more liberal attitudes, the relationship between education and conservatism is negative. Finally, education might affect the personality measures: self-actualization,

1. We examined additional background variables such as region, size of community, race, sex, and so on. These variables are unimportant in the multivariate model and their exclusion does not affect the parameter estimates.

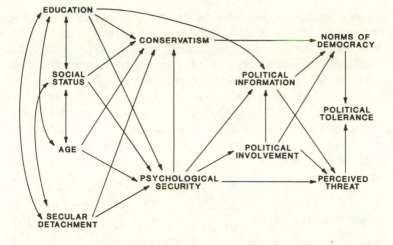

**Fig. 8-2. Fully Specified Model of Tolerance**

dogmatism, and self-esteem. Persons with higher levels of education should be more competent, generally better able to manipulate and understand the forces affecting them, and thus better able to close the gap between the ideal self and the perceived self, i.e., to have higher self-esteem. Learning about diverse points of view and ways of experiencing life should make them less dogmatic.

Social status should have an impact similar to education, although we do not expect any direct relationship with political information. Age should affect two of the political variables directly—older respondents should be more conservative (both on social and economic issues) and should be more dogmatic and have lower self-esteem.[2] Secular detachment should have basically the same impact as age.[3]

2. Erikson and Luttbeg (1973: 188–189) note that "on most standard poll questions older people are found to be somewhat more conservative than young adults . . . On 9 out of 10 issues, the younger generation is the most liberal, by margins of from 8 to 21 percentage points."

3. As noted in Chapter 5, we coded religion as a secular detachment variable: 1 = Baptists; 2 = other religions; 3 = no religion. This ordering is purely empirical and is used to maximize the impact of religion on tolerance. Little impact is discovered, and any other coding scheme would only diminish this minor impact. The skeptic might argue that the paths between religion and personality, and religion and ideology, in Figure 8-2, should be reversed: that it is certain personality characteristics and ideologies that cause some respondents to be non-religious, rather than vice versa. We present secular detachment as the prior determinant, although the process is undoubtedly more complicated. Few respondents have become Baptists because of personality or political ideology, although many Baptists have undoubtedly developed their personality traits

The model presented in Figure 8-2 presents the variables we expect to have direct and significant impact on one another. It is not a fully recursive model because several possible recursive relationships have been deleted since they were not expected to be significant. In fact, we estimate a fully recursive model, but generally we report only those coefficients that are statistically significant. In this way, our *a priori* expectations can be compared with the modeling results, making clear which of the hypothesized direct paths, in Figure 8-2, are erroneous and should not have been specified, and which unspecified paths between variables do appear to exist. The next section presents our methodology for parameter estimation and our empirical results.

### Parameter Estimation

There are numerous ways to "test" the model in Figure 8-2. Perhaps the simplest is to perform a series of regression analyses, treating the model as recursive, and reporting the standardized path coefficients or the unstandardized regression coefficients.[4] This procedure is simple enough, involving a series of assumptions, most of which are reasonable. Yet there are two serious problems which can be handled better by different statistical procedures. The first is the problem of measurement error. We have specified a theoretical model in Figure 8-2, but as noted in Table 8-1, the empirical analysis must rely on operational measures of theoretical constructs. Even if we could assume that all measurement error is random, the parameter estimates obtained using ordinary least-squares regression would be biased.[5] A second problem is that multiple indicators of the theoretical constructs are available, producing problems of overidentification. More information is available than could be used effectively by ordinary regression procedures.

Fortunately, recent developments in maximum-likelihood confirmatory factor analysis treat these problems satisfactorily. The problem of measurement error is solved by allowing the specification of a set

and political ideologies as a result of their religious doctrine. No doubt the development of both religion and personality generally proceeds concomitantly during childhood socialization, from common causal processes.

4. There is considerable debate over the relative advantages and disadvantages of standardized and unstandardized coefficients. Since almost all of the variables in this analysis are attitude or personality scales that have arbitrary units of analysis—and since the major concern is a comparison of the relative impact of different sets of variables—we have relied on standardized coefficients. See Tukey (1956: 38–39).

5. As Bohrnstedt and Carter (1971) show, random measurement error in the independent variables of a multivariate regression equation will produce biased parameter estimates.

**Table 8-1**          **Measures Used in Analysis of Political Tolerance**

| Theoretical Variable | Empirical Measures |
| --- | --- |
| Education | Education |
| Social Class | Income |
| | Occupation |
| Age | Age |
| Religion (Secular Detachment) | Religious Affiliation |
| Personality (Psychological Security) | Dogmatism (Rokeach) |
| | Self-actualization (values) |
| | Self-esteem (McClosky) |
| | Faith in People |
| Ideology (Conservatism) | Self-identification |
| | Domestic Issues |
| | Ideological Position of Least-Liked Group |
| Political Information | Political Information Scale |
| Political Involvement | Talk Politics |
| | Interested in Politics |
| General Norms of Democracy | One Prothro-Grigg item |
| | Five McClosky items |
| Perceived Threat | Five Semantic Differential Items |
| Political Tolerance | Tolerance Scale (six-item scale) |

of theoretical relationships among unmeasured, theoretical constructs, and of a set of measurement relationships between these theoretical constructs and their empirical indicators. Using only information about the relationships among indicators, we can obtain estimates of the relationships among the theoretical constructs (called *structural parameters*) and estimates of the relationships between each theoretical construct and its empirical indicators (called *epistemic correlations*).[6] Some of the details of these statistical procedures are presented in Appendix 8-A.

For purposes of illustration and simplicity, we present the results in stages.[7] We begin with a reduced portion of the fully specified model

6. The epistemic correlations are the square roots of the reliability coefficients. Thus, even in the absence of traditional estimates of the measurement reliability of an indicator—such as measures based on test-retest correlations, measures of internal consistency, and so on—the techniques discussed in Appendix 8-A derive estimates of the reliability of the indicators. See Sullivan and Feldman (1979).

7. We present the results in stages simply because it allows us to present each concept and its measures, and to discuss the relationships between them. It makes the discussion more manageable. This is not the way the model was created, however, nor does the LISREL model proceed in this fashion. See Appendix 8-A.

of political tolerance. Figure 8-3 specifies the relationships among four theoretical constructs: the general norms of democracy, the perceived threat of respondents' target groups, their political ideology, and their tolerance of these target groups.

Most of the theoretical constructs are measured by several empirical indicators. The epistemic correlations help both to determine which indicators are the most reliable measures of each construct, and to assess the "true nature" of the construct. We therefore elaborate each set of partial results before presenting the full model.[8]

For political ideology (conservatism), the arrows connect the abstract concept with its measures, or indicators, including self-placement on the ideological spectrum and the ideology of the respondents' least-liked groups. The numerical entries on the arrows are the epistemic correlations, indicating the "goodness" with which each indicator measures the hypothesized theoretical construct. The *size* of the correlations indicates the quality of measurement; the *pattern* of the epistemic correlations suggests interpretations of the underlying constructs. In the case of ideology, both indicators are moderately reliable measures of the underlying construct, although the ideology of the least-liked group is somewhat better than ideological self-placement. In previous chapters, we used a third measure of ideology based on four

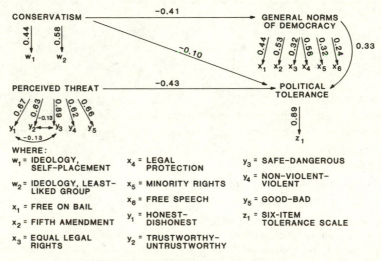

WHERE:

$w_1$ = IDEOLOGY, SELF-PLACEMENT

$w_2$ = IDEOLOGY, LEAST-LIKED GROUP

$x_1$ = FREE ON BAIL

$x_2$ = FIFTH AMENDMENT

$x_3$ = EQUAL LEGAL RIGHTS

$x_4$ = LEGAL PROTECTION

$x_5$ = MINORITY RIGHTS

$x_6$ = FREE SPEECH

$y_1$ = HONEST-DISHONEST

$y_2$ = TRUSTWORTHY-UNTRUSTWORTHY

$y_3$ = SAFE-DANGEROUS

$y_4$ = NON-VIOLENT-VIOLENT

$y_5$ = GOOD-BAD

$z_1$ = SIX-ITEM TOLERANCE SCALE

**Fig. 8-3. Tolerance Model: Stage I**

8. For readers versed in factor analysis, the epistemic correlations can be interpreted as factor loadings and the abstract constructs as factors. The pattern of loadings helps to label and interpret the factors.

domestic issues. During our modelling it became clear that it would be inappropriate to use simultaneously the three measures of ideology, since including the issue index unduly affects the "goodness of fit" of the entire model to the data. (We elaborate on this below.)

The perceived threat variable is measured with five semantic differential items noted in Chapter 7. They are equally reliable measures of perceived threat, although the safe-dangerous adjective pair defines the concept somewhat more clearly than the other four pairs. Two arrows directly connect some of these indicators, representing correlated errors that undoubtedly result from the fact that the semantic differential items share a common format. The error for safe-dangerous correlates − .13 with the error terms for both honest-dishonest and for trustworthy-untrustworthy. These pairs were contiguous on the questionnaire, explaining their correlated errors.

For the general norms of democracy variable, see, once again, Table 7-14, where we used seven items from the Prothro and Grigg and McClosky studies. One of these items was dropped from our analysis because it does not correlate strongly enough with the other items to assume that it measures the same underlying construct. Although it is tempting to delete the items with the lower epistemic correlations, the marginals in the more abstract questions are highly skewed, and hence these "less good" measures must be included to assure stable variation on the general norms construct.[9] For political tolerance, we rely on our six-item tolerance scale, which has an epistemic correlation of .89.[10]

The estimates of the structural parameters (partial path coefficients, corrected for measurement error) are also presented in Figure 8-3. Perceived threat has the strongest direct impact on political tolerance; the coefficient of − .43 shows that the greater the respondents' perceived threat, the less their political tolerance. General norms of democracy also has a strong impact (.33), confirming our suspicion that general norms affect respondents' specific applications of tolerance. Conservatism has little direct impact on political tolerance. There is a slight tendency for conservatives to be less tolerant, all things equal, but the coefficient is small (− .10) and is the only statistically insignif-

9. There are several correlated error terms among $x_1$ through $x_6$, but they are excluded from Figure 8-3 because the figure would become excessively complicated.

10. The epistemic correlation between the political tolerance scale and the underlying construct is obtained by taking the square root of the scale's estimated reliability. (See note 6.) Coefficient alpha for the political tolerance scale is .79, so the epistemic correlation is fixed at .89. The other epistemic correlations are estimated with the excess information, provided by the overidentified model, using the LISREL program. The epistemic correlation for the political tolerance scale is thus a fixed parameter, whereas the others are free parameters to be estimated.

icant one in Figure 8-3. We delete it from further consideration and assume that the only reason conservatives are less tolerant than liberals is that they are less supportive of the general norms of democracy. In fact, conservatism and support for general norms are strongly negatively related (−.41). These results are consistent with the hypothesized model in Figure 8-2, which, because of our content-controlled measure, does not specify a direct link between ideology and political tolerance.

In Figure 8-4, two abstract concepts and their indicators, psychological security and political involvement, are added to the model. The indicators and epistemic correlations for the variables previously discussed—conservatism, perceived threat, general norms, and political tolerance—are deleted. The path coefficients (estimates of structural parameters) among these abstract constructs are presented again, however. The reader should recall that, although each succeeding figure includes additional variables, the parameter estimates will not change, because they were derived from the fully specified, fully recursive model. The results are presented in stages, although the statistical estimation was not conducted in these stages because to do so would cause the initial and intermediate models to be badly misspecified and the resulting parameter estimates to be biased.

For the personality (psychological security) construct, the dogmatism scale is by far the "best" indicator. It practically defines the construct, although the self-esteem scale also has a large epistemic correlation. The other two variables—self-actualization and faith in people—are

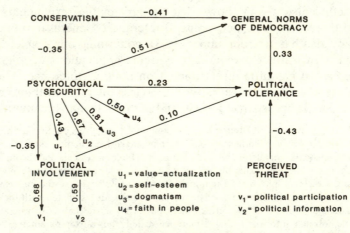

Fig. 8-4. Tolerance Model: Stage II

less important than dogmatism and self-esteem in defining the personality construct. Thus, although we label the construct "psychological security," it is closely related to the traditional dogmatism-authoritarianism syndrome. A lack of self-esteem is often thought to underlie this syndrome, and the epistemic correlations suggest that this is true. The dogmatism scale also has the highest correlation coefficient with political tolerance.[11]

The original model (see Figure 8-2) included *two* constructs designed to examine the participatory democracy thesis: political information and political involvement. A political information scale was used to measure the former, and three measures—political interest, talking about politics, and a political participation scale—were used to measure the latter. However, these two constructs are so highly correlated that portions of the analysis were plagued by multicollinearity, causing very large standard errors for the parameter estimates. (The "corrected" correlation between information and involvement is .84). The most sensible solution is to collapse the information and involvement factors into one political involvement construct. Because of computer limitations on the number of endogenous indicators in the model, only two of the four involvement indicators could be included. We chose the two most reliable measures, political participation and political information. As the epistemic correlations in Figure 8-4 indicate, the participation scale loads higher on the involvement construct, although they both have high loadings.

The path coefficients among constructs in Figure 8-4 indicate that political involvement has only minimal impact on political tolerance—the same as political ideology—and is not statistically significant. Psychological security, on the other hand, has a significant *direct* impact on political tolerance, as well as a strong *indirect* impact through support for general norms of democracy. Support for general norms of democracy results more from personality than from ideology, and even political ideology is strongly influenced by personality. People who are

11. The various personality measures included in the survey should in principle permit an evaluation of the alternative psychological explanations of tolerance, presented in Chapter 6. A preliminary look at the intercorrelations among these measures points to a major problem in this respect. Once corrected for attenuation due to unreliability these psychological characteristics are strongly intercorrelated, invalidating attempts to separate their individual effects on tolerance. In such situations, even small fluctuations based on sampling error or missing data could completely revise any conclusions drawn from variance partitioning procedures. These variables will, however, be used jointly to determine the overall impact of this readily observable psychological syndrome on political tolerance. No specific comments can be made about the relative merits of the various underlying psychological theories.

less dogmatic and higher in self-esteem are more likely to be involved in political activities, are more likely to be liberals (although not necessarily on economic questions; see below), and are *much* more likely to adhere to the general norms of democracy than people who are more dogmatic and lower in self-esteem. The indirect impact of personality on tolerance is as great as its direct impact, and the fact that both ideology and support for general norms derive to some extent from personality vitiates a purely cognitive, political explanation of tolerance. Including political factors as intervening variables between psychological security and political tolerance does not totally attenuate the direct impact of personality on tolerance. For clarity of presentation, we delete the direct impact of political involvement on political tolerance, as we did for political ideology, since both paths are very weak.[12]

In Figure 8-2 direct relationships between political involvement and perceived threat, and between political involvement and general norms, are posited, but neither of these paths survives empirical estimation; their path coefficients are very small. Thus perceived threat is an independent variable, although we conceptualized it as an intervening variable, part of a perceptual process affected by psychological and political variables.[13] Another difference between the hypothesized model of Figure 8-2 and the empirical results of Figure 8-4 is that the effects of psychological security on general norms of democracy and on political tolerance are direct. This is not surprising since information and involvement fail to connect psychological security with norms and tolerance. The initial expectation—that personality would relate to norms and tolerance—is correct, but its effects are not mediated by political involvement.

12. The parameter estimates presented in these figures are derived from a model that excludes political involvement, because of limitations of the computer program on the number of endogenous indicators that can be analyzed simultaneously. The coefficients directly involving political involvement were obtained from fitting a model that deleted some indicators for general norms. The LISREL IV program does not have these limitations, but this analysis was completed before it was generally available. The analysis reported in this chapter was performed using LISREL III.

13. More technically, perceived threat was conceptualized as an *endogenous* variable but is really an *exogenous* variable. We simplify the discussion in the text by using the terms *dependent* variable to describe political tolerance; *intervening* variable to describe any variable that is both "caused by" and "causes" other included variables; and *independent* variable to describe any variable not "caused" by any of the variables in the model, but "causing" at least one other included variable. Endogenous variables include both dependent and intervening variables, while exogenous variables include independent variables. Although our use of terms in the text is oversimplified, it is easier for the general reader to understand. We use the more correct terms in Appendix 8-A.

In Figure 8-5, four independent variables are added to the model—secular detachment, education, social status, and age. All but the third are single indicator variables for which we must assume perfect measurement. The social status variable is measured by occupational status and income, although income defines the abstract construct better than occupation; the epistemic correlations are .87 for income and .53 for occupation. There is one significant correlation among error terms, between income and age. Since age is assumed to be perfectly measured, the correlated error is between the error term for the indicator, income, and the construct, age.

None of these independent variables has *any* significant direct impact on general norms, political tolerance, or perceived threat. In terms of impact on the other three intervening variables, political involvement is affected about equally by age, status and education; the three path coefficients are .28, .27, and .33, respectively.[14] Both education and status also have a significant indirect impact on involvement, through psychological security. As expected, respondents who are older, of higher social status and level of education, are more involved in politics. The $R^2$ for political involvement is .64, quite respectable.

Psychological security is strongly influenced by education (.28) and social status (.34). Surprisingly, social status consistently has a greater

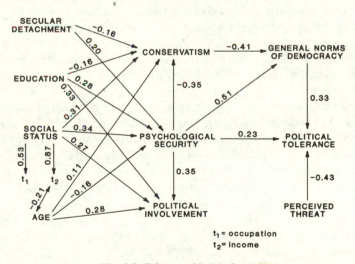

t₁ = occupation
t₂ = income

**Fig. 8-5. Tolerance Model: Stage III**

14. We again note that these coefficients are path coefficients, which summarize the direct impact of one independent variable on a dependent variable, controlling for the impact of all other variables in the equation.

impact than education on the intervening variables. It appears, however, that a flexible and confident personality is more a function of income and occupational status than of education, suggesting that personality, as analyzed here, is as much affective as cognitive in nature. The $R^2$ for psychological security in our model is .42 ($R = .65$), and the major unspecified factor is probably child-rearing practice within the parental family. Finally, both age and secular detachment have a minor direct impact on psychological security, with younger respondents and those from less traditional religions exhibiting a more flexible and open personality structure (path coefficients of $-.16$ and .20 respectively, both statistically significant, although quite small).

Conservatism is affected primarily by psychological security ($-.35$), as noted earlier, and by social status (.31). Respondents with higher social status tend to be more conservative, a finding consistent with many previous studies. This is reversed, however, for education; although the tendency is weak, those with higher education tend to be more *liberal* ($-.16$) contrary to the conventional wisdom. But our measures of political ideology do not include the more traditional domestic issue items often used in studies of ideological constraint or issue voting. Our liberalism-conservatism scale is probably a weighted average of respondents' perceptions of their degree of liberalism on both traditional economic and newer social issues. And the ideological nature of respondents' least-liked groups—whether they dislike two left-wing groups, two right-wing groups, or one of each—is probably much more affected by social than economic liberalism-conservatism. Thus, these findings are more consistent with past research if one thinks of our political ideology construct as based more on social than economic ideology.

Other studies have shown that personality and political ideology (on traditional economic issues) are not highly correlated, but that personality and position on social issues *are* more highly correlated.[15] To examine these assumptions, we replaced our "least-liked groups" measure of political ideology with the domestic welfare issues scale, discussed in Chapter 7. The most noteworthy changes in path coefficients were between psychological security and conservatism, a drop from $-.35$ to $-.25$; between socioeconomic status and conservatism, an increase from .31 to .45; and between conservatism and general norms of democracy, a decrease from $-.41$ to $-.26$. Although the signs were

15. Although surprisingly little work has been done to link personality with political ideology, the most striking examples with positive results have involved issues such as patriotism, attitudes toward treatment of criminals, sex role behaviors, and so on, issues more purely social than economic (Stone, 1974: ch. 8).

unchanged, and all of these coefficients are statistically significant, the changes in magnitude suggest that the ideology construct reflects mainly social ideology, and that when ideology is defined in economic terms, the results are different. First, personality is undoubtedly more highly related to social issues than to economic issues. Attitudes toward minorities, toward the use of drugs, toward alternative life styles, and toward women's liberation are more a function of personality and less a function of social status than are positions on economic issues; the latter tend to be highly related to status. Furthermore, support for the general norms of democracy is more likely to be a part of social liberalism than of economic liberalism. These findings are methodologically significant because they tend to validate our use of ideology, justifying the decision not to use economic issues along with the other two ideology measures.

A substantive point that deserves consideration involves the relationships among education, socioeconomic status, psychological security, and conservatism. First, the direct impact of social status on conservatism is, as expected, positive. Higher social class leads to ideological (social) conservatism.[16] However, the indirect impact of social status on conservatism, through psychological security, is negative. Higher levels of socioeconomic status produce a more flexible and open personality, which in turn produces ideological liberalism. To the extent that financial success and occupational status define a less dogmatic personality structure, high in self-esteem and self-actualization, social status leads to ideological liberalism.[17]

This finding may help explain the oft noted finding that socioeconomic status does not produce such ideological cleavages in the United States as it does in other industrialized nations (Alford, 1963). High social status in the United States tends to have counterbalancing, indirect effects on political ideology. Among some individuals, the desire to protect economic well-being, and the status quo that produced it, is undoubtedly increased by high levels of income and occupational status. But at the same time, among other individuals, a personality structure is created (or reinforced) which is conducive to liberalism and which vitiates conservative tendencies. Thus, on balance, the net impact of social status on ideology is attenuated.

Education, however, has a consistent (though small) impact on political ideology, leading both directly and indirectly to increased lib-

16. The relationship between social status and *economic* ideology is even stronger, however.

17. This indirect impact, which is opposite to the direct impact of socioeconomic status on political ideology, is approximately the same for both social and economic ideology.

eralism. To the extent that education and social status are associated, the conservatism of high status is further diluted, since education leads to liberalism. This finding applies equally to social and economic ideology. The coefficents in Figure 8-5 are path coefficients, representing the impact of one variable on another, controlling for all other variables; the fact that social status and education have opposite effects on conservatism must be interpreted in this light. Controlling for education, increases in social status (income and occupational status) bring about a strongly increased *conservatism*. The fact that education and social status are highly correlated, and that education leads to increased liberalism, complicates this picture. Among respondents at the same educational level, higher income and occupational status cause increased conservatism, while among respondents with the same income and occupational status, more education causes increased liberalism. Increased conservatism probably results from the desire to protect a privileged position in society, while increased liberalism probably results from the cognitive processes, instilled by education, discussed in Chapter 5.

Before moving to a more detailed discussion of the dependent variable, it is instructive to recall the discussion at the end of Chapter 3, where we noted that, prior to making a decision about how much to tolerate a particular target group, respondents had to go through a process of selecting a target group from among those available. This prior step, we argued, is primarily an ideological one, with liberals selecting right-wing and conservatives selecting left-wing groups. We have used that information in this chapter in deciding how to measure political ideology. Our two measures have been the ideology of the target groups selected by respondents as well as their self-placement on an ideology scale. The results in Figure 8-6 point to two additional factors which influence this first step, that of target selection. Personality, or psychological security, is a very important component of this step, as is social status. People with high status, other things (such as personality) equal, are more likely to select left-wing groups as targets; other things (such as social status) equal, people with less psychological security also select left-wing groups. Personal political ideology aside, then, the haves in society appear to recognize that threats to their privileged position come from the left, not the right. And, personal insecurity seems to predispose respondents somewhat more against the left than against right-wing threats. Perhaps this is because the right-wing is more likely to promise order, predictability, and traditional notions of security than the left. The left seems to offer, at least in the short run, a less predictable and ordered society. Whatever the case

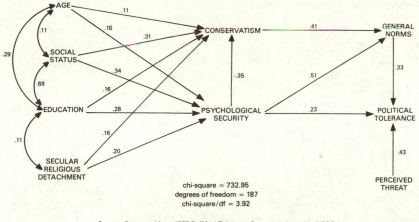

chi-square = 732.95
degrees of freedom = 187
chi-square/df = 3.92

Source: Computed from 1978 Political Tolerance Survey conducted by NORC.
Note: Disturbance terms have been omitted for the sake of clarity.

**Fig. 8-6. Political Tolerance Model**

may be, it is interesting to note the role of these non-ideological factors in target group selection. It is not *merely* a matter of one's personal ideology determining the selection of targets. The $R^2$ for conservatism is .22 ($R = .47$), lowest among the intervening variables. Although social status and psychological security have a moderately strong impact on conservatism, much of the latter's variance is not explained by the model. Both secular detachment and age have a minor direct impact on conservatism. For secular detachment the path coefficient is $-.16$, with the less fundamentalist religious groups being more liberal, as expected. For age, the path coefficient is .11, with the younger respondents being slightly less conservative.

Figure 8-6 presents the final, empirically specified, model of political tolerance ($R^2 = .57$). It includes the correlations among the exogenous variables, but deletes political involvement, which is not an intervening variable. Political involvement has no direct impact on political tolerance, general norms of democracy, or perceived threat. The model in Figure 8-6 thus adds only the exogeneous correlations to Figure 8-5. The only large correlation is between social status and education (.69). The goodness of fit statistics for the model are presented in Figure 8-6. The chi square to degrees of freedom ratio of 3.92 is a good fit (see Chapter 3).[18]

18. The reader should recall, however, that the model on which the goodness-of-fit statistics are based includes the measurement model reflected in the epistemic correlations, the correlations among error terms (noted in Figures 8-3 through 8-5), and the

## Internal and External Threat

As is evident from Figure 8-6, internal threat, based on personality characteristics, and external threat, based on perceived danger from the least-liked group, are powerful determinants of political tolerance. Furthermore, these two threats appear to be essentially independent of one another, although about half of the impact of psychological security is mediated by political ideology and by support for the general norms of democracy. Nevertheless, psychological security has considerable direct impact on political tolerance.

The combined impact of psychological security and external threat on political tolerance may not be linear and additive, as we assumed in Figure 8-6. To illustrate this, one might think of tolerance as something fragile and easily displaced by intolerance. If citizens lack psychological security, they are easily threatened and will react like authoritarian or dogmatic personalities: they will be intolerant. On the other hand, citizens who are internally secure—high in self-esteem, low in dogmatism, high in self-actualization—still may not be tolerant, because they may be vulnerable to an external threat. They may perceive that their least-liked group is indeed dangerous and untrustworthy, and thus not to be tolerated politically. In spite of their psychological security, then, they express intolerant attitudes.

In a sense, then, perhaps both internal security and external security are necessary conditions for political tolerance. If *either* is absent, an individual will be relatively intolerant. We therefore expect an interactive relationship among personality, perceived threat, and political tolerance, which causes most people to be politically intolerant— particularly since personality and perceived threat are uncorrelated.

Before examining this relationship, let us clarify the conceptual relationship between political tolerance and what we call external threat, or perceived threat. We have argued that there can be no tolerance in the absence of a real objection to a group or an idea. Indifference cannot be the basis for tolerance. Superficially, it may seem that our threat variable is a prerequisite for the existence of political tolerance,

---

additional correlated errors (mentioned in footnote 9). Furthermore, the goodness-of-fit statistics are based on the fully recursive version of the model in Figure 8-6, although with a few exceptions, we have not presented path coefficients under .20. Re-estimating the goodness of fit statistics with a model that deletes all of the paths with coefficients under .20 would only improve the fit because it would not significantly alter the ability of the model to explain variance in the dependent and intervening variables, but it would increase the degrees of freedom. We felt this would be "cheating" in a sense because it would involve fitting a model that we did not posit *a priori* and that in at least a couple of instances provided some unexpected results.

but we must distinguish clearly between an *objection* to a least-liked group, and a perceived *threat* from that group. Although we expect them to be highly related, empirically, they need not logically be considered identical. Plausibly, one may object strongly to a particular group, perhaps on principled grounds, but yet perceive little or no threat from that group. The group itself may be perceived as honest, trustworthy, safe, non-violent, and so on, all adjectives used to measure perceived threat. One objects to them because their ideas are simply wrong-headed, but one realistically notices that the group is not likely to prevail and is not a serious challenge to one's values or goals. The objection is present, the perception of external threat is absent. The question we addressed earlier was the relationship between perceived threat and political tolerance, and we discovered a rather strong empirical relationship. This need not have been the case, although an absence of a relationship would have raised some serious questions. Here, we wish to examine the relationships among internal threat, external threat, and political tolerance.

To examine this, the sample was divided into four groups, based on a fourfold typology of the two constructs that define internal and external threat (psychological insecurity and perceived threat). The groups are: (1) high on both insecurity and perceived threat, (2) high on insecurity but low on perceived threat, (3) low in insecurity but high on perceived threat, and (4) low on both insecurity and perceived threat. The above argument suggests that only the last group will be generally tolerant; the other three groups will be approximately equally intolerant, because either one of the threat conditions may be sufficient to trigger an intolerant response.

Table 8-2 presents the results of an analysis of the mean levels of political tolerance in the four threat groups, using the dogmatism scale to measure internal threat and the safe-dangerous adjective pair to measure external threat (the indicators with the largest epistemic correlations in Figs. 8-3, 8-4). Both variables are dichotomized at the mean, and in the case of dogmatism, which is normally distributed, this produces high and low groups of approximately equal size. The distribution for safe-dangerous is skewed, however, as most respondents are clustered on the "dangerous" end of the dimension (a ratio of about three to one), producing a very small "non-threatened" group, low on both dogmatism and perceived external threat.

Clearly, the relationships among threat, dogmatism, and political tolerance are additive and linear (Table 8-3). Moving from low to high dogmatism reduces the mean political tolerance score by about 3.7 points, from 17.4 to 13.7; shifting from low to high threat reduces the

Table 8-2          **Mean Political Tolerance Scores (Six-Item Scale), by Perceived Threat and Dogmatism**

|  |  | Perceived Threat (Safe-Dangerous) | | |
|  |  | Low | High | Row Means: |
|---|---|---|---|---|
| Dogmatism | Low | 19.2 (213) | 16.7 (512) | 17.4 (725) |
|  | High | 16.5 (165) | 13.4 (458) | 13.7 (723) |
|  | Column Means: | 18.0 (378) | 13.7 (1070) |  |

The N's are in parentheses.

mean political tolerance score by about 4.3 points, a similar change. The four groups may be ordered into three categories that produce a linear effect on political tolerance: those in the low threat group (low on both dogmatism and external threat) have a mean of 19.2, above the midpoint of the six-item political tolerance scale; those in the medium threat groups (high on either dogmatism or external threat but not both) have means of 16.5 and 16.7, almost identical; and those in the high threat group (high on both dogmatism and external threat) have a mean of 13.4. The latter three groups are below the midpoint of the scale, especially the high threat group, which is well toward the intolerant end of the scale. Thus these effects are cumulative, and adding an external threat to those who are internally insecure erodes their political tolerance even further. This need not have been the case; if the low-low group in Table 8-2 had a very high mean and the other three groups had lower means, which were essentially equal, an interaction could have occurred even given the independence of psychological security.

### Alternative Types of Perceived Threat

A possible objection to the analysis is that certain groups of respondents have had to fear for their very lives from some of the extremist groups on our list, while other respondents have not been personally threatened. In the latter cases, the respondents' least-liked groups must be considered abstract threats to their "way of life" or to their property or "freedom," and hence the processes involved may differ. Some analysts would claim that for Jews to be intolerant of the Nazis or fascists, and for Blacks to be intolerant of the Ku Klux Klan, is justified politically, since it represents a genuine defensive reaction to threatened physical harm to self or loved ones. On the other hand, it is entirely different for working class Whites to be intolerant of socialists or communists, groups they have not experienced at close hand, and that have not threatened them physically.

Certainly, some of the open-ended responses to the questionnaire support this notion. The external threat posed by least-liked groups to various respondents differs considerably, and the skeptic no doubt inquires whether these differences influence the multivariate analysis. For example, for respondents, such as Blacks and Jews, who have been the targets of physical attacks by the Klan and the fascists, external threat may be a more important determinant of political tolerance than psychological security. They should perceive a much greater danger from their least-liked groups than other respondents, and perhaps if we re-estimated the model for Blacks and Jews only, we would find that the perceived threat variable increased in importance while the psychological security variable decreased. For the other respondents, who have not experienced direct physical threat, perhaps psychological security would remain very important while perceived threat would become less important.

Table 8-3A presents the correlations between the personality and perceived threat measures, and political tolerance. Included are those personality and threat variables with the highest epistemic correlations (i.e., the most reliable). Columns one and two compare the correlations for Blacks and Jews with those for others.[19]

The pattern of correlations in the two columns is very similar. In each, there is little relationship between ideology and political tolerance, and a moderately strong relationship between perceived threat and political tolerance. Although the correlation for dogmatism is slightly stronger for Whites than for Blacks and Jews, and although the correlation for dangerous-safe is slightly stronger for the latter than the former, all the remaining differences are negligible. There is not sufficient difference to sustain the claim that for Blacks and Jews perceived external threat is the major determinant of political tolerance, while for others, political tolerance is mainly a function of psychological security.

To explore further the possibility that threat relates differently to political tolerance for these groups of respondents, Table 8-3B com-

19. Blacks and Jews are combined because the nature of the external threat should be similar; this does not distort the findings and it produces a larger sample size.

**Table 8-3**        **Correlates of Political Tolerance, by Subgroup**

| | Race | | Education[a] | |
|---|---|---|---|---|
| | Blacks and Jews | Other Whites | Low | High |
| A. Correlation of Political Tolerance with: | | | | |
| Ideology (self-placement) | − .08 | − .18 | − .10 | − .21 |
| Self-esteem scale | .34 | .31 | .24 | .28 |
| Dogmatism scale | − .36 | − .42 | − .35 | − .36 |
| Dangerous-safe | .35 | .23 | .28 | .24 |
| Dishonest-honest | .26 | .26 | .27 | .31 |
| Good-bad | − .27 | − .26 | − .31 | − .22 |
| B. Mean Scores on: | | | | |
| Political Tolerance | 15.3 | 16.2 | 15.5 | 18.8 |
| Dangerous-safe | 1.9 | 2.1 | 2.1 | 1.9 |
| Dishonest-honest | 2.6 | 2.9 | 2.8 | 2.8 |
| Good-bad | 6.4 | 6.1 | 6.1 | 6.3 |
| N = | 191–214 | 1108–1132 | 1100 | 250 |

[a] The high education group includes respondents with a college degree or more education; the low education group includes all other respondents.

pares mean scores on political tolerance and the measures of perceived external threat. Although other Whites are slightly more politically tolerant than Jews and Blacks, as one might expect since the threat to the former is less personal and direct, the difference is small. The other differences on the semantic differential adjective pairs are also in the correct direction—with Jews and Blacks perceiving their least-liked groups as marginally more dangerous, dishonest, and bad than the Whites perceive their least-liked groups—but small. These findings do not support the argument that Whites are generally politically tolerant and fail to perceive an external threat from their least-liked groups, while Blacks and Jews not only perceive a threat but also react to it with intolerance. All three groups—Jews, Blacks, and other Whites— are best characterized as perceiving a threat and being intolerant.

The skeptic would claim that, although the nature of the external threat does not have different consequences for the dynamics of political tolerance, different types of respondents may arrive at similar positions on the intolerance scale through entirely different processes. Perhaps, for example, the highly educated yet intolerant form their views differently than those who are less educated. Highly educated people may be influenced more by cognitive than affective factors.

Perceived external threat may lead educated people to become intolerant—they perceive a threat both to their fundamental values, and to the concept of political tolerance itself—and are thus led by such cognitive considerations to intolerance toward the threatening groups. Uneducated people, on the other hand, are influenced primarily by affective factors. They become intolerant because they are insecure personally—they have low self-esteem, are generally dogmatic, and so on. Education is related to personality, although it is not related to perceived threat (Figure 8-6).

In Table 8-3A, we present the correlations between several intervening variables and political tolerance for two different education groups. Although there is some tendency for the high education group to be influenced more strongly by ideology than the low education group, the only other difference between column three and column four is in the opposite direction. The low education group is slightly more strongly influenced by the perceived external threat variable than the high education group, particularly the "good-bad" adjective pair. The remaining differences in the correlations are negligible. In Table 8-3B, it is evident that the high and low education groups have virtually identical perceptions of the degree of external threat posed by their least-liked groups. Similar processes appear to operate for these different subgroups.[20]

## Political Elites and the Processes of Political Tolerance

Does the model of Figure 8-6, which can be used to explain political tolerance among the mass citizenry, also apply to political elites (defined as those who participate most actively in the political process)? Although the correlations between various intervening variables and political tolerance are not affected significantly by education, the latter is an imperfect indicator of membership in the political elite. Our analysis asked only whether the roles of internal and external threat differed according to educational grouping. Here the question is more difficult, since we have no direct data on political elites. As a result, we stratify our sample according to level of political involvement to examine whether the model applies to those among the mass public who participate most actively.

20. The variances of these variables do not differ significantly across these various subgroups. As a result, the correlations may be compared without the fear that they differ only because the variances differ. Comparisons based on regresson coefficients result in similar conclusions.

Chapter 7 demonstrated that the linear relationship between political participation and political tolerance is weak, although the percentage differences in political tolerance between the most elite group of participants (those who are engaged in at least five of the six political acts in our questionnaire) and the rest of the sample are substantial. The active participants represent only seven percent of the national sample so, although these percentage differences are large, they do not strongly influence the correlation coefficient. The multivariate analysis presented earlier in this chapter, and the bivariate controls introduced in Chapter 7, suggest that these differences largely result from selective recruitment not from a causal relationship between political participation and political tolerance.

In addition, we must ask whether the causal processes leading to political tolerance and intolerance are similar and have similar impact for both political elites and the mass citizenry. We have therefore applied the model in Figure 8-6 to that seven percent of the sample engaging in at least five of the six acts of political participation (Chapter 7). The pattern of correlations for this subgroup is notably different from the sample as a whole, in contrast to the other subgroups previously examined. The multivariate results differed in four significant ways from the standardized path coefficients for the full sample (presented in Figure 8-6): (1) There was severe multicollinearity between the general norms of democracy and the political tolerance constructs, so no distinction could be made between them; thus the general norms indicators were used as additional indicators of political tolerance; (2) Psychological security had a smaller direct impact on political tolerance (.10 vs. .23), but a greater indirect impact because it related significantly to perceived threat ($-.35$ vs. .00); (3) The direct impact of conservatism on political tolerance was greater ($-.45$ vs. $-.10$); (4) Social class had no impact on the other variables, while secular detachment had considerable impact, particularly on conservatism (.33) and psychological security (.34).

Before examining the implications of these findings, the technical problems of comparing analyses of the full sample and an elite subsample must be addressed. Since our LISREL analysis relies on standardized path coefficients among unmeasured concepts, the results can be affected by changes in the variances of the indicators, quite apart from differences in the causal processes underlying the model. Since it is likely that the high participation subsample has a restricted range and variance on several of the indicators used to estimate the model, it is also likely that the path coefficients among the constructs change merely because the variances change, not because the causal processes are different for the two groups.[21] For example, since the "elite" sample is small and preselected on the basis of political participation, we might expect a restricted range on variables such as education and support for the general norms of democracy, particularly in light of McClosky's findings about ideological consensus among the elites and the masses.

We therefore compared the variances on the 23 indicators for the more participatory subsample (our "elites") and the remainder of the sample and we examined the unstandardized coefficients from an ordinary multiple regression analysis, using the political tolerance scale as the dependent variable and the two indicators of each construct with the highest epistemic correlations as the independent variables.[22] Although there are differences in variances across the two samples, the direction of these differences is not always as expected. For example, in 12 of the 23 comparisons, the non-elites have greater variances, while 11 times they have smaller variances. In several instances, these differences are sufficient to render the standardized coefficients suspect. These will be discussed below, in conjunction with the unstandardized results (Table 8-4).

The first finding from the LISREL analysis, that the general norms of democracy constrain the elites more than the full sample, is supported by the unstandarized results. The unstandardized coefficients for the two indicators of general norms have greater impact on political tolerance in the "elite" subsample—1.4 vs. 0.9 for the legal protection question, and 2.9 vs. 0.4 for the majority vote question.[23] This suggests, of course, that the activists' specific attitudes toward political tolerance are strongly constrained by their level of support for the general norms of democracy. In a sense, this finding partially supports McClosky's (1964) analysis, which suggests that among the political elite, specific applications of the norms of democracy are, in some sense, congruent with their general support for these abstract norms, but that this does not hold for the mass public. The results presented here do not support

21. The maximum likelihood estimation techniques used by the LISREL program are large sample techniques. Since the size of the "elite" subsample is so small, the resulting parameter estimates are biased. Therefore when the standardized LISREL results conflict with unstandardized regression results, reported in the text, the unstandardized results should be given greater weight.

22. An unstandardized solution for the LISREL model can be obtained, but the results are based on an analysis of the relationships among unmeasured constructs, which have no inherent units of analysis. So even these results must be standardized in some fashion.

23. The former difference between regression coefficients is not statistically significant at the .05 level, but the latter is, by a considerable margin.

Table 8-4        **Unstandardized Regression Coefficients with Tolerance, High vs.
                  Low Participation Subsamples**

| Independent Variables | High Participation Subsample (N = 86) | Low Participation Subsample (N = 1092) |
|---|---|---|
| Self-Placement (Ideology) | 0.03 | −0.1 |
| Groups Picked (Ideology) | −1.3 | −1.0* |
| Legal Protection (General) | 1.4* | 0.9* |
| Majority Vote (General) | 2.9* | 0.4* |
| Dishonest-Honest (Threat) | −0.8* | −0.4* |
| Dangerous-Safe (Threat) | −0.4 | −0.6 |
| Dogmatism (Personality) | −0.3* | −0.2* |
| Self-Esteem (Personality) | 0.2 | 0.1* |
| Education | 0.2 | 0.2* |
| Income (Social Class) | −0.1 | −.01 |
| Occupation (Social Class) | −.02 | −.01 |
| Age | −.04 | −.01 |
| Secular Detachment | 2.53* | 0.85* |
| Adjusted $R^2$ | .36 | .35 |

*Significant at the .05 level

the precise form of McClosky's conclusion, however, since both elites *and* masses are constrained in applying these more general norms; the results merely support McClosky's finding that there are differences between the elite and the mass public, since although both groups are constrained, the elite group is more tightly constrained in its attitudes of political tolerance.

The second finding—that psychological security has a smaller direct, but greater indirect, impact on political tolerance in the "elite" sample— is partially confirmed and partially refuted by the unstandardized results. It is clear from Table 8-4 that the direct impact of psychological security on political tolerance is about the same in both groups (in fact, the unstandardized coefficients for the "elite" group are slightly larger, contrary to the pattern of the standardized coefficients).[24] With respect to the indirect impact, through perceived threat, of psychological security on political tolerance both standardized and unstandardized results reveal an impact only in the "elite" sample. The standardized coefficient between psychological security and perceived threat is about zero in the full sample, but −.35 in the high participation sample;

24. As noted in footnote 21, the standardized estimates for the "elite" sample are biased. Furthermore, the variances for both personality and tolerance differ between the two groups, so the unstandardized results should be accepted in this instance.

the unstandardized coefficients are $-0.2$ and $-1.0$ respectively.[25] It is perplexing to find a relationship between internal and external threat among the active participants only. As noted in Figure 8-2, the initial theoretical model specified a relationship between personality and perceived threat in the full sample, based on the expectation that the personally insecure would project their insecurity onto political targets (their least-liked groups), and would therefore perceive these groups as dangerous, bad, and so on.

Speculatively, we suggest that the findings make sense in the following way. Among the entire sample, the level of political involvement and information is low. It is generally acknowledged that politics is of low salience to the average citizen. As a result, when average respondents think about their least-liked groups, they probably lack a completely realistic perception of that group's role in the political process, and do not carefully assess the group's ability to realize its goals. Most respondents may conclude, unrealistically, that their least-liked group is dangerous, untrustworthy, and so on. There is no greater tendency for those high or low on dogmatism to perceive danger because both personality types have inaccurate perceptions. On the other hand, those actively involved in politics, who have considerable knowledge about the political process, should make more realistic assessments of their least-liked groups, and thus perceive them as less dangerous and unpredictable. However, activists who lack internal security may be more inclined to project personal feelings of insecurity onto their least-liked targets, in spite of their activism and knowledge—or perhaps their psychological insecurity interferes with the development of more realistic perceptions.

The third finding, that ideology is much more important as a determinant of political tolerance among the activist sample, is not entirely validated by the unstandardized results. Although the group ideology measure shows a larger coefficient with political tolerance among the "elites," the coefficient is statistically significant only in the non-elite sample. This is probably not because of differences in variances, which are similar in both groups, but most likely is the result of the relationship between ideology and support for general norms of democracy. Since the multicollinearity between general norms of democracy and political tolerance was so great in the high participation sample, the indicators of both constructs were used to measure the

25. The unstandardized coefficients relate the honest-dishonest adjective pair to the dogmatism scale—the indicators with the highest epistemic correlations. The zero order correlations between these two variables are $-.09$ in the non-elite sample, and $-.32$ in the "elite" sample.

dependent variable, political tolerance. Therefore, in the activist analysis, the impact of political ideology on political tolerance and on general norms was combined, producing a greater direct effect of ideology
on political tolerance. We are uncertain whether to treat this as a substantively important finding. Is combining general norms items with
political tolerance items among the "elites" substantively meaningful?
We argue that it is. The very strong relationship between these two
groups of items (among activists) suggests that the dependent variable,
political tolerance, is legitimately conceptualized as something more
abstract among the "elites" than among the remaining respondents.
As such, among the most politically active, ideology has a more direct
impact on political tolerance, as part of the same abstract system of
thought. Among the less politically active, ideology and general norms
of democracy are more abstract than political tolerance and only operate to constrain political tolerance within broad limits. Therefore,
the standardized coefficients imply a meaningful difference in the processes leading to political tolerance among "elites" than among non-
elites.

It is not surprising that for the activists, political ideology is more
strongly related to political tolerance. As noted earlier, political tolerance is inherently a liberal concept, originating in liberal thought,
and more important in liberal than conservative democractic theories.
(See Chapters 1 and 7.) Political activists are, by definition more directly involved in politics and government in the United States. As a
result, they are more directly exposed to liberal and conservative
thought, and once they choose between them they are more likely to
subscribe to their preferred ideology's norms of political tolerance.
Thus activist liberals and conservatives should differ more in political
tolerance than the mass public as a whole, since the latter are less
likely to divide neatly into two opposing ideological camps. This is
precisely what we find—there is a powerful tendency for liberal activists
to be more politically tolerant than conservative activists. As in the
whole sample, among the most active ideology is affected by psychological security, vitiating the argument that the entire process is somehow more "rational" for activists than for the rest of the sample.

The fourth finding using standardized coefficients is that, among the
elites, social class has a smaller impact on the intervening variables,
while secular detachment has a greater impact, particularly on psychological security and conservatism. The unstandardized results show
no difference in the impact of the social class variables, income and
occupation, on these factors, while secular detachment clearly has a

greater impact on political tolerance for the activists (2.53) than for the remaining respondents (0.85). Additional regression analyses (not shown) support this general conclusion: secular detachment has a greater impact in the "elite" sample on self-esteem (2.9 vs. 1.2), on dogmatism ($-2.6$ vs. $-1.2$), and on self-identified liberalism-conservatism (.28 vs. .17).[26] These findings indicate that the non-religious activists differ considerably from the more conventionally religious activists, whereas these differences are less pronounced among the non-activist groups.

In summary, this analysis suggests that the model specified for the mass sample may not apply to contemporary political elites. There are some significant differences in the processes generating political tolerance between the most participatory segment and the electorate as a whole, differences both in degree and in kind, as the impact of various independent variables on political tolerance varies considerably for these two groups. Although there is no certainty that the model that fits best for the most participatory segment of the electorate also applies to political candidates and leaders, it is likely to be a better guide than the model that fits the entire electorate.

## Social Tolerance

Chapter 4 describes tolerance in American society, emphasizing *political* tolerance. Subsequently, a six-item *political* tolerance scale was analyzed. Respondents were also asked three questions about social activities of their least-liked groups: would they invite a member of that group for dinner, would they be upset if a member of that group moved in next door, and would they feel positively about their son or daughter dating a member of that group. (See Tables 3-3 and 3-4.) Although respondents were generally intolerant of *political* activities on the part of these groups, they were even less tolerant of these groups' *social* activities. For example, in the Twin Cities sample, only 4 percent were tolerant on the dating question, 31 percent on the dinner question, and 34 percent on the neighbor question. In the national sample, these percentages were 4, 18, and 37, respectively. Thus while the average percent tolerant on the political tolerance questions was 35 percent, the average on the social tolerance questions was 20 per-

26. Five of these six coefficients are statistically significant at the .05 level. Only .28 is not. None of the differences between the pairs of coefficients is statistically significant, but the pattern is clear.

cent. The two highest ratios of strongly intolerant to strongly tolerant responses were on the dinner and dating questions (Table 4-1).[27]

Why are more respondents politically than socially tolerant? Even though the American electorate has been characterized as politically intolerant, it is obviously even more socially intolerant. While the electorate need not tolerate certain groups of people socially, a significant proportion of respondents appears willing to set aside intolerance when it comes to political activities. One obvious explanation is that some respondents subscribe to the general norms of civil liberties and tolerance. They do not approve of particular groups and ideas, and as a result they have no desire to socialize or to express social approval of such groups. They do, however, believe that the rights of citizenship accrue to all citizens, and that in keeping with the creed of democracy, they they must inhibit any desire to repress these groups. Although this explanation appears to be inconsistent with the arguments of Prothro and Grigg (1960) and McClosky (1964), support for the general norms of democracy does have a significant direct impact on political tolerance, as we noted earlier. Perhaps these norms have little or no impact on social tolerance, because, quite correctly, many respondents recognize that the norms do not cover all spheres of human activity; rather they are meant to apply more narrowly to explicit political activity.

To test this explanation, our final tolerance model (Figure 8-6) was re-estimated, substituting a three item social tolerance scale for the six-item political tolerance scale as the dependent variable. (Data not shown.) The reliability coefficient (alpha) for this scale is .62. The results of the analysis confirm the line of reasoning outlined above. The path coefficients between the independent variables and social tolerance are .05 for psychological security, − .08 for conservatism, .14 for general norms of democracy, and .65 for perceived threat. None of the other independent variables has any direct impact on social tolerance. Social tolerance is unrelated to anything except perceived threat, whose impact is even greater than it is on political tolerance. Although there is not much variation in social tolerance, what variation

27. The social items refer to activities that involve the respondents themselves, whereas the political items are more distant from personal situations. This undoubtedly accounts for some of the difference in responses. Political activities are not part of the everyday life of most respondents whereas social activities are. Our social items are what Bogardus (1925) called social distance measures, so another way to interpret these findings is that respondents wish to maintain maximum social distance between themselves and their least-liked groups. Even respondents who are politically tolerant wish to maintain this distance, and "social distance" is by no means a violation of any conceptions of democracy or tolerance of which we are aware.

exists appears to be mostly a function of perceived threat. The less a least-liked group threatens one's values and way of life, the more one is willing to tolerate that group both politically *and* socially. However, when there appears to be some threat, social tolerance falls by the wayside, regardless of whether the respondent professes support for the general norms of democracy; such support does, however, allow some respondents to remain politically tolerant in spite of their social intolerance and their perceptions of threat.

## Tolerance and Stouffer's Content-Biased Measures

We have repeatedly pointed out that the original Stouffer and Stouffer-based measures contain a serious content-bias and therefore do not validly measure political tolerance. Since the Stouffer measures are biased (they specify only left-wing targets), political ideology ought to have a more powerful impact on them than on the content-controlled measure. Furthermore, the general norms of democracy may constrain specific applications of political tolerance less for the Stouffer measures than for ours. It will be easier for liberals than for conservatives to appear tolerant on Stouffer's questions, regardless of their support for the abstract norms of civil liberties. On Stouffer's questions, liberals who fail to support the abstract norms may be politically tolerant while conservatives who support them may or may not be politically tolerant.

To examine these possibilities, the model of Figure 8-6 was reestimated using a dependent variable based on Stouffer's four questions about atheists and communists (Tables 3-3 and 3-4). Whereas with the content-controlled dependent variable, the path coefficient between conservatism and political tolerance is non-significant, using the Stouffer measure, it is a statistically significant $-.18$. Thus liberals are more tolerant than conservatives on Stouffer's measures, even controlling for the fact that liberals have more secure personalities and give greater support to the general norms of democracy. This result is not the case with our measure. Conversely, using Stouffer's measure of political tolerance, the path coefficient between support for the general norms and political tolerance is .19, whereas with our measure it is .33, a considerable difference. Clearly, we have measured something closer to a general concept of tolerance than have Stouffer and those who adopted his measure.

Another set of differences between the models is that the impact of perceived threat is stronger using our measure ($-.43$ vs. $-.25$) while the impact of psychological security is weaker (.23 vs. .32). Although our measure of perceived threat is based on least-liked groups, this path coefficient was estimated for Stouffer's measure using that subset of respondents who selected communists, socialists, or atheists as their least-liked group. We conclude that Stouffer's measure, in addition to being content-biased and only weakly related to support of the general norms of democracy, is considerably more a function of internal (i.e., psychological) than of external threat.

## Summary and Conclusions

In this chapter, we specified a multivariate model of political tolerance, including sets of social, psychological, and political independent and intervening variables, and tested it, using a national opinion survey. The results demonstrate that, although the social background variables have no direct impact on political tolerance, both psychological and political variables do.[28]

Psychological security has a considerable direct impact, as well as an indirect one through support for the general norms of democracy. Political ideology has a considerable indirect impact, as liberals are more likely than conservatives to support these general norms; the general norms in turn serve as a powerful constraint on political intolerance, contrary to the generally accepted findings of previous research; and perceived threat has a strong direct impact on political tolerance. Finally, political variables such as participation, information, and other measures of political involvement have no impact, direct or indirect, on political tolerance.

We also briefly examined the argument that, for various subgroups in the population, different processes influence political tolerance. There are no significant differences in these processes among Blacks, Jews, Whites, highly educated, and uneducated groups in the national sample. The same model seems to fit each subgroup equally well. There is, however, an elite group of the most active participants that differs from the sample as a whole. The best explanatory model for political tolerance among this elite differs from the one for the general population, but the process represented does not appear to be more "rational" for the high participants, since personality plays a role as powerful in that subsample as among the less politically active subsample.

28. The indirect effects of the social background variables on political tolerance are not very large. For example, education has a first-level indirect effect of .06 on tolerance through personality; its second-level indirect effect on tolerance through personality is .05. The indirect effects of the other social variables are smaller. (See Greene, 1977 for an algorithm for tracing the various indirect causal effects.)

Finally, we examined the fit of our model to a social tolerance scale and to a scale based on the Stouffer questions about communists and atheists. The electorate is less socially tolerant than politically tolerant, perhaps because support for general norms acts to increase political tolerance over its "natural" level. Most respondents are probably predisposed to be intolerant because of psychological insecurity or the threat perceived from their least-liked group; they express this intolerance socially, but some of them inhibit it in the political arena because they believe in the democratic creed. For the Stouffer items, we found a greater role for political ideology and for personality, but a lesser role for perceived threat and for general norms, supporting our measurement strategy.

In the previous five chapters we presented detailed results and analyses, having significant implications for the political system and for understanding democratic theories. We have not discussed these consequences in any depth, although in Chapter 1 we established a foundation for such a discussion. The final chapter addresses these broader questions and attempts to place the empirical analysis in a broader theoretical context.

## Appendix 8-A. Statistical Procedures

We faced two related problems in testing the multivariate explanation of political tolerance set forth in Figure 8-2: the estimation of the structural parameters of the model, and the associated difficulties resulting from measurement error in the variables. Random measurement error leads to attenuation of bivariate correlation coefficients and to less predictable biases in coefficients from multivariate analyses. Since measurement error is typically high in surveys, such biases can significantly affect the parameter estimates in a complex model.

Various solutions have been suggested to this measurement problem (Blalock, Wells, and Carter, 1970); one that has received a great deal of recent attention is the use of multiple indicators of the theoretical constructs (Costner, 1969; Namboodiri, Carter, and Blalock, 1975: 555–609). This technique is flexible, effective in deriving accurate parameter estimates, robust in relation to other methods of dealing with measurement error, and especially clear in presenting the theoretical relationships underlying the indicator model. The last is accomplished through the development of an "auxiliary theory" (measurement theory) that links the empirical indicators with the abstract, theoretical constructs. The "auxiliary theory" is added to the main, or structural, theory that specifies the hypothesized relationships among the theoretical constructs (Blalock, 1968). The latent variables are unobserved, but their indicators are measured, allowing derivation of distinct estimates for the structural coefficients and of the epistemic correlations that link the indicators with the latent constructs. In addition, it is possible to assess the adequacy of the auxiliary theory, testing hypotheses about both the concept-indicator relationships and the presence of non-random measurement error.

While in theory this is a useful solution to the problem of random measurement error, in practice a major problem remains in all but the simplest of models: parameter estimation for the combined main and auxiliary models. Estimation difficulties result from overidentification in the structural equations, present in most multiple indicator models. Overidentification leads to multiple estimates of each parameter, and the number of estimates varies depending on the complexity of, and the restrictions placed on, the model. The problem arises because, even if the model is theoretically correct in every respect and would therefore fit perfectly in the population, the parameter *estimates* are derived from a sample and would not necessarily equal the parameters because of sampling error. There are, therefore, several estimates of each parameter, all of which are unbiased (given correct specification) but all of which are probably different. What is required, therefore, is a single, most efficient, unbiased estimate from the individual values obtained. A properly weighted average of the individual estimates is needed, weighted inversely by their standard errors (Hauser and Goldberger, 1971). Since such an average is usually not available for a path analysis, some other method is needed to obtain the "best" parameter estimates.

One solution to this problem, developed by Joreskog and his associates (Joreskog, 1969, 1970, 1973; Werts, Linn, and Joreskog, 1971), is to apply maximum likelihood estimation to a confirmatory factor analysis structure. While several forms of this analysis have been presented, the most general approach, and the one used here, is that of analysis of linear structural equations with measurement error (LIS-REL), as discussed by Joreskog (1973) and Joreskog and Sorbom (1975). This procedure permits the specification of three sets of equations. The first gives the (hypothesized) relationships among the true or latent variables, and is similar in form to a standard path analysis or econometric model, except that these variables are not directly observed.

To define these latent variables, two other sets of equations are necessary. One specifies the indicators of the endogenous (dependent) variables as functions of these variables plus a random error component for each indicator. (This is also the source of a major difference between confirmatory factor analysis and the more widely known and used exploratory factor analysis. In the confirmatory case zero loadings are specified *a priori* for those latent variables hypothesized *not* to have a direct effect on the indicator. In exploratory analysis this is approximated by various rotations of a more or less arbitrary solution.) The second set of equations does the same for the indicators of the exogenous (independent) variables. Thus, these three sets of equations permit specification of the relationships in the main and auxiliary theories as one of three types: free parameters (to be estimated), fixed parameters, and constrained parameters (unknown but set equal to some estimated coefficient.)

In this form, it is not possible to estimate directly any of the free or constrained parameters, since there are too many unknowns in these equations. It is possible, however, to derive the variance-covariance matrix for the indicators (or the correlation matrix if the variables are standardized) on the basis of the hypothesized factor structure. This is a fairly straightforward, if tedious, exercise (see Joreskog, 1973, or Long, 1976). This hypothesized (generated) variance-covariance matrix should then equal the observed matrix, assuming correct specification of the model. The problem then becomes one of estimating the values of the free and constrained parameters to maximize the fit between the hypothesized and the observed variance-covariance matrices.

If the model is identified, there are several methods available to estimate the parameters, including least squares and maximum likelihood. The maximum likelihood estimation procedure is preferable for several reasons. First, for large samples the estimates are consistent (unbiased), efficient (have as small a variance as any other estimator), and are approximately normally distributed. Second, the maximum likelihood estimators are scale invariant. That is, if the units of measurement have no real significance (the case here), the correlation matrix may be analyzed instead of the variance-covariance matrix. And finally, maximum likelihood estimation also generates a convenient statistical test for evaluating the adequacy of the model. This is the likelihood ratio test, which for large samples, is distributed as a chi-square distribution and tests the null hypothesis that the model specified by the fixed and constrained parameters is a perfect fit to the observed data. A large (significant) chi-square indicates that the hypothesized model does *not* fit. In practice, however, rather than maximizing the likelihood function, a related function is minimized since its value is more useful in the statistical test (Joreskog, 1969). A scalar function between the observed covariances (correlations) and the covariances generated from the hypothesized latent structure is minimized.

There are several considerations involved in fitting and modifying a latent factor model (assuming of course that the initial specification was made on theoretical grounds). First, examination of the chi-square statistic indicates the model's overall goodness of fit. However, if a poor fit is suggested, this statistic does not help to locate the problem. The computer program provides a matrix of residuals (the difference between the actual correlations and the values generated by the model). But as Costner and Schoenberg (1973) have shown, in many cases these patterns of residuals may be misleading and care should therefore be exercised in examining them. A more reliable procedure is to examine the latent variables in pairs, to detect possible correlated errors or misspecifications between the indicators of the two constructs. In this way the source of a poor fitting model may be more accurately detected.

A less obvious consideration in developing a good model relates to the theoretical interpretation of the latent constructs. Ideally, these constructs should be determined solely by the relative magnitude of the correlations among indicators of *each* construct and not by the correlations across constructs. However, since maximum likelihood estimation is a full information technique, the loadings of the indicators on a construct *may* be affected by the correlations across constructs. This can result in misleading interpretations of the latent constructs (Burt, 1976). One way to detect this is to re-examine the constructs in pairs, noting changes that appear in the epistemic correlations. If the epistemic correlations remain approximately stable throughout this process, it is safe to conclude that the theoretical meaning attached to the latent construct is determined solely by the relationships among its indicators. If the epistemic correlations vary greatly, the source of the problem must be detected and remedied to insure a reasonable interpretation of the model.

Our model estimation proceeded as follows. In all cases where theoretical constructs were measured by multiple indicators, there was no evidence of significant variation in the epistemic correlations. On the basis of pre-test results (Sullivan, Marcus, Pierson and Feldman, 1979) and prior research (summarized above), we separated education from socioeconomic status. In the pre-test analysis, we discovered that, given the empirical relationships among indicators, the impact of education on other variables could not be explained by assuming it is merely an indicator of socioeconomic status. Education is therefore treated as a separate exogenous variable, along with social status, age, and secular detachment. Three measures of socioeconomic status, including occupation, income, and a measure of subjective class, were originally used. The epistemic correlation between the social status construct and the subjective social class self-placement index was so low that the latter could not be considered a measure of social status as income and occupation could. So three of the four initial exogenous variables are measured by single indicators and are assumed to be perfectly reliable: education, age, and secular detachment. The fourth, social status, has two measures.

The first endogenous variable in the model is personality, initially measured by the five scales: dogmatism, self-actualization, self-esteem, trust in people, and other directedness. The epistemic correlation for the last was so low that it was dropped from the analysis.

The second endogenous variable in the model is political ideology. As noted in Table 8-1, there were three measures of political ideology, including ideological self-placement, a domestic issues scale, and a measure of the ideological location of the respondent's least-liked groups. Although the epistemic correlations for each measure were acceptable, the structural parameters among unmeasured variables were significantly affected by the particular combination of measures used for the ideology construct. Whenever ideological self-placement and the groups measure were used, the impact of ideology on both general norms and political tolerance was much greater than when the issues index was used. See the text for further discussion.

The third and fourth endogenous variables in Figure 8-2 are political involvement and political information. There are three measures of involvement, noted in Table 8-1: talk politics, interest in politics, and political participation. The measure of political information is the information scale discussed earlier. Separating political involvement and information conceptually made a great deal of sense. Empirically, however, the two concepts are highly correlated, resulting in multicollinearity with unstable parameter estimates whose values, in several instances, failed to make substantive sense. For example, high information levels were negatively associated with support for general norms of democracy. This is implausible in light of prior research on the impact of political information on various political variables. As a result, these two variables were combined into one, involvement in politics. Based on their epistemic correlations, the two single-item indicators, talk politics and interest in politics were eliminated. The two indicators used were the political participation and political information scales. The latter is conceptualized as an indicator of a broader factor of involvement, including both active physical participation and also psychological involvement in politics.

The next endogenous variable in the model is general norms of democracy measured by six items used by Prothro and Grigg, and by McClosky (Table 8-1). Since the items elicit great agreement from the American electorate, this construct is unstable unless all the measures are used simultaneously. For example, because of a limit on the number of endogenous indicators that can be used in the computer program LISREL III, on several occasions only the two or three general norms items with the highest epistemic correlations were used. The result was considerable alteration in the pattern of parameter estimates. Further investigation showed that these altered results were nonsensical and that the abstract construct is very sensitive to the particular combination of indicators. The factor is stablized by using as many indicators as possible.

Another variable conceptualized as endogenous in Figure 8-2 is perceived threat. The measures include the five semantic differential items noted in Table 8-1, and all five have high epistemic correlations. Perceived threat, however, cannot be used as an endogenous variable, at least given these particular indicators. None of the five measures of threat correlate with any other variable except the dependent variable, political tolerance. It must be presented as a fifth exogenous variable, independent of both personality and the political variables in the model.

After the measurement model was established in this manner, the coefficients of the complete model were estimated simultaneously. The structural model was specified initially as fully recursive; i.e., we did not estimate the model in Figure 8-2 but rather the fully recursive version of that model. Our "test" of this model in Figure 8-2 was to see whether all of the missing arrows from the hypothesized model would be non-significant and whether all of the specified relationships would be significant. The results are presented in Figures 8-3 through 8-6. In these figures, most coefficients less than .20 have been deleted. Several discrepancies between the hypothesized model and the empirical results are discussed in the text.

There are other statistical and methodological considerations. First, in a technical sense, it is inappropriate both to specify a model and to estimate its parameters on the same data set. Some form of cross validation is required, most commonly two independent data sets, one for model specification and one for parameter estimation. In a pretest, we first specified the model using the same dependent variable presented in this analysis, a political tolerance scale based on respondents' least-liked groups. The parameters were then estimated, not on a second sample of respondents, but on a scale based on respondents' second least-liked groups. The results were identical, confirming that the findings reported here are not totally idiosyncratic, and providing a crude form of cross validation. In addition, the national sample of 1509 respondents was randomly divided into two groups and the patterns of correlations among variables compared. There were no significant differences between them, certainly none large enough to generate different parameter estimates. Thus if we had divided the larger sample into two independent samples, one to specify the model and the second to estimate its parameters, the results would have been the same as those reported in this chapter.

Rather than risk a drastically reduced sample size, the correlations used as input for the LISREL analysis were based on pairwise, not listwise, deletion. The differences in the size and direction of the correlations produced by the two methods of deletion were minimal. Of the 528 correlations among indicators, in only 28 instances was the absolute difference in correlatons between the listwise and pairwise coefficients .05 or greater. The largest difference was .09: the listwise correlation between faith in people and information was .18 while the pairwise correlation was .27.

# Political Tolerance: Implications for Democratic Theory

**9**

The previous chapters have approached the problem of tolerance from several empirical and theoretical standpoints. It goes without saying that other theories might have been discussed and that more variables might have been analyzed, more findings reported, and more data presented with even finer discriminations. But we have discussed those theories and reported those findings that we judged most important. In the present chapter, we summarize the major findings and develop their implications for democratic theories. In doing so, we move beyond our findings to speculate on their larger meaning.

From the standpoint of previous work on tolerance, this research may appear as either innovative or eccentric. We have, in any case, adopted a different measure of tolerance from that used in earlier studies, and this has led to conclusions at variance with those reported in these studies. From Stouffer's *Communism, Conformity, and Civil Liberties* (1955) to the Nunn, Crockett, and Williams (1978) replication of his work, research on tolerance produced a consistent body of generalizations, among the most important of which are the following:

> The public was intolerant, especially of dissident groups on the left, such as communists and socialists; they are now tolerant.

> The educated are significantly more tolerant than the uneducated.

> The active participant in politics is more tolerant than the inactive and apathetic.

> Political leaders are far more tolerant than the public at large.

> Processes are at work in advanced societies that will

248

eventually produce more tolerant citizens; this has already taken place to a significant degree.

Such findings seemed to imply that political leaders should be trusted to protect civil liberties and to abide by the "rules of the game." This conclusion, accepted by many,[1] may not be completely fair to Stouffer, who was more optimistic because he saw many factors that would, over time, produce a more tolerant society. Yet it is still fair to say that the main impact of his work was to reinforce concern for the "tyranny of the majority." It must be noted, though, that the tyrannical majority envisioned here was a conservative public stamping out opposition on the left; there was little concern about the possibility of a liberal majority attacking opposition on the right, or of a consensual majority antagonistic to both extremes.

The clearest problem with these studies is that they measure only tolerance and intolerance of the left. Since tolerance means a willingness to "put up with" groups that people may oppose or dislike, this approach at best yields only a partial description and, at worst, it produces misleading conclusions. These initial suspicions were confirmed when we adopted a "content-controlled" measure of tolerance that allowed respondents to select the group or groups to which they were opposed. Since many people selected target groups on the right, and were unwilling to tolerate these groups, our findings diverged from those of studies that conceptualized tolerance more narrowly. Most importantly, our study shows that the targets of intolerance are ideologically diverse and that several factors that have been shown to be related to tolerance, such as education and political participation, are of lesser importance when viewed from a causal standpoint. These findings warrant a reconsideration of various empirical claims that have been made about the relationship between tolerance and democracy in America. Before proceeding to these broader and more controversial questions, however, a summary of our empirical conclusions is in order.

## Summary of Findings

The findings may be grouped into three categories, which involve: (1) distribution on tolerance across the sample as a whole and across important sub-groups within the sample; (2) causal relationships most important for explaining why people select particular target groups; and (3) causal relationships accounting for individual differences in tolerance and intolerance. In terms of the causal relationships, it is

1. Greenstein (1970, ch. 3), Flanigan and Zingale (1979, pp. 180–183).

generally true that the sociological variables (age, religion, race, class, sex, and education) are more important in explaining the target groups picked, while certain political and psychological variables (e.g. perceptions of threat, dogmatism, self-esteem, and ideology) are more helpful in understanding variations in levels of tolerance. In other words, some variables designated in earlier studies as causes of tolerance or intolerance are actually more important as causes of target group selection. A brief summary of our more important findings:

1. Distributions in the Sample:

   Most people are intolerant of some group or groups when given the opportunity to select groups they oppose. (Chapter 3)

   Claims that the public is now more tolerant than in the 1950s are either untrue or greatly exaggerated. (Chapter 3)

   In the 1950s, there was probably greater agreement that communists were a threat. In the 1970s, there was more diversity of targets for intolerance. (Chapter 4)

   People are nearly as intolerant of groups on the extreme right as of groups on the extreme left, though people are more intolerant of communists than of other groups. (Chapter 4)

   People justify their intolerance as a defense against undemocratic groups that threaten their rights—that is, they do not tolerate groups they view as intolerant. (Chapter 7)

2. Sources of Target Groups Selected:

   There is a strong relationship between ideology and the groups selected as targets, as those on the left select targets on the right, and those on the right select targets on the left. (Chapters 3 and 7)

   There are differences among religious groups in the targets selected: Protestants and Catholics are more likely to select groups on the extreme left, while Jews and those with no religious affiliation are likely to select groups on the far right. (Chapter 4)

   Education is also related to target groups selected, as those with more education are more likely to select groups on the right, while those with less education are more likely to select groups on the left. (Chapter 4)

   Blacks and Whites also differ, the former tending to select right-wing groups (generally the Ku Klux Klan), while the latter are more likely to select left-wing groups. (Chapter 4)

   When given a chance to select two groups, a minority of respondents (41%) selected two groups from the same end of the ideological spectrum, while most people (59%) mixed their selections between the left, right, and center. (Chapter 4)

3. Sources of Tolerance and Intolerance:

While those who participate a great deal in politics are more tolerant than those who participate less, the relationship is spurious and results from other factors, related both to participation and tolerance. (Chapters 7 and 8)

Education is very weakly related to tolerance, when the relationship is controlled for other variables. While the highly educated are more tolerant than the less educated, this relationship also results from other factors. (Chapters 5 and 8)

Those who profess no religious affiliation are significantly more tolerant than those who profess some affiliation, but there are few significant differences among Catholics, Protestants, and Jews in levels of tolerance. The independent influence of religion on tolerance is therefore weak. (Chapters 5 and 8)

The degree to which respondents endorse the abstract principles of democracy is independently related to our measure of tolerance, which is based on hypothetical responses to specific situations. Abstract principles thus constrain responses to specific situations. (Chapters 7 and 8)

The factors most strongly and consistently related to tolerance are perceptions of threat from target groups and two psychological constructs, self-esteem and dogmatism. The greater the perceived threat from a group, the more likely a person is to be intolerant of the group. The greater a person's psychological security, the more likely that person is to be tolerant. (Chapters 5 through 8)

As extensive as these findings may appear, they still leave many questions unanswered. For example, we do not know the relationship between attitudes and behavior in this area. Given the nature of the study, we can speak of attitudes and predispositions only; we cannot be certain that these attitudes and predispositions will have a great deal to do with actual behavior. In addition, we cannot tell how universal, or how limited, our findings may be, since they may be dependent on the nature of the political environment when our survey was conducted. Nor do we know very much about the stability of these attitudes, or about the process through which the salience of target groups may change. All of these issues must remain open, and they may be regarded as subjects for future investigation.

In addition, we recognize that our results are to some extent regime dependent, and that an entirely different pattern of relationships might be found in a society in which tolerance is not considered an important value. In the United States, tolerance is associated with a series of desirable characteristics—for example, psychological security and commitment to democratic principles. But in a society with different political values, these particular relationships may not hold.

Our results may be interpreted narrowly or broadly. Looking at this study narrowly, readers may be interested in our measure of tolerance, the distributions found on this measure in the sample as a whole and across important sub-groups in the sample, and the causal relationships reported between tolerance and other independent variables. They may also place our research in the context of previous work on tolerance, and evaluate its importance in relation to its contribution to understanding the public's support for civil liberties. From this standpoint, the results of the research, though limited, may be satisfactory.

From a broader standpoint, however, we have raised more questions than we have been able to answer. By showing that most Americans are intolerant of some groups, we either weaken the connection between pure tolerance and democracy, or we suggest that the United States is not fully democratic. By questioning claims about the impact of education and participation on tolerance, we imply that there is no developmental sequence that will produce greater tolerance. And by assuming that tolerance implies the acceptance of intolerant groups, we suggest that the principle may be internally contradictory, and that complete tolerance is either unobtainable or undesirable. Such questions need to be kept open, especially in a liberal society that tries to solve all questions through neutral procedures, because they remind us that there is a point at which procedures must be justified by some substantive standard. The search for that standard, and its justification, goes well beyond the scope of empirical research.

It is also worth noting that the judgments people make during times of "normal" politics are likely to differ from those they make during crises. It is easy to endorse the principle of tolerance when its immediate beneficiaries are weak; it is harder to do so when significant political consequences are likely to follow. There is a sense in which we have given respondents a difficult test, since we have asked them about groups they dislike or oppose; yet, at the same time, none of these groups is presently very powerful.

Yet empirical results are not irrelevant to these broader questions of democracy and politics. They can help to validate, or to render invalid, theoretical claims about democracy. Since such claims are usually political and normative, empirical findings may not reach the level of discourse at which such claims are argued. Nevertheless, to the extent that theories of democracy rest on empirical assertions, they cannot be adequately evaluated without taking into account empirical findings that bear on such assertions. According to Thompson (1970), theoretical claims about citizenship are advanced, justified, and evaluated at three different levels of discourse, which he calls (1) conditions, (2) constructive ideals, and (3) reconstructive ideals.

> Conditions concern citizenship as it exists, constructive ideals concern citizenship at it could be in present social and political structures, and reconstructive ideals concern citizenship as it might be in a new structure. Evidence from social science (in its present state of development) is most relevant for justifying a condition, less relevant for a constructive ideal, and least relevant for a reconstructive ideal (pp. 38–39).

Insofar as democratic theories prescribe standards that must be met if democracy is to exist, it is possible to assess the standards using empirical findings. Assuming that pure tolerance is a democratic ideal— a highly problematic assumption—it is possible to measure the level of tolerance in a democratic regime and to compare it with the requirements of a particular theory. In addition, one can assess the likelihood that future trends will strengthen or undermine the standard or, once the factors that reinforce the standard are discovered, one can suggest constructive steps to achieve it. Thus, Stouffer argued that the link between education and intolerance meant that American society would become more tolerant over time, since educational opportunity was becoming more widely available. In brief, though the standard—tolerance—was not met under existing conditions, developments in the society led him to conclude that it would be met in the future within existing political institutions.

Had Stouffer found high levels of intolerance and no evidence of favorable trends to justify the constructive ideal, he might have moved to the reconstructive level of argument. That is, he might have concluded that under the existing regime the standard of tolerance could not be met without instituting different political arrangements. Here the theoretical implications are not based on the empirical findings, since they cannot demonstrate that the standard would be met under the hypothetical arrangements. Nor can the findings justify the standard itself. All that can be said on the basis of the findings is that there is no prospect of the criterion being met under existing arrangements. Alternatively, given the failure to meet the standards, one might abandon the ideal of a tolerant citizenry. Thus, one might conclude, with Prothro and Grigg (1960), that democracy does not require a tolerant citizenry. But this would require an alternative theory of democracy, one that dispenses with tolerance.

These considerations suggest how our empirical findings relate to the theoretical approaches outlined in Chapter 1. Given what has been said, these findings can not address every theoretical assertion, but they can treat questions that arise on Thompson's first two levels of discourse discussed above. There is a sense in which our presentation will distort these theories. We have had to adapt them to the issue of tolerance and to modern controversies that may not have been so important when they were formulated. Thus, readers should not view this brief presentation as a rigorous reconstruction of these theories.

## Implications for Democratic Theory

The findings presented in Chapters 3 through 8 bear directly on both the assumptions and predictions about tolerance implicit in each variety of democratic theory. In reviewing these assumptions and predictions, it will become apparent that there are real limitations to the analysis and, indeed, to any attempt to match broad theories of democracy with the results of empirical investigations. We will acknowledge these limitations as they arise, since they qualify the conclusions drawn about tolerance and democratic theory. In addition, it should be noted that most theorists distinguish between the level of tolerance that is desirable or possible and the level that is required to sustain a liberal regime. Obviously, the level of tolerance that some think desirable can go well beyond what they think is necessary to maintain a representative system.

Dennis Thompson develops a useful analytic scheme that is well suited to our discussion of democratic theories. Although developed for a study of J.S. Mill, the schema can be applied to the varieties of democratic theory we considered in Chapter 1. Thompson argues that two principles underlie the work of J.S. Mill (*Considerations on Representative Government*), the principle of participation and the principle of competence. Mill argued that the principle of participation required that the greatest effort be made to extend participation so that the educative value of participation is as extensive as possible and that the representative function of participation is broadly met. Mill balanced this principle of participation with the principle of competence. Those participating in the political system must meet general standards to ensure that governmental policy is responsive to the *general* (or common) interests of the society. Mill did not expect that the raw aggregation of self-interests would reflect the common interests of the community. To realize the principle of competence, to ensure that sufficient competence is available to the government, Mill considered a variety of methods (such as the Hare system of voting and various plural voting schemes) to "weight" the influence of the competent (presumably the more educated)[2] though not so much that the weighted competent can overcome a majority. This apparent conflict of principles is resolved by Mill in the following way.

In liberal democratic theories the principle of participation is the more enduring principle for two reasons. First, it is the principle of participation that provides the primary legitimacy of the government as a representative government. Second, the principle of participation is the more enduring principle because Mill argued for a developmental sequence through which the need for the principle of competence declines. The developmental sequence that Mill envisioned relies upon the beneficial results of greater education and greater participation among the electorate. The educative consequences of formal education and of political experience will lead to a more informed and more responsible electorate. Thus, we can anticipate that the protective purpose of the principle of competence will recede as the beneficial consequences of the developmental process are realized. Hence, liberal theories gain support from any evidence that the electorate meets these democratic standards or from trends and relationships that suggest that they could or will meet them.

The major alternative to liberal theories of democracy, which we have labeled the "conservative" theory, is based largely on the writings of Joseph Schumpeter. Schumpeter was skeptical about the developmental potential of the electorate since he believed that human nature was more or less fixed, at least within the limits of a liberal society. Thus, if the standards of competence are not met at present, there is no compelling reason to suppose that they will be met in the future. The restraints implied by the competence principle are therefore not only justified for the present, but they are necessary and permanent features of a stable democracy. In addition, these restraints on citizens provide more authority and latitude of action for political leaders, who are presumed to be more competent than any other group.

In brief summary, the liberal theories of democracy require the highest levels of tolerance among both the political elites and the mass citizenry; these theories are optimistic and place their faith in both education and political participation as sources of ever increasing levels

---

2. Mill eventually fails to confirm a faith in any method of institutionalizing the principle of competence, since he could find no certain way of identifying the competent class.

of political tolerance. Conservative theories require less tolerance, and place their faith in political elites to protect democratic processes. Conservative theories do not require the center to tolerate the ideological extremes, but they do require tolerance of an alternative leadership class that shares, with the current political incumbents, faith in the rules of the game. The conservative variants of democratic theory do not assert that increasing levels of education and participation will necessarily increase tolerance, although they do assert that tolerance will strongly reflect social status and political position.

The third variant of democratic theory to be discussed is the Federalist position, as it was developed by Madison in numbers 10 and 51 of *The Federalist*. Though Madison does suggest in the tenth paper that the process of representation will "filter" public opinion so that enlightened opinion will rise to the top, he does not claim special talents for leaders in the new regime. Instead, he defends the Constitution on the ground that it provides a framework through which the common good may be discovered through the conflict of interest and ambition. By establishing a system of checks and balances and separated powers, the framers hoped to minimize the danger of majority tyranny, so that the benefits of an energetic government could be enjoyed in a republican regime. This institutional framework, combined with the social diversity that was to be found in a continental system, represented the core of Madison's theory of the "extended republic." Applied to the present concern (and thus wrenched out of its context), this theory might well have anticipated high levels of intolerance both among citizens and leaders, though the targets of this intolerance would be as diverse as the society itself. Thus, the regime is protected by the diversity of target groups and by a constitutional order that disperses political power. At the same time, neither the theory nor the Constitution provides a hard and fast guarantee that a consensus cannot emerge from the process that is hostile to some particular group. Indeed, if such a consensus does emerge and is able to impose its will, there is a presumption that it is legitimate and that its target poses a threat that can be legitimately suppressed.

It is of course difficult to apply these theories, especially those of Mill and Madison, to the problem formulated in this book. We are concerned with tolerance and intolerance of extremist groups on the left and the right, a concern that certainly did not preoccupy either Madison or Mill, since anti-liberal ideologies had not yet made their forceful appearance when they were writing. Madison was primarily concerned with the protection of propertied groups against a coalition that might have an interest in plundering them. It is hard to see how he could have worked up much sympathy for the communists, who now represent precisely the kind of interest that he most feared. Mill wanted to defend the claims of individual conscience against the conformity sometimes required by society, on the ground that the society has much to learn from those who disagree with it. The political claims that Madison and Mill wanted to protect are not equivalent to those that are being studied here. When we adapt their theories to the present concern, then, we are primarily adapting the processes they developed to defend different ends. Since ends are more important than means in most political theories, we might be accused here of elevating what is less important in their theories and casting aside what is most important. As there is a good deal of truth in this, we shall proceed tentatively.

What, then, do our empirical results say about these theoretical formulations? Our most important finding was that once one ascertained that the target group was indeed disliked (and hence a candidate for intolerance), then nearly every segment of the society was quite likely to be intolerant. While the majority sentiment supported the restriction of civil and social liberties, the majority sentiment was not directed against a specific target. Instead, the targets of intolerance are diverse and heterogeneous, ranging across a full ideological spectrum. Only the communists and the Ku Klux Klan were selected by more than one respondent in ten (29% and 24% respectively of the national sample). Moreover, this diversity was also found within the various segments of the local and national samples.[3] The prospects for a "tyranny of the majority" would have been much greater if we had found considerable agreement on the potential targets of intolerance. Thus, the diversity of the targets selected works against and mitigates to some extent the rather high levels of intolerance we found in our sample.

Some of the fears of "mass society" theorists that industrialization and modernization will lead to a politically homogeneous society are not supported by this study.[4] In a somewhat different sense, the high levels of intolerance we found may actually characterize a developed democratic system rather than give evidence of an unrealized democratic culture. The prevention of "tyranny" in a democracy may not come solely, or even primarily, from a universal belief in the norms of tolerance. Instead, the defense of political and civil rights may come from the diversity of opinions and the anchoring of this diversity in

3. The only exception to this would be the tendency of Blacks to choose the KKK as a target.

4. See Halebsky (1975) for an excellent historical overview of the mass society approach to social behavior.

strongly held opinions that are not likely to be abandoned for a mass political movement. We have called this kind of situation "pluralistic intolerance."

In addition, it appears from our study that there is a selective recruitment process that yields more tolerant individuals at the higher levels of political involvement.[5] However, this process is not so strong as to yield a majority of "more tolerant" individuals at the highest level of political involvement. Still, this result is suggestive and it does lend some support to claims that political leaders are the strongest defenders of the norms of tolerance. How and in what fashion this selective recruitment process operates is unclear. Since we did not have an elite sample, we could not address the question with sufficient rigor to answer it.

The multivariate model describes the relationships between various factors and the impact of these variables on one another. The model does not describe how institutional or other system level characteristics affect the level of tolerance. Still, a good deal can be learned from the multivariate model, and its findings have a good deal to suggest to the democratic theorists.

The paths between education and tolerance, mediated by personality, ideology, and the general norms of tolerance, suggest that higher levels of education may produce increases in tolerance among the general population. But given the high levels of intolerance in our sample and the considerable attenuation of the relationship due to the number of mediating variables, the prospects for substantial increases cannot be very great. Thus, while the spread of formal education may influence the mediating variables, these changes will only marginally affect the levels of tolerance in the population.

More importantly, the educative consequences of increased political experience and involvement on political tolerance are so slight as to eliminate any paths from these factors to tolerance. The traditional expectation that education and more secure personalities improve the

5. Although the full range of scores on political participation is not closely related to the full range of scores on political tolerance, the smaller number of respondents who are involved in political activities are more tolerant than the rest of the respondents. This suggests some sort of threshold effect, consistent with the developmental process discussed in the text. Unless total political involvement occurs, participation variables have no impact on tolerance. The difficulty is that the number of citizens so involved is so small that the effects of participation on the aggregate level of intolerance are very limited indeed. If one discusses a reconstructive ideal (Thompson, 1970), based not on the status quo but on a complete redefinition of political participation, then perhaps the liberal theorists are correct. Such reconstructive ideals are beyond the scope of empirical investigations such as ours.

extent of political involvement and this in turn produces a more informed public is substantiated by the model. The developmental process is likely to yield a more involved and more informed public as education and economic development (the path from status to political involvement) are enhanced across the population. However, the political competence of the electorate, at least with respect to the application of norms of tolerance to objectionable groups, does not vary with the level of political involvement or of political information. This finding goes to the heart of the developmental process and the prospects for full participation. The degree of tolerance does not depend upon either the level of political involvement or the extent of political information as we have measured them. It is cetainly possible that other forms of political experience than those commonly found in the United States might have the ability to produce a more tolerant individual. These findings do not preclude that possibility. Nonetheless, there is no evidence that the degree of tolerance is affected one way or the other by the modes of participation that are found in the United States and the range of political information of the kind we consider here.

Two major propositions of the conservative theories are (1) that the "carriers" of the democratic creed are found in the higher social strata and are disproportionately represented among political elites, and (2) that the public at large is generally intolerant and does not understand the requirements of democratic politics. A third feature of these theories is the suggestion that the relationships between tolerance, on the one hand, and education and participation, on the other, are spurious and are in fact caused by differences in social status.

Regarding the claims about social status, our analysis in Chapter 8 demonstrated that status, as measured by income and occupation, has only a small and indirect impact on tolerance. Indeed, one of these indirect paths works in the opposite direction: higher levels of social status are related to higher levels of conservatism, which in turn produce lower levels of tolerance. It appears then, from our findings, that conservative claims for a tolerant political stratum, which defends democratic processes, are as illusory as liberal claims for a developmental sequence that will strengthen tolerant norms among citizens at large.[6]

Our evidence supports in part the conservative claim that the mass public is authoritarian, to borrow a term, and therefore intolerant.

6. The appropriate test of this hypothesis would involve a sample of political elites. Our conclusions are thus tentative because of the nature of our sample, though it is not unreasonable to expect the class or status variables to be related to tolerance in a mass sample if the conservative hypothesis about the "carriers" of the democratic creed is correct.

Though we cannot assess with our data the permanence or immutability of the personality characteristics which are so strongly related to tolerance, it does appear that the various dimensions of personality are so closely inter-related as to constitute some syndrome of traits (see Appendix 8-A). Education, religion, status, and age are related to personality, but other factors not incorporated into our model, such as family socialization processes, are probably more closely related to it. All this is consistent with the assumptions of the more conservative democratic theorists, though it by no means proves them.

In a sense, then, our results suggest that both the liberal and the conservative theorists were too optimistic. The liberal theorists assumed that a truly liberal regime will eventually develop tolerant and democratic citizens. The evidence reviewed here suggests that the processes these theorists posited to produce greater tolerance—education and participation—do not do so in American society. Though the conservative theorists were more pessimistic, they were sufficiently optimistic to believe that a political elite, insulated from the pressures that produce mass intolerance, might promote or defend democratic institutions and practices. Again, our evidence indicates that even the more active citizens are generally intolerant, though perhaps less so than those who are less active. However, the former tend to select somewhat different targets for their intolerance than the latter—that is, they are more sensitive to challenges from the right than they are to challenges from the left.

The final formulation to be discussed, the federalist theory, is more pessimistic about these prospects than the other two theories. It assumes that the potential for intolerance exists among all citizens, and is likely to be activated if their interests are threatened sufficiently. There is no particular group that can be trusted to protect the rights of other groups; and there is no developmental process that is expected to perfect public opinion. Given this formulation, one might expect to find high levels of intolerance, combined with substantial diversity in the groups that are potential targets of this intolerance. This is, of course, consistent with our findings at a very general level. Americans are generally intolerant of extremist groups on the left and the right, which perhaps comes as no surprise to those who study the classic texts in American politics. In addition, the selection of target groups generally follows along class, status, religious, and ideological lines, even though these variables do not predict levels of tolerance very well. Finally, our findings concerning the importance of external threat are consistent with the belief that people are likely to be intolerant of groups that are thought to pose a substantial threat to their interests.

However, this proposition is so general, and perhaps so obvious, that it cannot be regarded as the unique property of any of these theorists.

This conclusion regarding the prospects for development was further reinforced by our findings with respect to social tolerance. This question is, of course, somewhat tangential to our major concerns in the book, and much less central to democratic theory than the question of political tolerance. Nevertheless, there are many who believe or hope that the expansion of educational opportunity or political involvement will reduce the extent to which political conflict spills over into the social sphere. Leaving aside the question of whether or not this is desirable, it is clear from the results reported in Chapter 8 that none of the independent variables usually designated in this context (political involvement, education, personality, political beliefs) bears a very strong relationship to social tolerance. The model, in fact, was a very simple one: "threat" was the only variable related in a significant way to social tolerance. Given those results, then, levels of social tolerance will only be increased by removing or substantially reducing levels of perceived threat from target groups.

In general, we think our findings are more consistent with a federalist interpretation of democratic theory. Madison's views on this question might be contrasted with those of some modern liberal theorists who assume that tolerance is good and that any deviation in the society, or among individuals, from an absolute standard of tolerance is undesirable. In this sense, such claims rest on a normative view of democracy that resembles Holmes's position in his dissent in *Abrams v. United States* (1919), which was discussed in Chapter 1:

> . . . when men have realized that time has upset many fighting faiths, they come to believe even more than they believe in the very foundations of their own conduct that the ultimate good desired is better reached by free trade in ideas—that the best test of truth is the power of the thought to get itself accepted in the competition of the market, and that truth is the only ground upon which their wishes safely can be carried out (p. 60).

Leaving aside the abstract merits of this view, it seems to us that any theory of democracy that relies on the widespread acceptance of this doctrine, or of something similar to it, is unrealistic and, in any case, unnecessary to the functioning of a democratic system.

The framers did not base the Constitution on the idea that political truth emerges from the competition of the market; nor did they believe that it was necessary that citizens accept this doctrine for a republican system to survive. Madison (Federalist 51), as we noted in Chapter 1, put his faith in more practical safeguards:

> In a free government, the security for civil rights must be the same as for religious rights. It consists in the one case in the multiplicity of interests, and in the other, in the multiplicity of sects; and this may be presumed to depend on the extent of the country and number of people comprehended under the same government (1961: 351–352).

For Madison, then, the safeguards consist in the processes of politics and the requirements of coalitions, not in the acceptance by citizens of an abstract creed of the sort that Holmes advocated. To be sure, Madison recognized that this was only a problematic solution and not a hard and fast safeguard.

When the political process provides many convenient targets for intolerance, the result is what we have called "pluralistic intolerance." Our results thus suggest that even though *levels* of intolerance are now quite high in American society, the *diversity* of the targets of intolerance prevent, for the time being, a concerted effort to eliminate any of these groups. But we do not mean to imply that this is a permanent condition.

The extent to which the American political system tolerates extremist political groups is thus better explained by Madison's formulations than by Holmes's or by those of liberal or conservative theorists generally. If we assume that a democratic system should be at least partly open to such groups, and that this is one of the conditions of democracy, to use Thompson's term, then we can say that this condition is currently met according to processes stipulated by Madison rather than by those stipulated by the other theorists discussed. This is hardly an accident, since Madison's formulations have influenced political practice in the United States far more than those of Holmes, Mill, or Schumpeter.

Those (such as members of the American Civil Liberties Union) who defend the value of complete procedural tolerance may well find this a shaky foundation on which to rest the principle, since any particular group may be put in danger if a consensus emerges that it is dangerous. Given the sometime mercurial character of American public opinion, the Madisonian solution may appear unreliable. The surest foundation for liberty, they might argue, lies in getting the public to understand and to accept the pure principle of tolerance. This might be understood as a "constructive" ideal, again to borrow Thompson's terminology. As we have already noted, the processes of education and political participation are often thought to broaden and strengthen the public's commitment to the tolerance principle. However, our study does not demonstrate that these processes are strongly connected to the acceptance of tolerant beliefs among individuals. The attempts to achieve this ideal through these particular processes thus seems likely to fail, at least if our results are to be believed.

The attempt to connect empirical results with broad theoretical formulations of the kind considered here must stop some distance short of a declaration that one theory is true and another one false. In the nature of things, theories which purport to describe political reality are bound to be more accurate, in the narrow empirical sense, than those which criticize or are designed to alter that reality. Thus, theories which have a heavy reconstructive component are less likely to be "verified" by empirical research than those which focus on the conditions of democracy or on some proximate constructive ideal. Of the three theories considered above, Mill's is certainly the most descriptive, at least insofar as the issues discussed here are concerned. Schumpeter's theory was meant to be heavily descriptive, but he was also trying to sustain a form of liberal democracy against the scientific sociology of Pareto and Mosca as well as of Marx.

Theoretical formulations also differ in the extent to which they have actually shaped the reality that is the subject of empirical investigation. In this sense, all theories are not equal, a consideration that empirical researchers sometimes forget when they set about to test one or another proposition derived from the tradition of political theory. Madison's formulations in *The Federalist* have certainly shaped political practice in the United States more decisively than those of Mill or Schumpeter or Holmes. As the classic commentary on the Constitution, *The Federalist* has influenced the thought and practice of generations of judges, politicians, and political writers. The formulations contained in that work are therefore not wholly independent of the institutions and opinion that are the current subjects of empirical research in the United States. For this reason, the theory set forth in *The Federalist* cannot be tested as if it were just one of a number of accounts of political life in the United States.

## Concluding Comments

As we have noted throughout this volume, people disagree about the role that tolerance either does or should play in democratic societies. At one extreme, some argue that tolerance is an absolute value, and that all claims have the right to be heard in the "free market of ideas," even those which repudiate the market in ideas. Alternatively, in the American context, others argue that limits must be placed on these claims in order to protect the regime of democracy against those who use its protections to destroy it. We have not stated a position on this dispute, and see no need to do so here. However, this dispute does raise a difficult question about liberal politics: How does a regime defend itself against threats posed by those who act to undermine it if the regime itself is defined by procedures which require tolerance of all views as an absolute or a universal value?

Many of our respondents seemed to recognize the problem, and many proceeded to assert both of the above views of tolerance. They generally endorsed the abstract norms of tolerance, and since these norms do constrain intentions to act, they push the public in the direction of greater tolerance. On the other hand, people do recognize political threats posed by objectionable groups, and these perceptions also influence intentions to act, but in this case they limit the extension of procedural claims to these groups. The abstract norms and the perceptions of threat work in opposing directions.

The levels of tolerance in the society, and among individuals, at a given time may reflect some kind of balance between these conflicting claims and calculations. Thus, levels of tolerance probably fluctuate as levels of threat and support for the norms of tolerance fluctuate, though we do not want to suggest any mechanical relationship among these factors. As a practical matter, the result of this process brings the public down on the side of a prudential view of tolerance, since the abstract norms are endorsed but they are compromised in the face of perceived threats. In this sense, tolerance is not treated as a value of such importance that it is pursued above and before all other values. Since, in practice, tolerance is in conflict with other values, it has not achieved the status that the proponents of pure tolerance claim for it. The generally accepted proposition that tolerance is necessary to sustain political opposition to the leaders in office thus does not lead the electorate to conclude that any and all forms of opposition must be permitted.

One of the dangers of this position is that it lends itself to abuse by those in power who may attack their opponents under the guise of defending the regime. In addition, once this prudential construction is adopted, there is no hard and fast guarantee that real threats to democracy will be distinguished from truly democratic forms of opposition, because the very standards by which such a distinction might be made are established by the political process and are not engraved in stone. A prudential approach to tolerance only guarantees that the various claims that are part of the political process itself will be brought to bear on particular circumstances though it does prescribe in a normative way what claims can be legitimately weighed. From a certain point of view, arguments for pure tolerance as an absolute standard are themselves designed to shape the process through which such conflicts are resolved, since they are intended to shape the opinion that will settle the conflicts.

Normative assumptions about the importance or desirability of tolerance have in truth never been far from the surface since the beginning of this inquiry, and each step that we have advanced the subject has been accompanied by nagging questions that we could not resolve. But the ideas presented in the foregoing pages may enlighten future discussions of these questions, and, for some readers, they may encourage deeper reflection about the character of American democracy. In any event, this volume is not the last word on this subject, but only the most recent one, and as such it was written more to continue a discussion than to conclude one.

# Bibliography

Abrams v. United States. 1919. 250 US 616.

Adorno, T.; Frenkel-Brunswick, E.; Levinson, D.; and Sanford, N. 1950. *The Authoritarian Personality.* New York: Harper.

Alford, Robert. 1963. *Party and Society: the Anglo-American Democracies.* Chicago: Rand McNally.

Anderson, Walt. 1973. *Politics and the New Humanism.* Pacific Palisades, Cal.: Goodyear Publishing Co.

Barber, James David. 1972. *The Presidential Character: Predicting Performance in the White House.* Englewood Cliffs, N.J.: Prentice-Hall.

Berelson, Bernard; Lazarsfeld, Paul; and McPhee, William. 1954. *Voting.* Chicago: University of Chicago Press.

Berns, Walter. 1976. *The First Amendment and the Future of American Democracy.* New York: Basic Books.

Blalock, Hubert M. 1968. "The Measurement Problem: A Gap Between the Languages of Theory and Research," in H. M. Blalock and A. B. Blalock (eds.), *Methodology in Social Research.* New York: McGraw-Hill.

Blalock, Hubert M.; Wells, Caryll S.; and Carter, Lewis F. 1970. "Statistical Estimation with Random Measurement Error," in E. Borgatta (ed.), *Sociological Methodology 1970.* San Francisco: Jossey-Bass, ch. 5.

Bogardus, E. S. 1925. "Measuring Social Distance," *Journal of Applied Sociology,* 9, pp. 299–308.

Bohrnstadt, G., and Carter, T.M. 1971. "Robustness in Regression Analysis," in H. L. Costner (ed.), *Sociological Methodology 1971.* San Francisco: Jossy-Bass, pp. 118–146.

Brown, Steven R., and Taylor, Richard W. 1973. "Frames of Reference and the Observation of Behavior," *Social Science Quarterly,* 54, No. 1 (June), pp. 29–40.

Burt, Ronald S. 1976. "Interpretational Confounding of Unobserved Variables in Structural Equation Models," *Sociological Methods and Research,* 5 (August), pp. 3–52.

266

Calder, B. J., and Ross, M. 1973. *Attitudes and Behavior.* Morristown, N.J.: General Learning Press.

Campbell, D. T. 1963. "Social Attitudes and Other Acquired Behavioral Dispositions," in S. Koch (ed.), *Psychology: A Study of Science,* 6. New York: McGraw-Hill, pp. 94–172.

Christie, Richard, and Jahoda, Marie (eds.). 1954. *Studies in the Scope and Method of "The Authoritarian Personality."* Glencoe, Illinois: The Free Press.

Converse, Philip E. 1972. "Change in the American Electorate," in Angus Campbell and Philip Converse, (eds.), *The Human Meaning of Social Change.* New York: Russell Sage Foundation.

Cooke, Jacob (ed.). 1961. *The Federalist.* Middletown, Connecticut: Wesleyan University Press.

Costner, Herbert L. 1969. "Theory, Deduction and Rules of Correspondence," *American Journal of Sociology,* 75, pp. 245–263.

Costner, Herbert L., and Schoenberg, Ronald. 1973. "Diagnosing Indicator Ills in Multiple Indicator Models," in A. S. Goldberger and O. D. Duncan (eds.), *Structural Equation Models in the Social Sciences.* New York: Seminar Press, pp. 167–199.

Crick, Bernard. 1973. *Political Theory and Practice.* New York: Basic Books.

Cutler, Stephen J., and Kaufman, Robert L. 1975. "Cohort Changes in Political Attitudes: Tolerance of Ideological Nonconformity," *Public Opinion Quarterly,* 39 (Spring), pp. 69–81.

Dahl, Robert. 1956. *A Preface to Democratic Theory.* Chicago: University of Chicago Press.

———. 1961. *Who Governs? Democracy and Power in an American City.* New Haven, Connecticut: Yale University Press.

Davis, James A. 1975. "Communism, Conformity, Cohorts, and Categories: American Tolerance in 1954 and 1972–73," *American Journal of Sociology,* 81 (November), pp. 491–513.

Elms, Alan C. 1976. *Personality in Politics.* New York: Harcourt, Brace, Jovanovich.

Erikson, Robert S., and Luttbeg, Norman R. 1973. *American Public Opinion: Its Origins, Content and Impact.* New York: John Wiley and Sons.

Erskine, Hazel, and Siegel, Richard L. 1975. "Civil Liberties and the American Public," *Journal of Social Issues,* 31, No. 2, pp. 13–29.

Eysenck, Hans Jurgen. 1954. *The Psychology of Politics.* New York: Praeger.

Fishbein, Martin. 1967. *Attitude Theory and Measurement*. New York: Wiley.

Fishbein, Martin, and Ajzen, Icek. 1975. *Belief, Attitude, Intention and Behavior*. Reading, Mass.: Addison-Wesley.

Flanigan, William H., and Zingale, Nancy H. 1979. *Political Behavior of the American Electorate*. Boston: Allyn and Bacon.

Forster, Arnold, and Epstein, Benjamin R. 1964. *Danger on the Right*. New York: Random House.

Freedman, Anne E., and Freedman, P.E. 1975. *The Psychology of Political Control*. New York: St. Martin's.

George, Alexander. 1968. "Power as a Compensatory Value for Political Leaders," *Journal of Social Issues*, 24, pp. 29–50.

George, Alexander L., and George, Juliette L. 1956. *Woodrow Wilson and Colonel House: A Personality Study*. New York: Dover Publications, Inc.

Gibson, James L., and Bingham, Richard D. 1979. American Political Science Association paper, "Conditions of Committment to Civil Liberties: Libertarian Behavior of American Elites." Washington Hilton, September 1979.

Greene, Vernon L. 1977. "An Algorithm for Total and Indirect Causal Effects," *Political Methodology*, vol. 4, no. 4, pp. 369–382.

Greenstein, Fred I. 1970. *The American Party System and the American People*. Englewood Cliffs, N.J.: Prentice-Hall.

Gitlow v. New York. 1925. 268 US 652.

Halebsky, Sandor. 1975. *Mass Society and Political Conflict: Toward a Reconstruction of Theory*. New York: Cambridge University Press.

Hamilton, Richard F. 1972. *Class and Politics in the United States*. New York: Wiley.

Hartz, Louis. 1955. *The Liberal Tradition in America*. New York: Harcourt-Brace.

Hauser, Robert M., and Goldberger, Arthur S. 1971. "The Treatment of Unobservable Variables in Path Analysis," in H. L. Costner (ed.), *Sociological Methodology 1971*. San Francisco: Jossey-Bass, pp. 183–202.

Herson, Lawrence J. R., and Hofstetter, C. Richard. 1975. "Tolerance, Consensus, and the Democratic Creed: A Contextual Exploration," *Journal of Politics* 37 (November), pp. 1007–1032.

Hofstadter, Richard. 1955. *The Age of Reform*. New York: Knopf.

———. 1964. *Anti-Intellectualism in American Life*. New York: Vintage Books.

Inglehart, Ronald. 1977. *The Silent Revolution: Changing Values and Political Styles*. Princeton, N.J.: Princeton University Press.

Jackman, Mary. 1977. "Prejudice, Tolerance, and Attitudes Toward Ethnic Groups," *Social Science Research,* 6 (June), 145–169.

———. 1978. "General and Applied Tolerance: Does Education Increase Commitment to Racial Integration?" *American Journal of Political Science,* 22 (May), pp. 302–324.

Jackman, Robert. 1972. "Political Elites, Mass Publics, and Support for Democratic Principles," *Journal of Politics,* 34 (August), pp. 753–773.

———. 1977. "Much Ado About Nothing," *Journal of Politics,* 39 (February), pp. 185–192.

Jefferson, Thomas. 1944. "First Inaugural Address," in *Basic Writings of Thomas Jefferson,* edited by Philip S. Foner. New York: Wiley.

———. 1944. "Notes on the State of Virginia," in *Basic Writings of Thomas Jefferson,* edited by Philip S. Foner. New York: Wiley.

Joreskog, K. G. 1969. "A General Approach to Confirmatory Maximum Likelihood Factor Analysis," *Psychometrika,* 34 (June), pp. 183–202.

———. 1970. "A General Method for Analysis of Covariance Structures," *Biometrika,* 57, pp. 239–251.

———. 1973. "A General Method for Estimating a Linear Structural Equation System," in A. S. Goldberger and O. D. Duncan (eds.), *Structural Equation Models in the Social Sciences.* New York: Seminar Press, pp. 85–112.

Joreskog, K. G., and Sorbom, Dag. 1975. "Statistical Models and Methods for Analysis of Longitudinal Data." Research Report 75–1. Uppsala University, Statistics Department.

Key, V. O. 1961. *Public Opinion and American Democracy.* New York: Knopf.

Knutson, Jeanne. 1972. *The Human Basis of the Polity.* Chicago: Aldine-Atherton.

Korman, A. K. 1971. "Environmental Ambiguity and Locus of Control on Interactive Inferences on Satisfaction," *Volume of Applied Psychology,* 55, pp. 339–342.

Korman, A. K. 1963. "Selective Perception Among First Line Supervisors," *Personnel Administration,* 26, pp. 31–36.

Kornhauser, Arthur. 1959. *The Politics of Mass Society.* New York: The Free Press.

Kramer, Michael S., and Levy, Mark R. 1972. *The Ethnic Factor: How America's Minorities Decide Elections.* New York: Simon and Schuster.

Ladd, Everett C. 1978. Where Have All the Voters Gone? New York: Basic Books.

Lane, Robert E. 1962. *Political Ideology.* New York: Free Press.

————. 1969. *Political Thinking and Consciousness.* Chicago: Markham.

LaPiere, R. T. 1934. "Attitudes vs. Actions," *Social Forces,* 13, pp. 230–234.

Lasswell, Harold D. 1948. *Power and Personality.* New York: Viking Press.

Lawrence, David. 1976. "Procedural Norms and Tolerance: A Reassessment," *American Political Science Review,* 70 (March), pp. 80–100.

Lippman, Walter. 1955. *Essays in the Public Philosophy.* Boston: Little, Brown.

Lipset, Seymour Martin. 1960. *Political Man: The Social Bases of Politics.* New York: Doubleday.

Lipset, Seymour Martin, and Rabb, Earl. 1970. *The Politics of Unreason.* New York: Basic Books.

Locke, John. 1963. *Letter On Toleration,* edited by Mario Montuori. The Hague: Martinus Nijhoff.

Long, J. Scott. 1976. "Estimation and Hypothesis Testing in Linear Models Containing Measurement Error," *Sociological Methods and Research,* 5 (November), pp. 157–206.

Lowi, Theodore. 1969. *The End of Liberalism.* New York: Norton.

Mansbridge, Jane. 1980. *Beyond Adversary Democracy.* New York: Basic Books.

Mapp v. Ohio. 1962. 367 US 643.

Marcus, G. E.; Piereson, James; and Sullivan, J. L. "Rural-Urban Differences in Tolerance: Confounding Problems of Conceptualization and Measurement," *Rural Sociology,* 45 (Winter), pp. 731–737.

Marsh, Alan. 1977. *Protest and Political Consciousness.* Beverly Hills, Cal.: Sage Publications.

Martin, John G., and Westie, Frank R. 1959. "The Tolerant Personality," *American Sociological Review,* 24, no. 4 (August), pp. 521–528.

Mayo, Henry B. 1960. *An Introduction to Democratic Theory.* New York: Oxford University Press.

McClosky, Herbert. 1964. "Consensus and Ideology in American Politics," *American Political Science Review,* 58 (June), pp. 361–382.

McClosky, H.; Hoffman, P.J.; and O'Hara, R. 1960. "Issue Conflict and Consensus Among Party Leaders and Followers," *American Political Science Review,* 54, pp. 406–429.

Macpherson, Crawford B. 1977. *The Life and Times of Liberal Democracy.* New York: Oxford University Press.

Milgram, S. 1963. "Behavioral Study of Obedience," *Journal of Abnormal and Social Psychology,* 67, pp. 371–378.

Mill, John Stuart. 1956. *On Liberty.* Indianapolis: Bobbs-Merrill Company.

———. 1958. *Considerations on Representative Government.* Indianapolis: Bobbs-Merrill Company.

Milton, John. 1644. *Aeropagitica.* London.

Mosca, Gaetano. 1939. *The Ruling Class.* New York: McGraw-Hill.

Namboodiri, N. Krishnan; Carter, Lewis F.; and Blalock, Hubert M. 1975. *Applied Multivariate Analysis and Experimental Designs.* New York: McGraw-Hill.

Nunn, Clyde Z.; Crockett, Harry J; and Williams, J. Allen. 1978. *Tolerance for Nonconformity.* San Francisco: Jossey-Bass.

Nunnally, Jum C. 1976. *Psychometric Theory.* New York: McGraw-Hill.

Oskamp, Stuart. 1977. *Attitudes and Opinions.* Englewood Cliffs, N.J.: Prentice-Hall.

Pateman, Carole. 1970. *Participation and Democratic Theory.* London: Cambridge University Press.

Pennock, J. Roland. 1979. *Democratic Political Theory.* Princeton, N.J.: Princeton University Press.

Pierce, John C., and Sullivan, John L. 1980. *The Electorate Reconsidered.* Beverly Hills, California: Sage Publications.

Prothro, James W., and Grigg, Charles W. 1960. "Fundamental Principles of Democracy: Bases of Agreement and Disagreement," *Journal of Politics,* 22 (May) pp. 276–294.

Renshon, Stanley Allen. 1974. *Psychological Needs and Political Behavior: A Theory of Personality and Political Efficacy.* New York: The Free Press.

Rogin, Michael. 1967. *The Intellectuals and McCarthy: The Radical Specter.* Cambridge, Mass.: MIT Press.

Rokeach, M. 1960. *The Open and Closed Mind.* New York: Basic Books.

Rosenberg, Morris. 1956. "Misanthropy and Political Ideology," *American Sociological Review,* 21, no. 6 (December), pp. 690–695.

St. Peter, Louis; Williams, J. Allen; and Johnson, David R. 1977. "Comment on Jackman's Political Elites, Mass Publics, and Support for Democratic Principles," *Journal of Politics,* 39 (February), pp. 176–184.

Sanford, Nevitt. 1973. "Authoritarian Personality in Contemporary Perspective," in J. Knutson (ed.), *Handbook of Political Psychology,* San Francisco: Jossey-Bass, pp. 139–170.

Schattschneider, E.E. 1960. *The Semi-Sovereign People.* New York: Holt, Rinehart, and Winston.

Schuman, Howard. 1972. "Attitudes vs. Actions *versus* Attitudes vs. Attitudes," *Public Opinion Quarterly,* 36, pp. 347–354.

Schuman, Howard and Presser, Stanley. 1977. "Question Wording as an Independent Variable in Survey Analysis," *Sociological Methods and Research,* 6 (November), pp. 151–176.

Schumpeter, Joseph. 1950. *Capitalism, Socialism, Democracy.* New York: Harper and Row.

Schwartz, S. H., and Tessler, R. C. 1972. "A Test of a Model for Reducing Measured Attitude-Behavior Discrepancies," *Journal of Personality and Social Psychology,* 24, pp. 225–236.

Sharkansky, Ira. 1970. *Regionalism in American Politics.* Indianapolis: Bobbs-Merrill.

Siegel, Peter H. 1971. "Prestige in the American Occupational Structure," unpublished Ph.D. dissertation, Department of Sociology, University of Chicago.

Sniderman, Paul. 1975. *Personality and Democratic Politics.* Berkeley: University of California Press.

Stone, William F. 1974. *The Psychology of Politics.* New York: The Free Press.

Stouffer, Samuel. 1955. *Communism, Conformity, and Civil Liberties.* New York: Doubleday.

Sullivan, John L., and Feldman, Stanley. 1979. *Multiple Indicators.* Sage University Papers on Quantitative Applications in the Social Sciences, 07-015. Beverly Hills: Sage Publications.

Sullivan, John L.; Marcus, George E.; Feldman, Stanley; and Piereson, James E. 1981. "The Sources of Political Tolerance: A Multivariate Analysis," *American Political Science Review,* 75 (March), pp. 92–106.

Sullivan, John L.; Marcus, George E.; Piereson, James; and Feldman, Stanley. 1979. "The Development of Political Tolerance: The Impact of Social Class, Personality and Cognition," *International Journal of Political Education,* 2, pp. 115–139.

Sullivan, John L.; Piereson, James E.; and Marcus, George E. 1978. "Ideological Constraint in the Mass Public: A Methodological Critique and Some New Findings," *American Journal of Political Science,* 22, No. 2 (May) pp. 233–249.

———. 1979. "An Alternative Conceptualization of Political Tolerance: Illusory Increases, 1950's–1970's," *American Political Science Review,* 73 (September), pp. 233–249.

Sutton, H., and Porter, L.W. 1968. "A Study of the Grapevine in a Governmental Organization," *Personnel Psychology,* 21, pp. 223–230.

Thompson, Dennis. 1970. *The Democratic Citizen*. London: Cambridge University Press.

Truman, David Bickness. 1951. *The Governmental Process: Political Interests and Public Opinion*. New York: Knopf.

Tukey, John W. 1956. "Causation, Regression and Path Analysis," in Oscar Kempthorne et al. (eds.), *Statistics and Mathematics in Biology*. Ames, Iowa: Iowa State College Press.

Walker, Jack L. 1966. "A Critique of the Elitist Theory of Democracy," *American Political Science Review*, 60 (June), pp. 289–295.

Weissberg, Robert, and Mark V. Nadel. 1972. *American Democracy: Theory and Reality*. New York: John Wiley and Sons.

Werts, C. E.; Linn, R. L.; and Joreskog, K. G. 1971. "Estimating the Parameters of Path Models Involving Unmeasured Variables," in H. M. Blalock (ed.), *Causal Models in the Social Sciences*. Chicago: Aldine, pp. 400–410.

Wheaton, Blair; Muthen, Bengt; and Summers, Gene F. 1977. "Assessing Reliability and Stability in Panel Models," in David Heise (ed.), *Sociological Methodology 1977*, pp. 84–136. San Francisco: Jossey-Bass.

Wicker, A.W. 1969. "Attitudes Versus Actions: The Relationship of Verbal and Overt Behavioral Responses to Attitude Objects," *Journal of Social Issues*, 25, pp. 41–78.

Wolff, Robert Paul; Barrington Moore, Jr.; and Herbert Marcuse. 1965. *A Critique of Pure Tolerance*. Boston: Beacon Press.

Zalkind, Sheldon; Gaugler, Edward; and Schwartz, Ronald. 1975. "Civil Liberties, Attitudes and Personality Measures: Some Exploratory Research," *Journal of Social Issues*, 31, pp. 77–91.

Zellman, G. 1975. "Anti-Democratic Beliefs: A Survey and Some Explanations," *Journal of Social Issues*, 31, pp. 31–53.

Zellman, G., and Sears, David. 1971. "Childhood Origins of Tolerance for Dissent," *Journal of Social Issues*, 27, pp. 109–135.

# Index

*Abrams v. United States* (1919), 8, 261
Act factors, 56, 59
Adorno, T., 16, 52n
Adorno's F scale, 152
Age, and target group selection, 100–101;
  and tolerance, 29, 131–35, 144, 225
Ajzen, I., 49
Alford, R., 124, 223
Alien and Sedition Acts, 7
American Civil Liberties Union (ACLU),
  9, 10, 82
Anderson, W., 148
Apathy, and action, 35–36
Atheism, tolerance of, 28–33, 54–61,
  63–76, 82–109, 167–75
Attentive publics, 106
Attitude-behavior correlation, 46–51
Authoritarianism, 16, 150–53
Autonomy, individual, 11–12
Auxiliary precautions, constitutional,
  21–22

Barber, J. D., 146
Belief system, 153–55
Berelson, B., 18, 40
Berns, W., 9n
Bias, mobilization of, 175
Bingham, R. D., 10
Black Panthers, 72–73, 82–109, 167–75,
  180
Blalock, H. M., 241, 242
Bogardus, E. S., 238n
Bohrnstadt, G., 214n
Brown, S. R., 37
Burt, R. S., 244

Calder, B. J., 50
Campbell, D. T., 49
Carter, L. F., 241
Carter, T. M., 214n
Checks and balances, system of, 21–23

Christie, R., 52n
Civil liberties, 27–33, 45
Class categories. *See* Social status
Class conflict, 13–14
Classical theory of democracy, 55
Cohort replacement, 55
Communism, 7, 17, 26–33, 48, 54–61,
  63–76, 82–109, 167–75
Competing elites, 15
Conservatism, as measure of ideology,
  216–18, 222–25. *See also* Ideology
Conservative democratic theory, 14–20,
  24–25
Costner, H. L., 241, 244
Crick, B., 2, 4, 9
Crockett, H. J., 26, 29, 33, 45, 54–56,
  115, 116, 126, 133, 136, 194, 209, 248
Crossovers, 74–76, 120
Cutler, S. J., 44, 131

Dahl, R., 18, 40
Davis, J. A., 26, 44, 54, 55, 132
Democratic norms of procedure: adherence to, 210–41; consensus on, 35–44;
  and education, 13–14, 35; support for,
  5–7, 26, 79, 84, 194, 202–7, 233–34,
  251. *See also* Rules of the game
Democratic theory: classical, 55; conservative, 14–19, 20, 24–25; federalist,
  19–23, 24–25, 260–62; liberal, 3, 11–14,
  20, 23–24, 255, 260
Demographic variables: effect on target
  group selection, 92–106; effect on tolerance, 92–106. *See also* Age; Race;
  Region
Dogmatism, 16, 153–56, 212–13, 219, 227
Dogmatism scale, 155

Education: and class, 94–96; and democratic norms, 13–14, 35; effect on political participation, 13–14; and target

group selection, 93–95, 103–6; and tolerance, 18–19, 28–29, 47, 53, 114–26, 143–44, 221–24, 251
Elites, political, and tolerance, 29–30, 39, 194–202, 231–37
Elms, A. C., 17
Epistemic correlations, 57n, 58–59, 215–16, 242, 244–46
Epstein, B. R., 100
Erikson, R. S., 96, 129, 212, 213n
Erskine, H., 33, 45
Exclusionary rule, federal, 42
Eysenck, H. J., 16

Factor analysis, 57n, 111, 188, 214–15, 216n
Fascism, 15–17, 72–74, 82–109, 167–75, 190, 229
*Federalist,* 5, 20, 36, 92, 256
Federalist democratic theory, 19–25, 260–62
Feldman, S., 215n, 244
First Amendment, 1, 8–10
Fishbein, M., 49
Flanigan, W. H., 249n
Forster, A., 100
Free market of ideas, 7–9, 28
Free speech, 41, 63–64, 204–7
Frenkel-Brunswick, E., 16, 52n

Gaugler, E., 146
Gender: and target group selection, 100; and tolerance, 29, 126–29
George, A. L., 146n, 148
George, J. L., 146n, 148
Gibson, J. L., 10n
*Gitlow v. New York* (1925), 8
Goldberger, A. S., 242
Greene, V. L., 240n
Greenstein, F. I., 249n
Grigg, C. W., 5, 18, 26, 29, 33–44, 47, 49, 51, 116, 202, 210, 238, 246, 253
Group factors, 56, 59, 61
Guttman scale, 115

Halebsky, S., 15, 257n
Hamilton, R. F., 96, 124
Hartz, L., 175, 176
Hauser, R. M., 242

Hedges, against excesses of power, 12–13
Herson, L. J. R., 48
Hierarchical control, 117
Hodge-Siegel Prestige Score, 124
Hofstetter, C. R., 48, 137

Ideology: measures of, 179–86, 216–18, 222–25; range of, 70–77; and tolerance, 77, 101, 175–86, 235–36, 240. *See also* Conservatism
Impulse control, 150–52
Information, political, 211, 219, 235, 240; measure of, 196–202
Inglehart, R., 149
Isolation, social, 17

Jackman, M., 5, 29n, 43n
Jackman, R., 29, 30, 30n, 195, 198
Jahoda, M., 52n
Jefferson, T., 7, 8, 9
John Birch Society, 61, 71–76, 82–109, 167–75, 177, 190
Johnson, D. R., 30n
Joreskog, K. G., 57n, 242, 243

Kaufman, R. L., 44, 131
Key, V. O., 40
Knutson, J., 145–48
Korman, A. K., 117, 123
Kornhauser, A., 16
Ku Klux Klan, 32, 48, 61, 72–76, 82–109, 167–75, 177, 188, 190, 229

Ladd, E. C., 212
Lane, R. E., 146, 147, 165
LaPiere, R. T., 40
Lasswell, H. D., 146n, 148
Latent factor model, 244
Lawrence, D., 26, 46, 122, 204, 210
Lazarsfeld, P., 18, 40
Learning process, 115–16, 150–53
Levinson, D., 16, 52n
Liberal-conservative scale, 71–76
Liberal democratic theory, 3, 11–14, 16, 20, 23–24, 255, 260
Liberalism, 175–76
Linn, R. L., 242
Lippmann, W., 16
Lipset, S. M., 17, 18, 176, 177

Localism, 142
Locke, J., 3, 10
Logrolling, 92
Long, J. S., 243
Lowi, T., 176
Luttbeg, N. R., 96, 129, 212, 213n

Macpherson, C. B., 11
Madison, James, 5, 20, 36, 92, 256, 262
Majority rule, 34, 38–39, 204–7. *See also*
   Tyranny of the majority
Mansbridge, J., 13
*Mapp v. Ohio* (1962), 42
Marcus, G. E., 64, 244
Marcuse, H., 4
Marsh, A., 149
Martin, J. G., 153
Marxism, 4
Maslow's need hierarchy, 146–50
Maximum likelihood estimation, 57–58,
   214–15, 233n, 244–49
Mayo, H., 10, 18
McClosky, H., 5, 6, 26, 33, 34, 47, 82,
   195, 202, 210, 233, 238, 246
McPhee, W., 18, 40
Measurement error, 241–42
Milgram, S., 50
Mill, J. S., 4, 8, 10, 11–14, 56, 254, 255
Minimalist democracy, 17
Minority rights, 34–36, 204–7
Mob rule, 13
Moore, B., Jr., 4
Mosca, G., 15
Multivariate analysis of tolerance,
   112–14, 209–47

Namboodiri, N., 241
National Opinion Research Center
   (NORC), 54, 56, 63, 66, 122
Nazi Party, of America, 1, 9, 15, 32, 79,
   82–109, 164n, 167–75
Neier, A., 9
Non-conformity, 27–33
Nunn, C. Z., 26, 29, 33, 45, 54–56, 115,
   116, 126, 133, 136, 194, 209, 248

Oblique rotation, 111–12
Occupational structures, 117
Oligarchy, 15
Oskamp, S., 49, 51, 207

Paradox of tolerance, 9
Pareto, V., 15
Participation, political: measure of,
   196–202; and personality, 19; Stouffer
   measure of, 239–40; and tolerance,
   18–19, 101–3, 194–202, 208, 219–20,
   235–36, 240, 251
Pateman, C., 17, 175
Personality, and participation, 19; and
   tolerance, 19, 212–14, 218–19, 234–35,
   240
Piereson, J., 64, 244
Pluralism, theory of, 176
Pluralistic intolerance, 77, 82–109, 258
Political information scale, 196–202
Political theory. *See* Democratic theory
Porter, L. W., 117
Presser, S., 117, 118, 122
Principles of democracy, fundamental,
   34–36, 39–44, 45, 52–53. *See also* Dem-
   ocratic norms of procedure; Rules of
   the game
Procedural rights scale, 158
Proletarian dictatorship, 8
Prothro, J. W., 5, 18, 26, 29, 33–44, 47,
   49, 51, 116, 202, 210, 238, 246, 253
Psychoanalytic theory, 152

Raab, E., 176, 177
Race: and target group selection, 96–99,
   103–6; and tolerance, 129–31, 144
Region, and tolerance, 29, 87, 141–44
Religion: and target group selection,
   99–100, 103–6; and tolerance, 3–4, 29,
   87, 127–29, 135–39, 144, 251. *See also*
   Atheism
Religious homogeneity, 11
Renshon, S. A., 146n
Rogin, M., 177
Rokeach, M., 16, 145, 153
Rosenberg, M., 153
Ross, M., 50
Rules of the game, 2, 18, 30, 39–44,
   52–53, 84, 249

St. Peter, L., 30n
Sanford, N., 16, 52n, 145, 151
Schattschneider, E. E., 175
Schoenberg, R., 146, 244
Schuman, H., 117, 118, 122, 207

Schumpeter, J., 15, 17, 255
Schwartz, S. H., 49
Self-actualization, 212–13. *See also* Maslow's need hierarchy
Self-esteem, 148–50, 157–60, 213
Self-interest, individual, 13, 21
Sexual inequality, 127
Sharkansky, I., 87
Siegel, P. H., 124
Siegel, R. L., 33, 45
Silent majority, 45
Situational thresholds, 49–50
Sniderman, P., 145, 157, 209, 212
Social learning theory, 156–60, 212
Social status, 95–96; and tolerance, 114–26, 144, 213–14, 222–24, 236
Social tolerance, 237–39
Social tolerance scale, 241
Socialism, 26–33, 54–60, 72–76, 82–109, 167–75
Socialization, 115–16, 150–53
Sorbom, D., 242
Stone, W. F., 222n
Stouffer, S., 6, 7, 26, 27–44, 51–53, 63, 115, 186, 187, 194, 209, 248
Stouffer items, 44, 54–60, 63–76, 93–94, 100, 105–7
Structural parameter, 57n, 59, 215, 242
Sullivan, J. L., 64, 215n, 244
Sutton, H., 117
Symbionese Liberation Army (SLA), 72–73, 82–109, 167–75

Target group, attitudes to, 48, 165–75
Target group selection, 70–77, 85–91, 224–25, 250–51, 256; effect of social and political variables, 92–106
Taylor, R. W., 37
Tessler, R. C., 49
Thompson, D., 253, 254, 258n
Threat, perceived, 79, 186–94, 208, 210–41; and dogmatism, 227; and education, 192–94; measure of, 187–94; and personality, 226–27; types of, 228–31
Tolerance, political: and age, 29, 131–35, 144; attitude-behavior link, 46–51; categories of, 112–14; and democratic norms, 5–6, 37, 52; and economic change, 31; and education, 18–19, 28–29, 47, 53, 114–26, 143–44, 221–24; and gender, 29, 126–29; levels of, 44–46, 83–84, 106–9, 111–44; model of, 56–60, 209–47; and political participation, 18–19, 101–3, 194–202, 211, 219–20; psychological sources of, 78–80, 145–62; and race, 129–31, 144; and region, 29, 87, 141–44; and religion, 3–4, 29, 87, 127–29, 135–39, 144; social sources of, 78–80, 110–44, 116–17, 221–24; in the United States, 54–60, 70–76, 77, 82, 110, 113, 259–60; and urbanization, 139–41, 144
Tolerance, political, measurement of, 6–7, 32–33, 46–49, 52–53, 77–78; content controlled, 60–76, 112–14; Stouffer measure, 28, 178, 182, 190–93, 239–40. *See also* Stouffer items
Tolerance, social, 237–39
Tough-tendermindedness, 16
Trait approach, 151
Truman, D. B., 176
Tukey, J. W., 214n
Tyranny of the majority, 20, 22, 84, 109, 249, 257. *See also* Majority rule

Urbanization, and tolerance, 139–41, 144
Utilitariansim, 11

Values, measurement of, 149

Wells, C. S., 241
Werts, C. E., 242
Westie, F. R., 153
Wicker, A. W., 49
Will, G., 9
Williams, H. J., 26, 29, 33, 45, 54–56, 115, 116, 126, 133, 136, 194, 209, 248
Williams, J. A., 30n
Wiretapping, 63–64
Wolff, R. P., 4

Zalkind, S., 146
Zellman, G., 156
Zingale, N. H., 249n